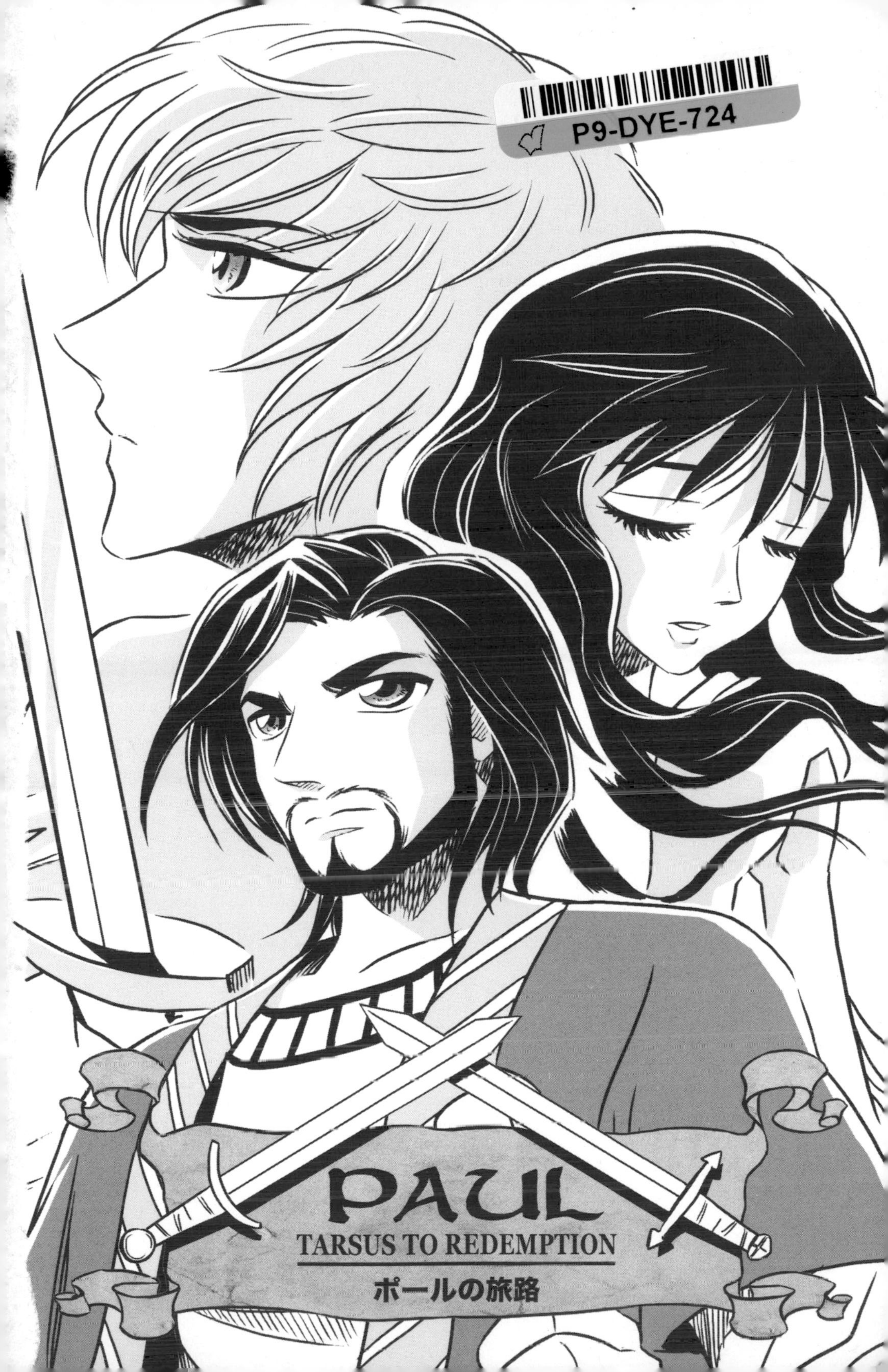
PAUL
TARSUS TO REDEMPTION
ポールの旅路

PAUL
TARSUS TO REDEMPTION

VOLUME I

Story by Matthew Salisbury
Art by Sean Lam

PAUL: TARSUS TO REDEMPTION (VOLUME I) by Matthew SALISBURY and Sean LAM
© 2010 ATIQTUQ
All rights reserved.

ISBN 978-0-9826538-0-7

0 9 8 7 6 5 4 3 2 1

Printed in the United States of America

Published by ATIQTUQ
817 Mission Ave., Suite 1A
San Rafael, CA 94901
www.atiqtuq.com

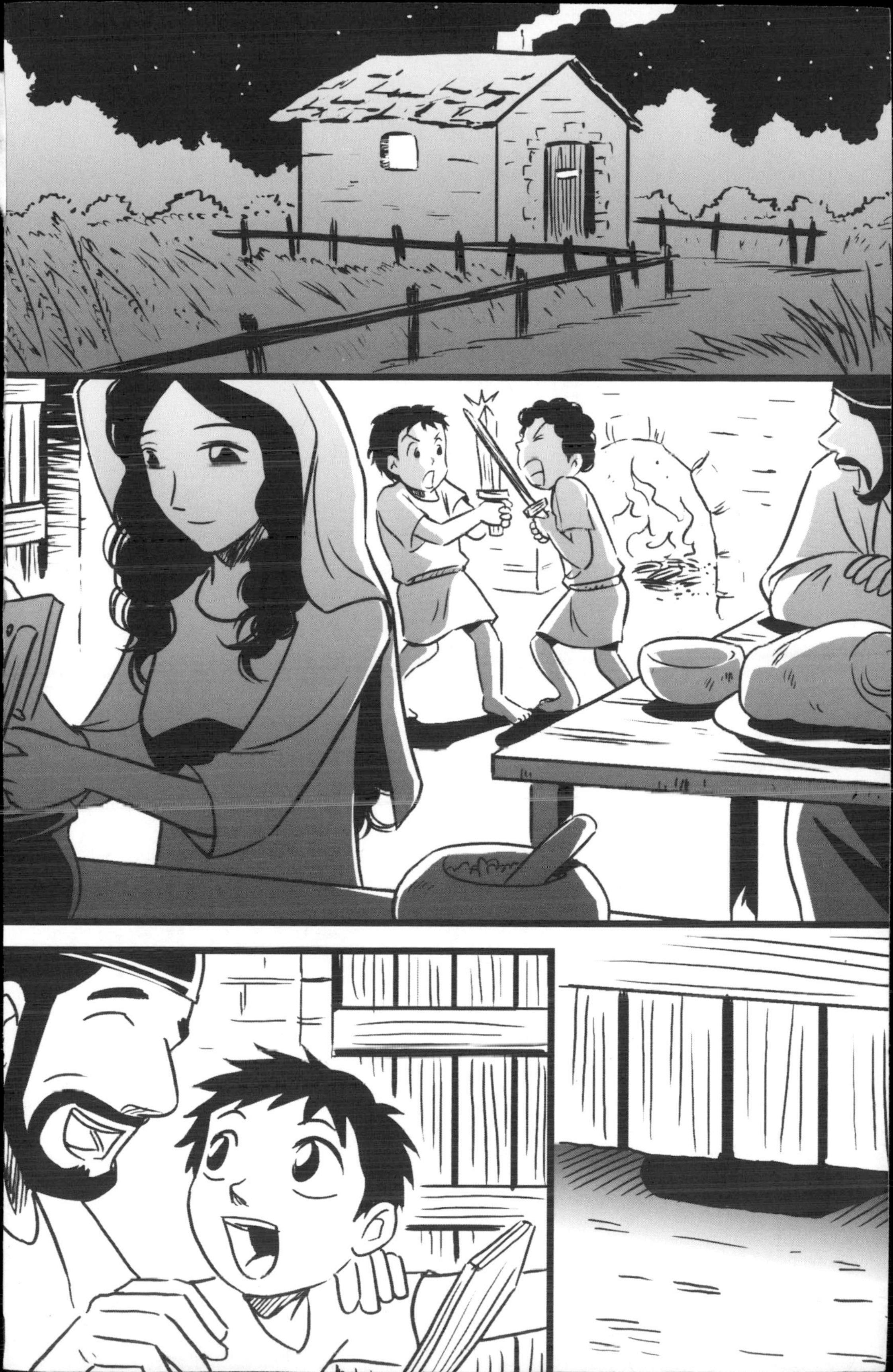

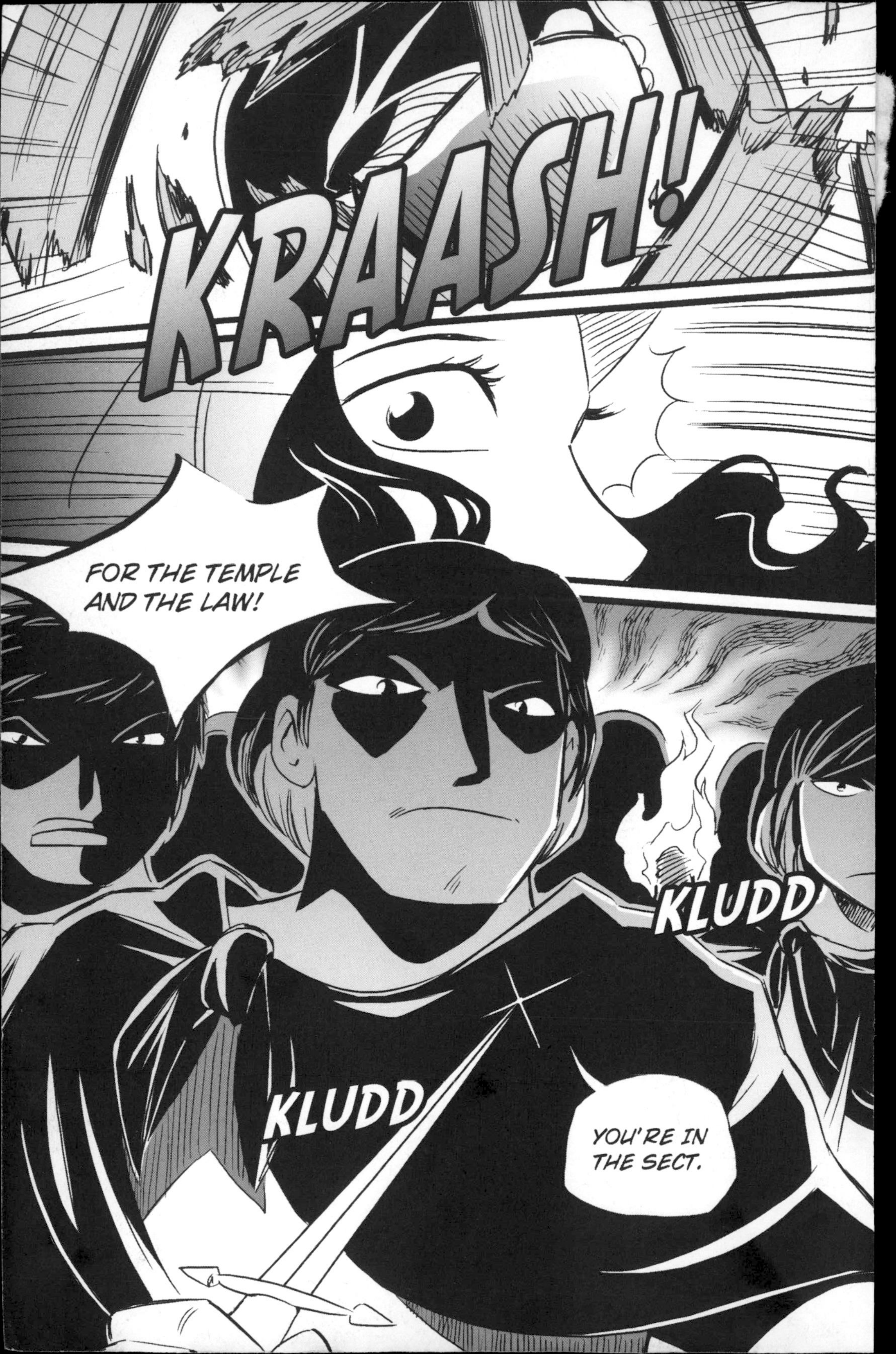
KRAASH!
FOR THE TEMPLE AND THE LAW!
KLUDD
KLUDD
YOU'RE IN THE SECT.

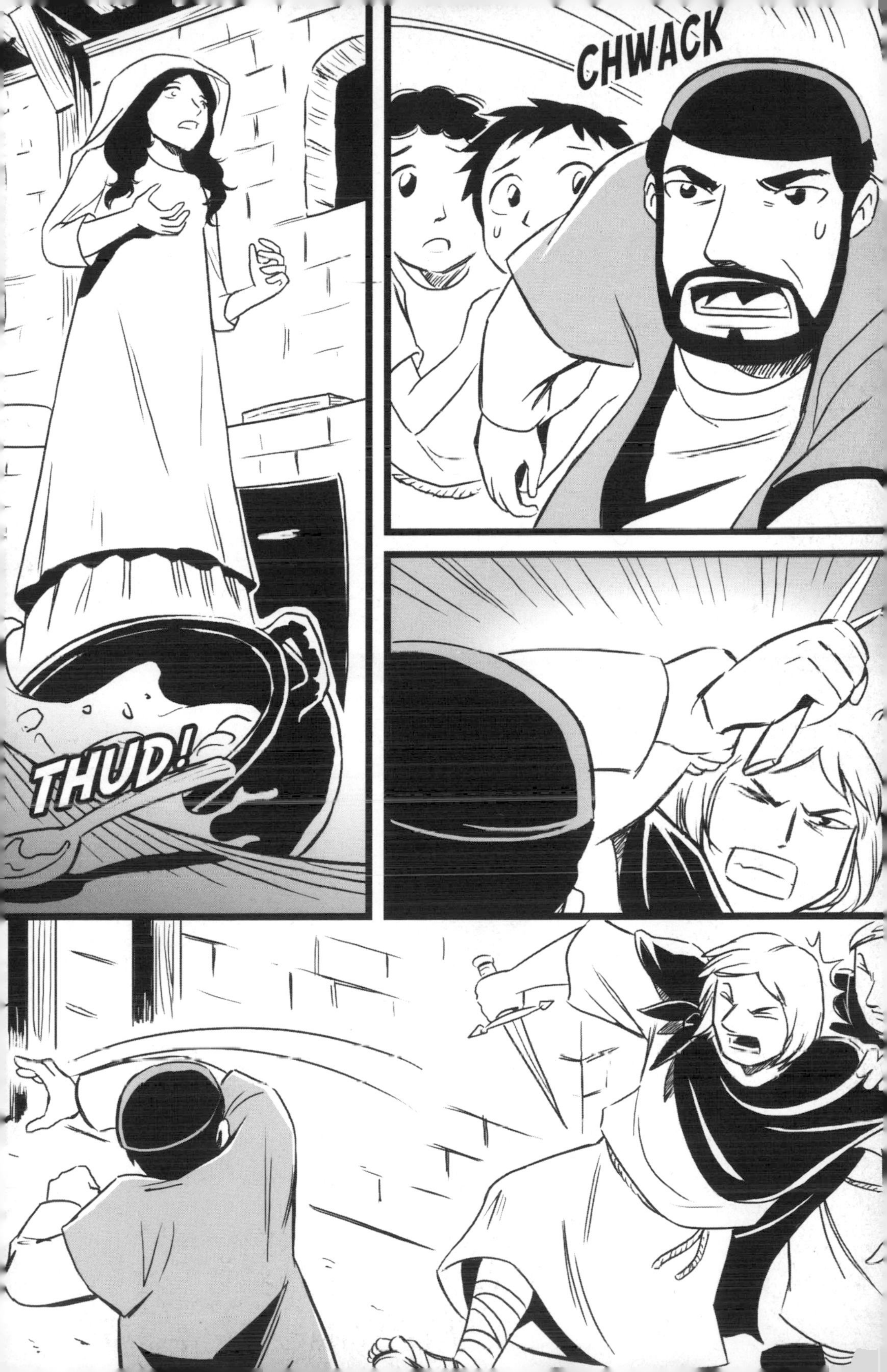
CHWACK
THUD!

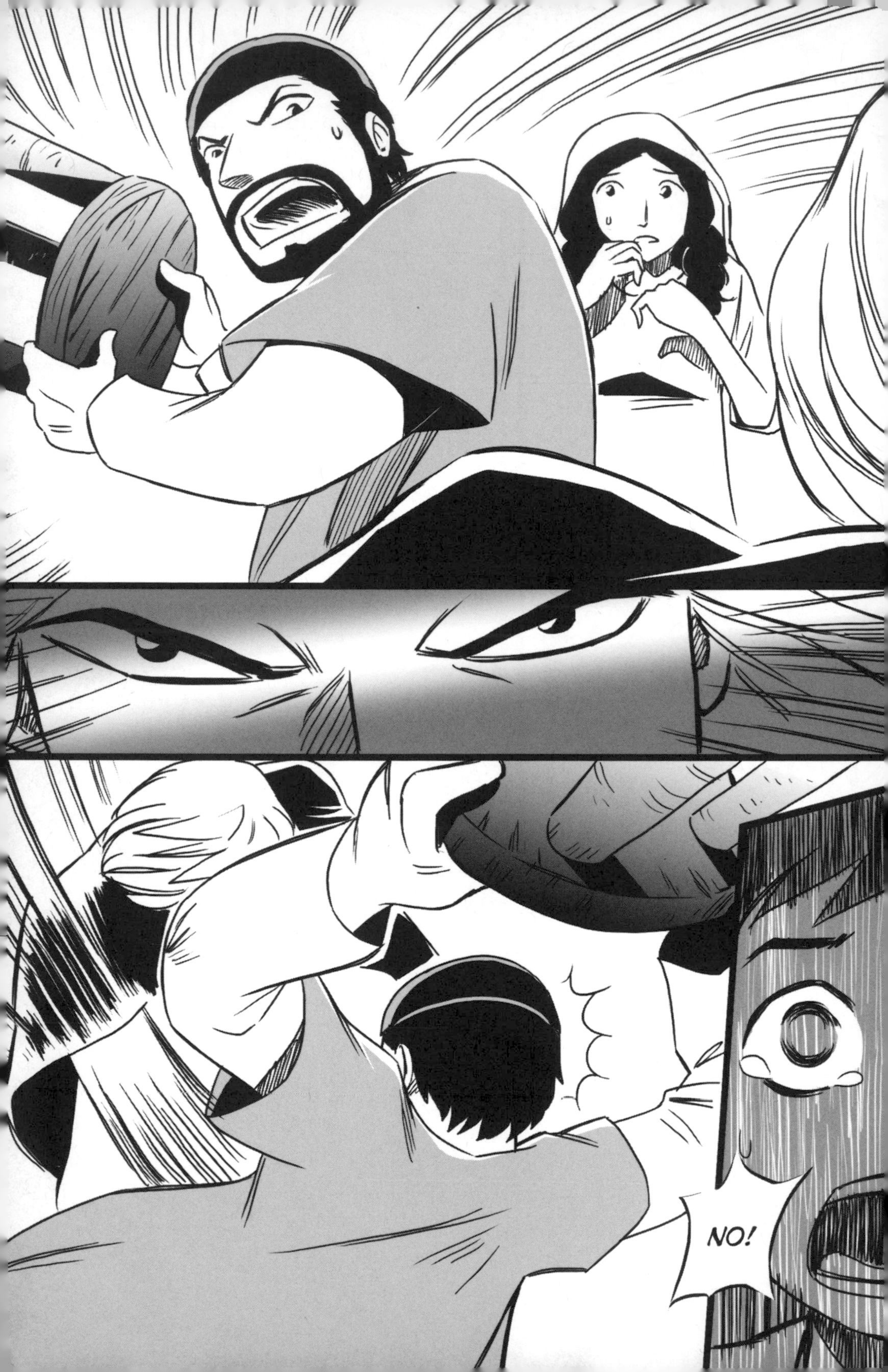
NO!

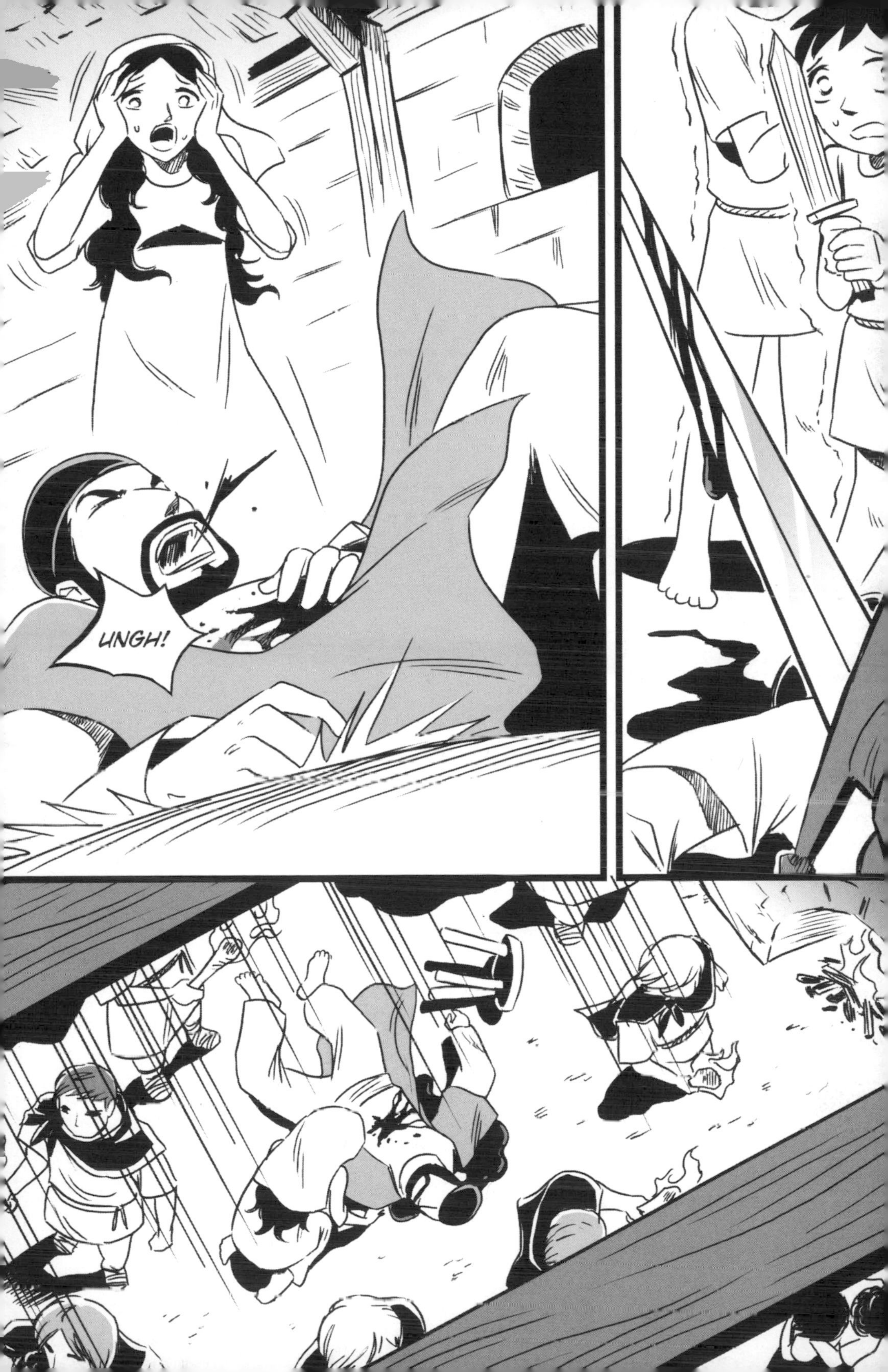
UNGH!

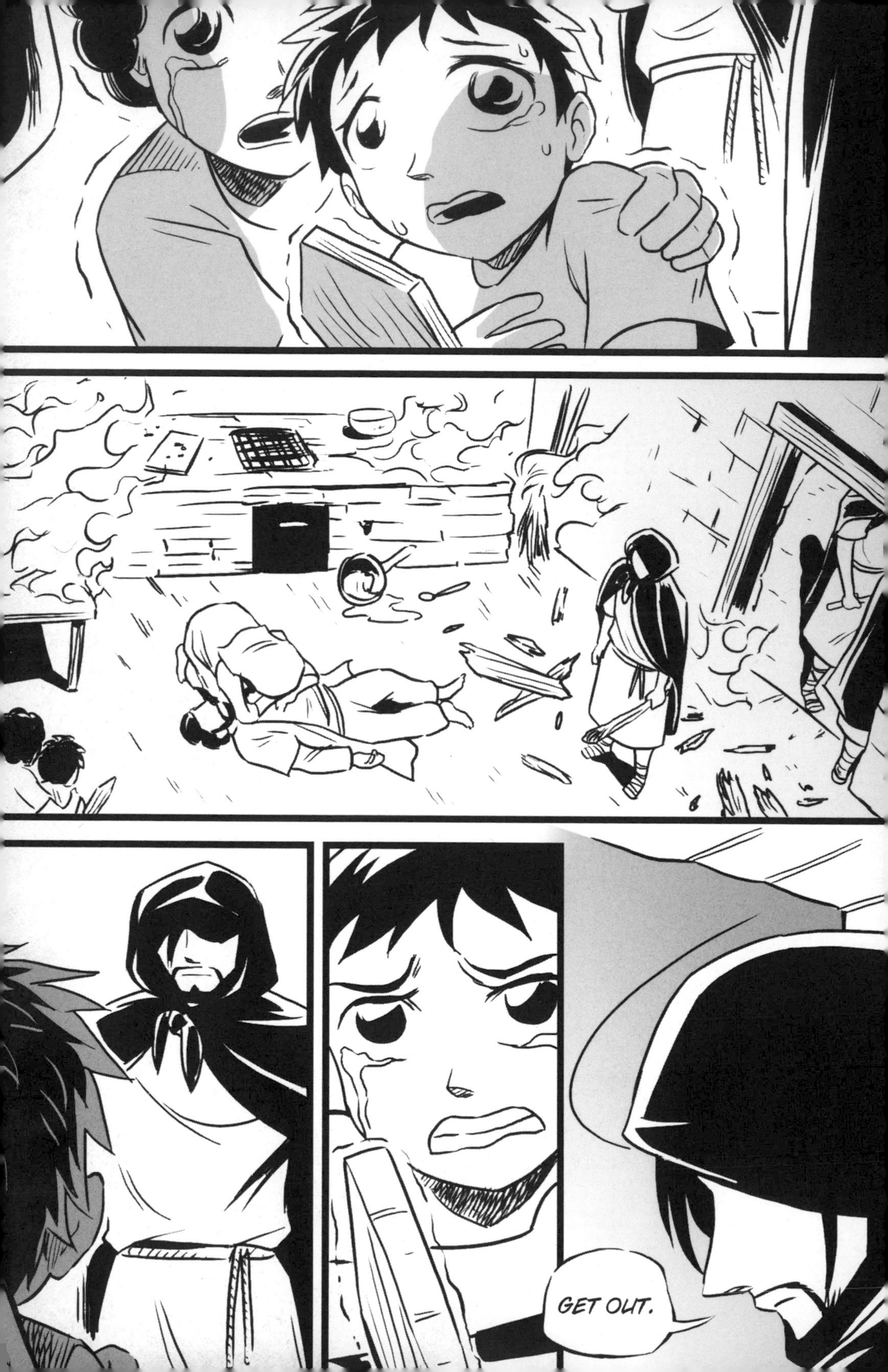
GET OUT.

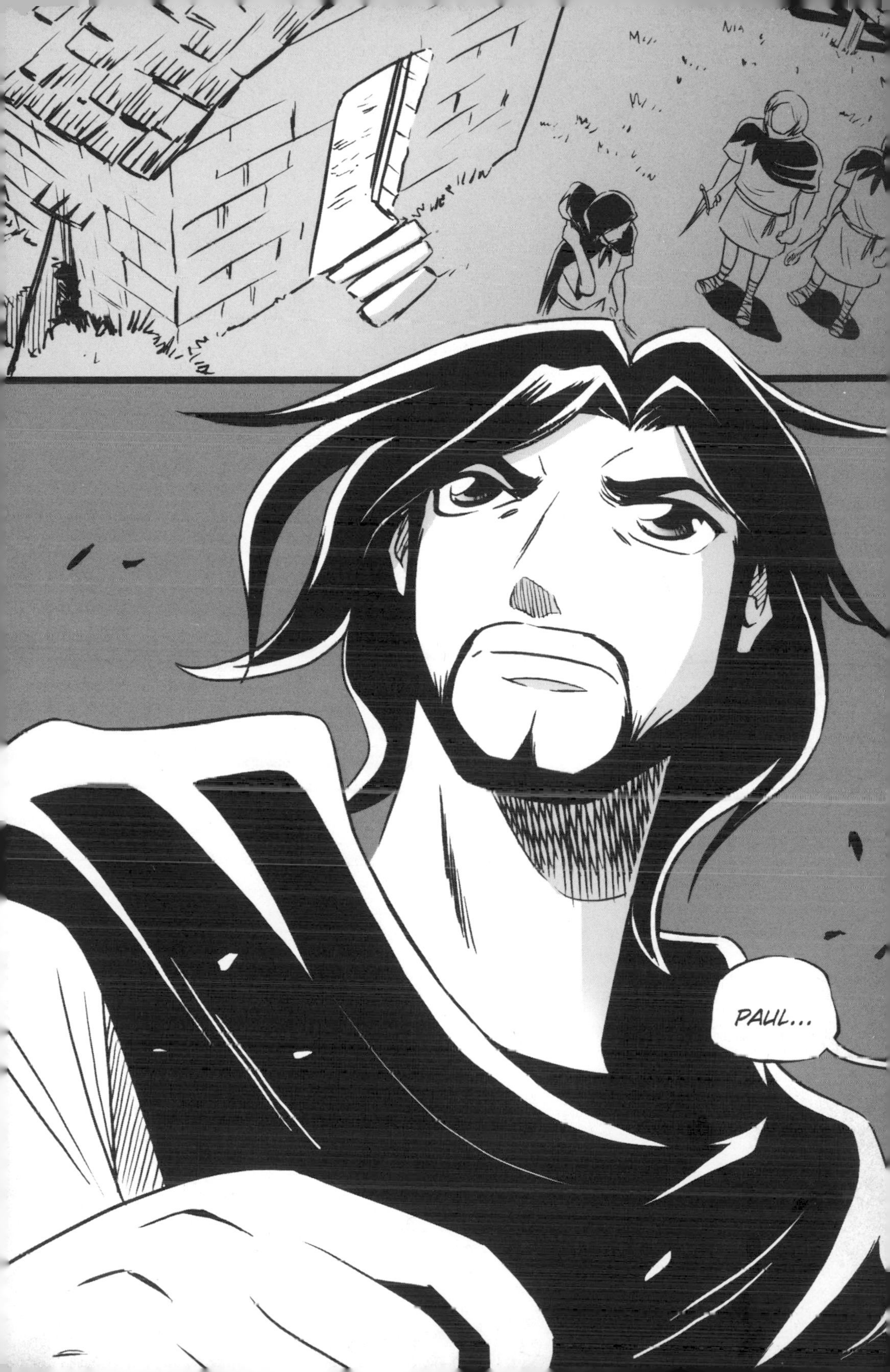
PAUL...

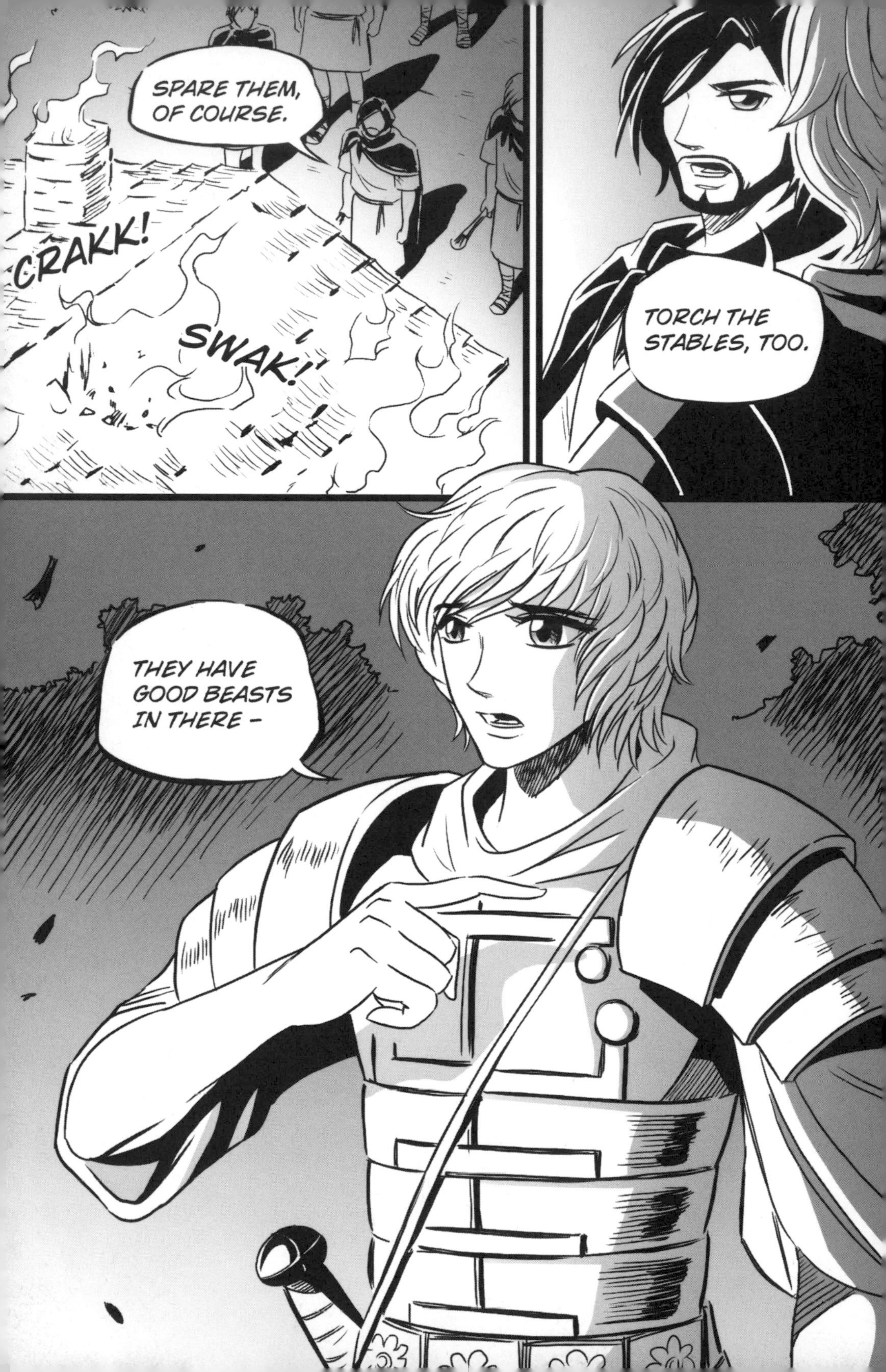
SPARE THEM, OF COURSE.
CRAKK!
SWAK!
TORCH THE STABLES, TOO.
THEY HAVE GOOD BEASTS IN THERE -

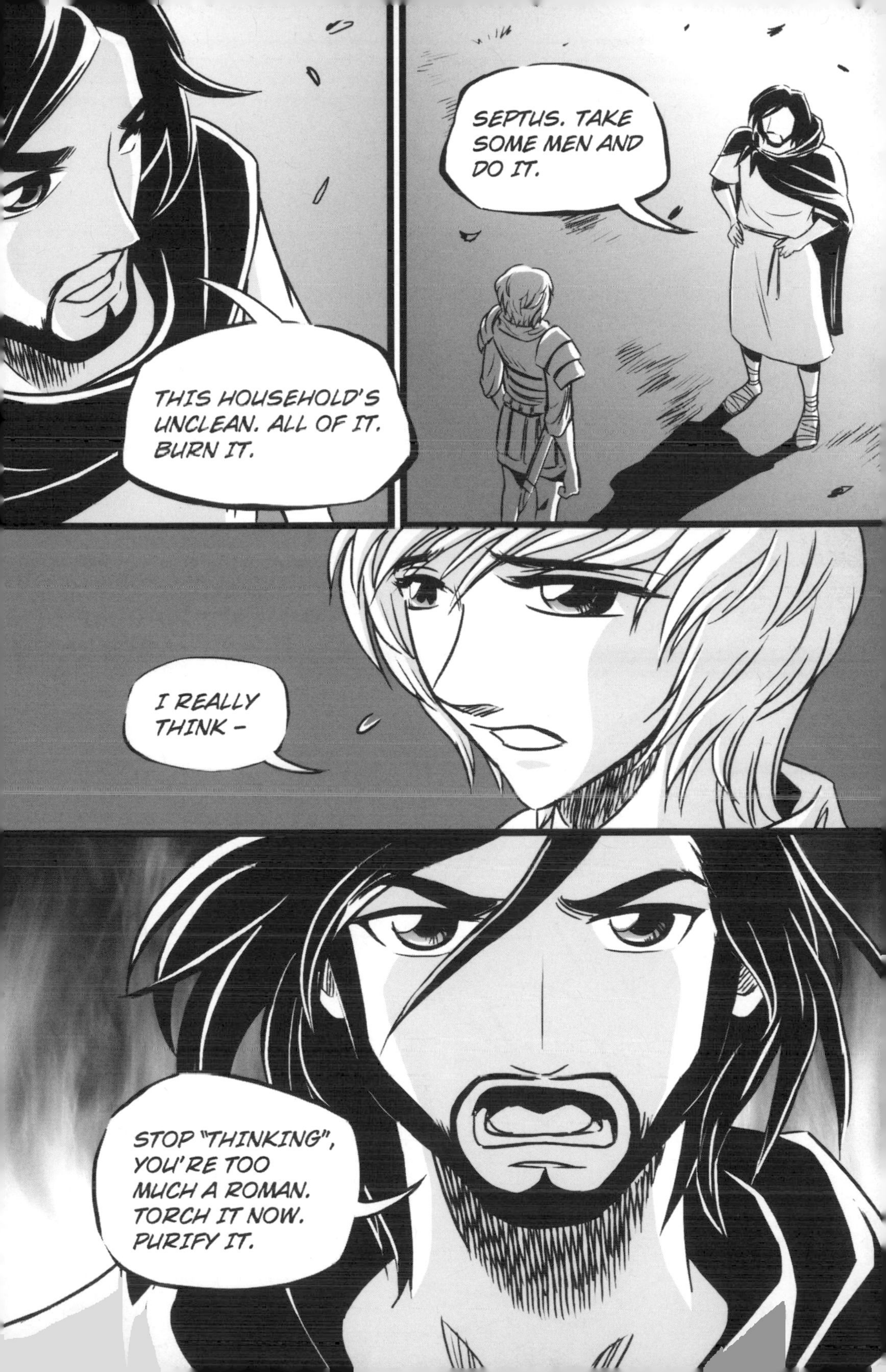
THIS HOUSEHOLD'S UNCLEAN. ALL OF IT. BURN IT.
SEPTUS. TAKE SOME MEN AND DO IT.
I REALLY THINK –
STOP "THINKING", YOU'RE TOO MUCH A ROMAN. TORCH IT NOW. PURIFY IT.

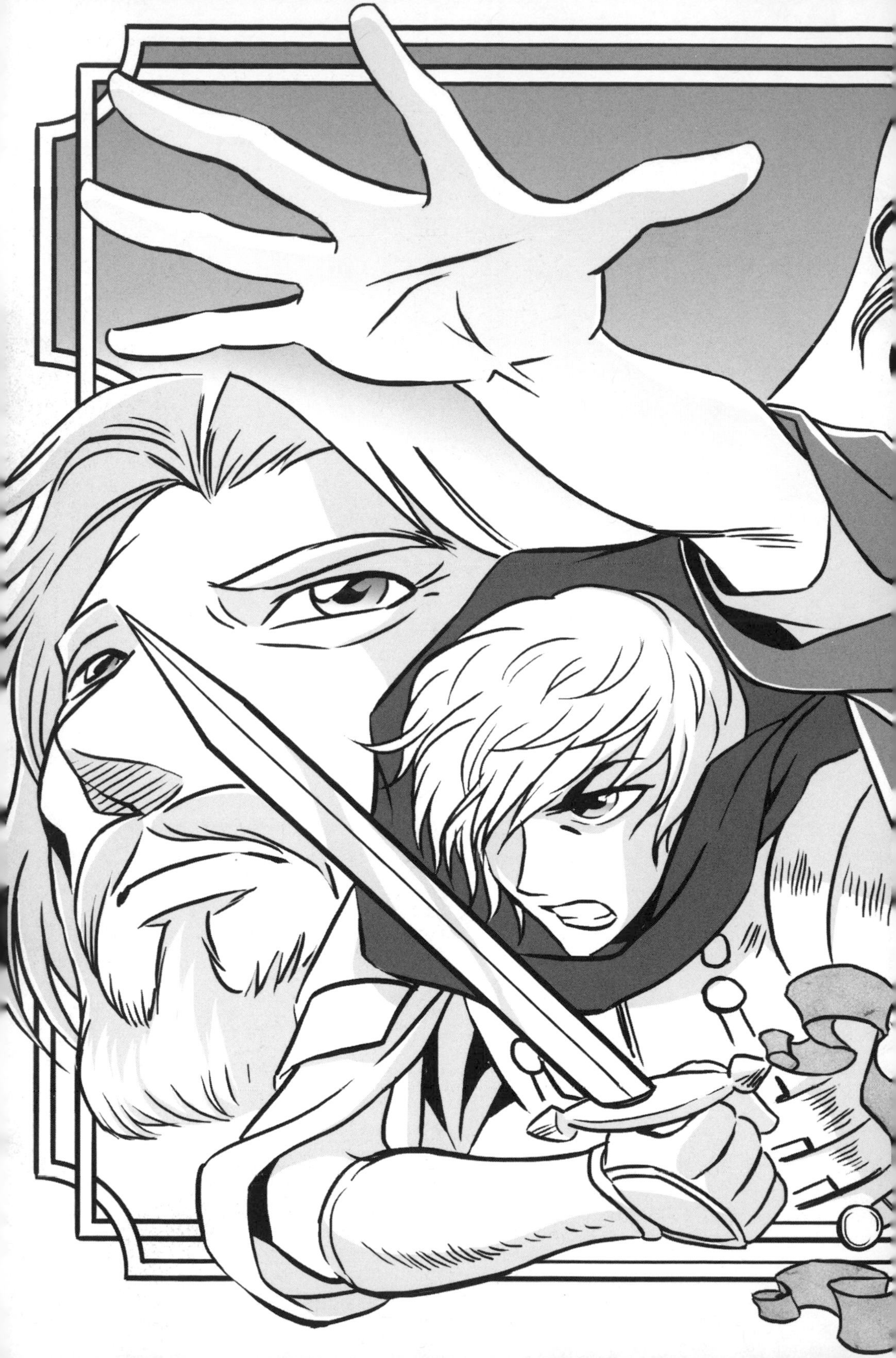

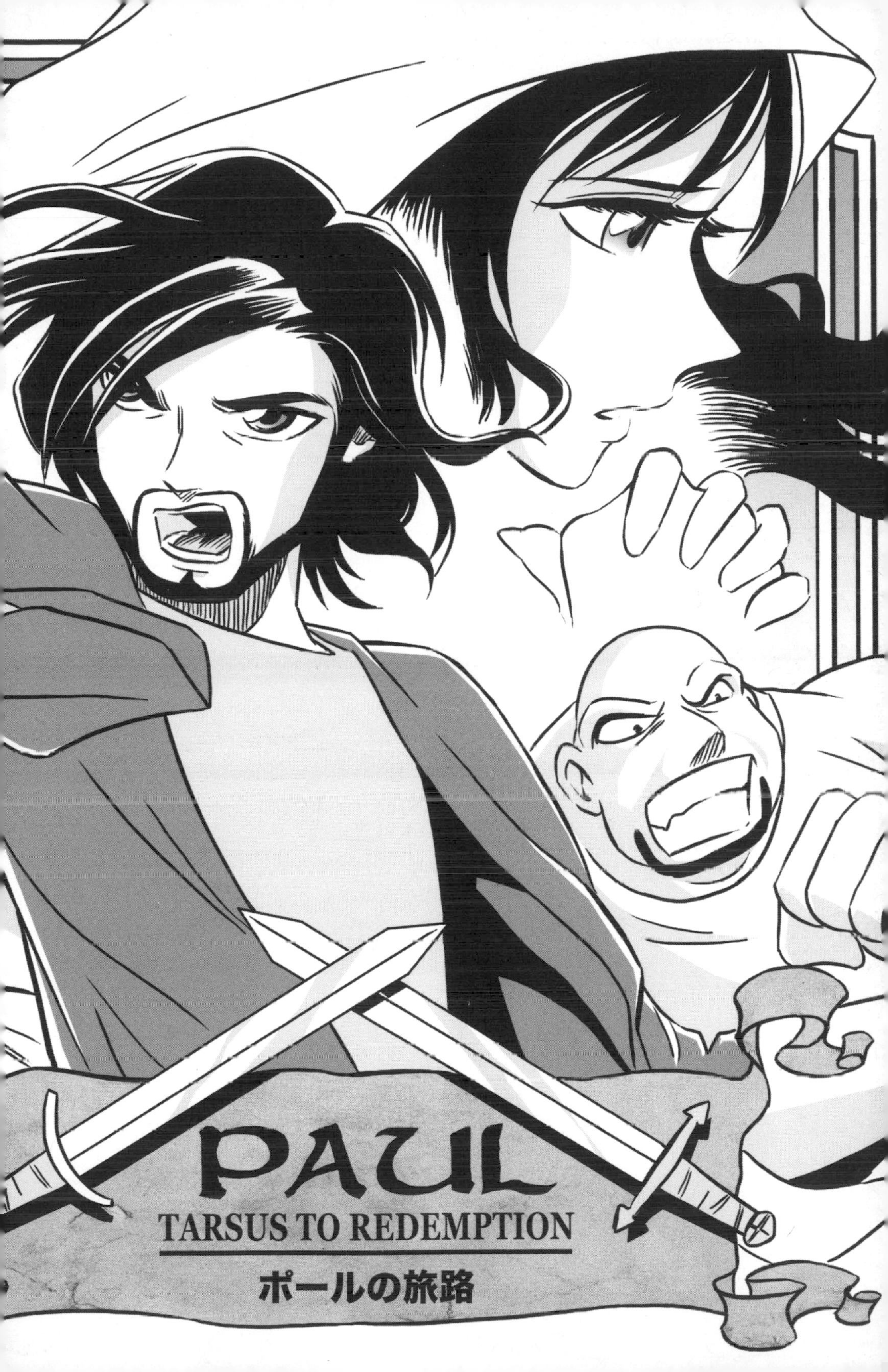
PAUL
TARSUS TO REDEMPTION
ポールの旅路

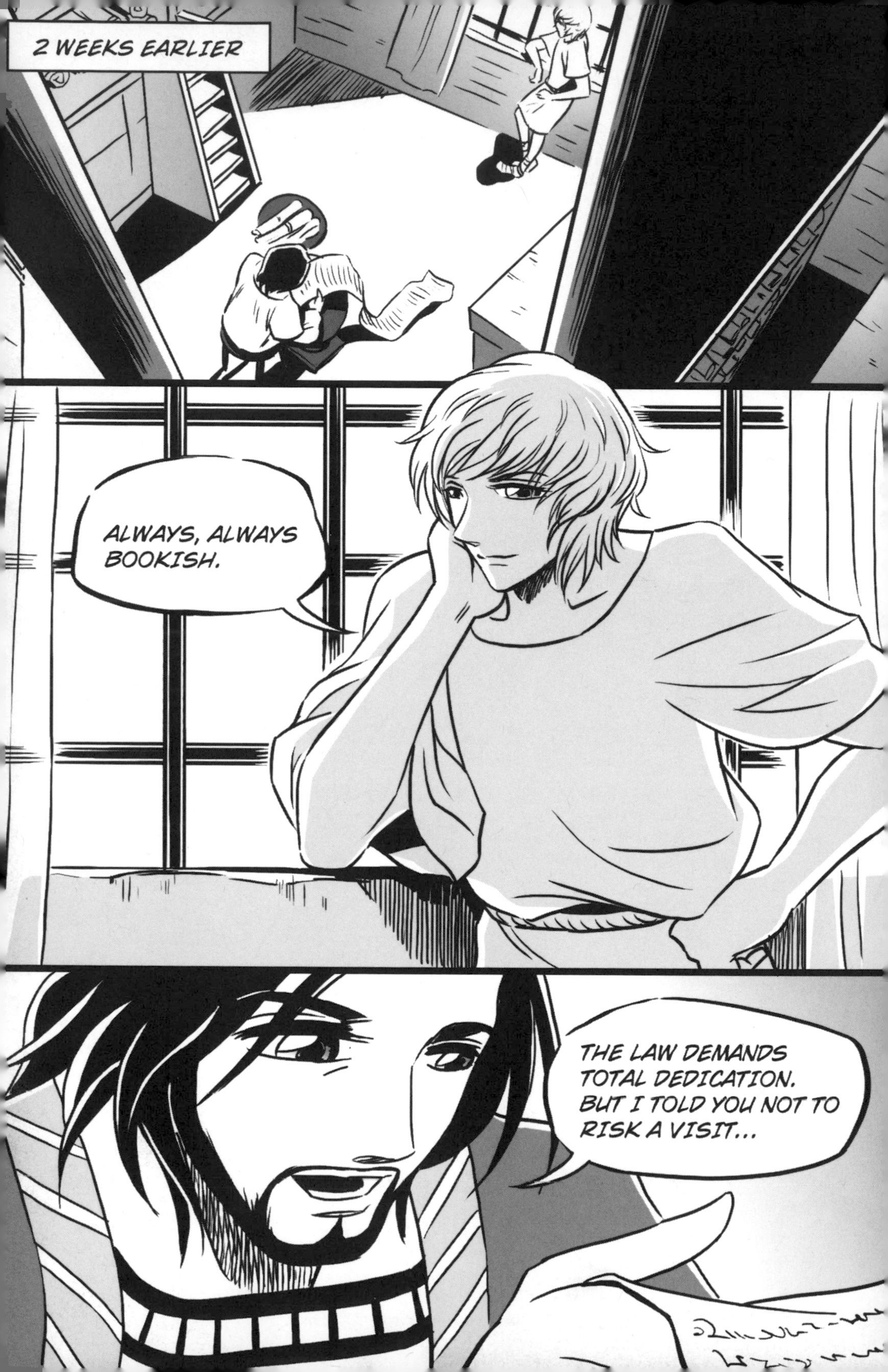
2 WEEKS EARLIER
ALWAYS, ALWAYS BOOKISH.
THE LAW DEMANDS TOTAL DEDICATION. BUT I TOLD YOU NOT TO RISK A VISIT...

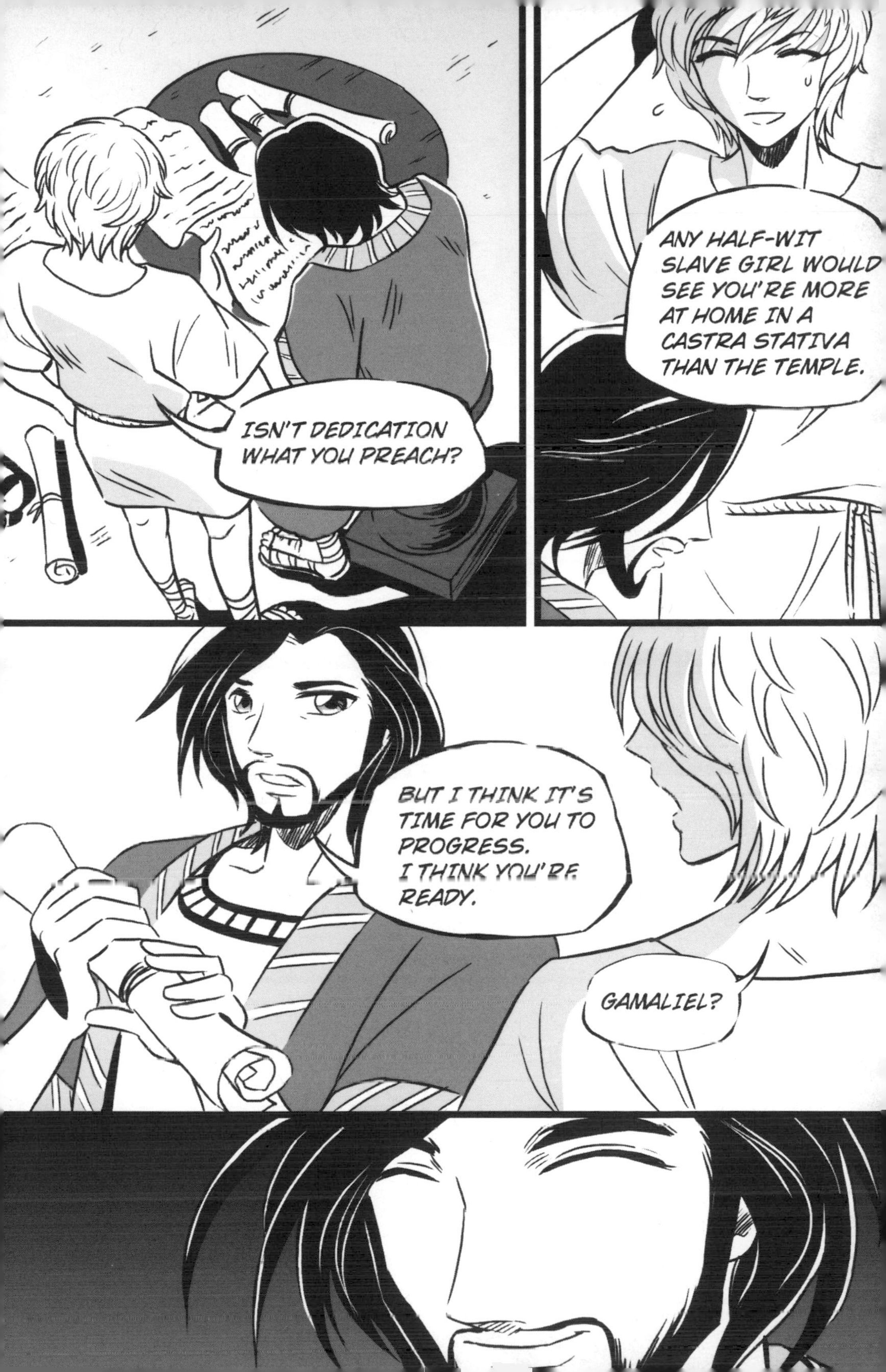
ISN'T DEDICATION WHAT YOU PREACH?
ANY HALF-WIT SLAVE GIRL WOULD SEE YOU'RE MORE AT HOME IN A CASTRA STATIVA THAN THE TEMPLE.
BUT I THINK IT'S TIME FOR YOU TO PROGRESS. I THINK YOU'RE READY.
GAMALIEL?

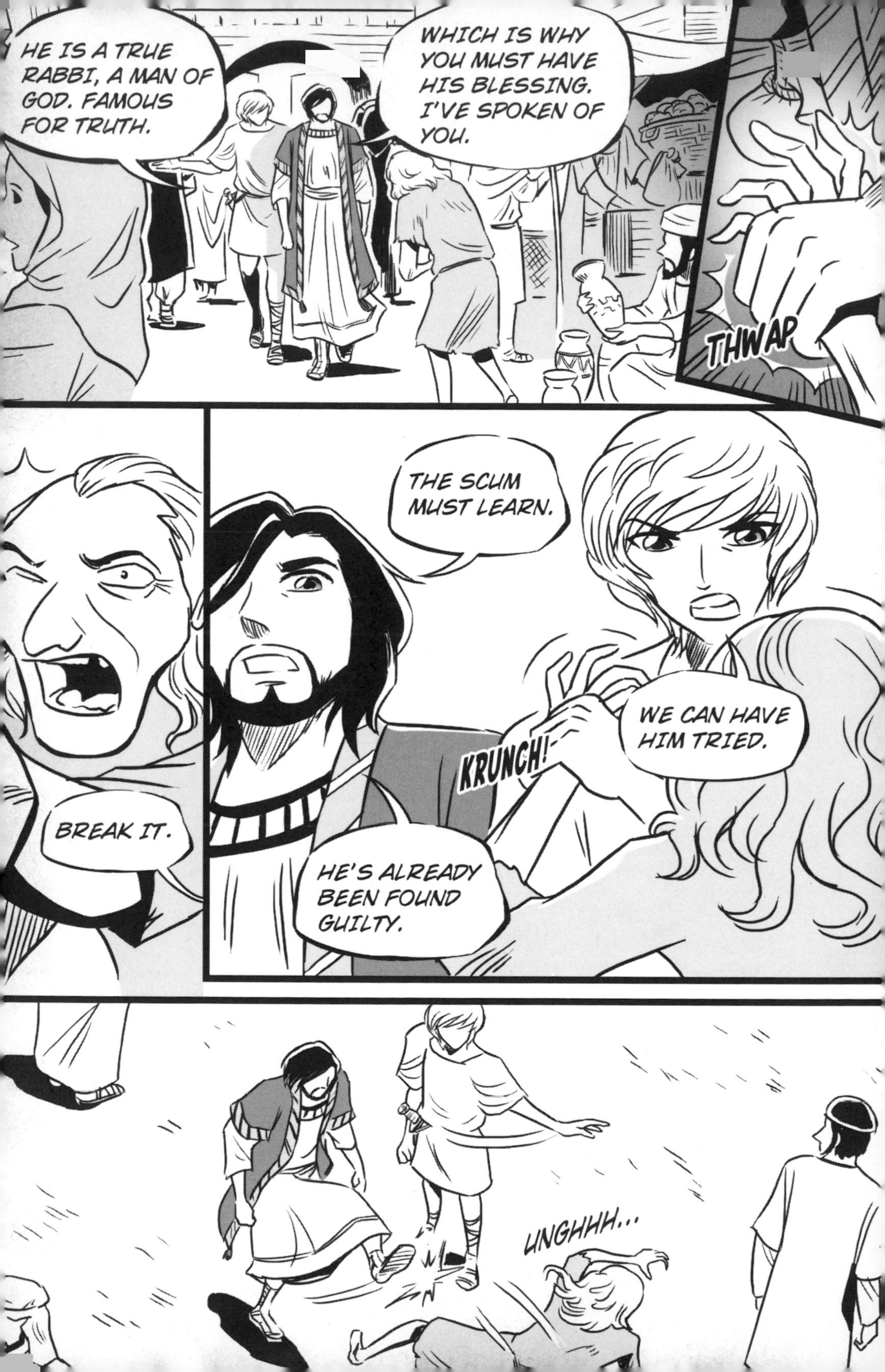
HE IS A TRUE RABBI, A MAN OF GOD. FAMOUS FOR TRUTH.
WHICH IS WHY YOU MUST HAVE HIS BLESSING. I'VE SPOKEN OF YOU.
THWAP
THE SCUM MUST LEARN.
BREAK IT.
KRUNCH!
WE CAN HAVE HIM TRIED.
HE'S ALREADY BEEN FOUND GUILTY.
UNGHHH...

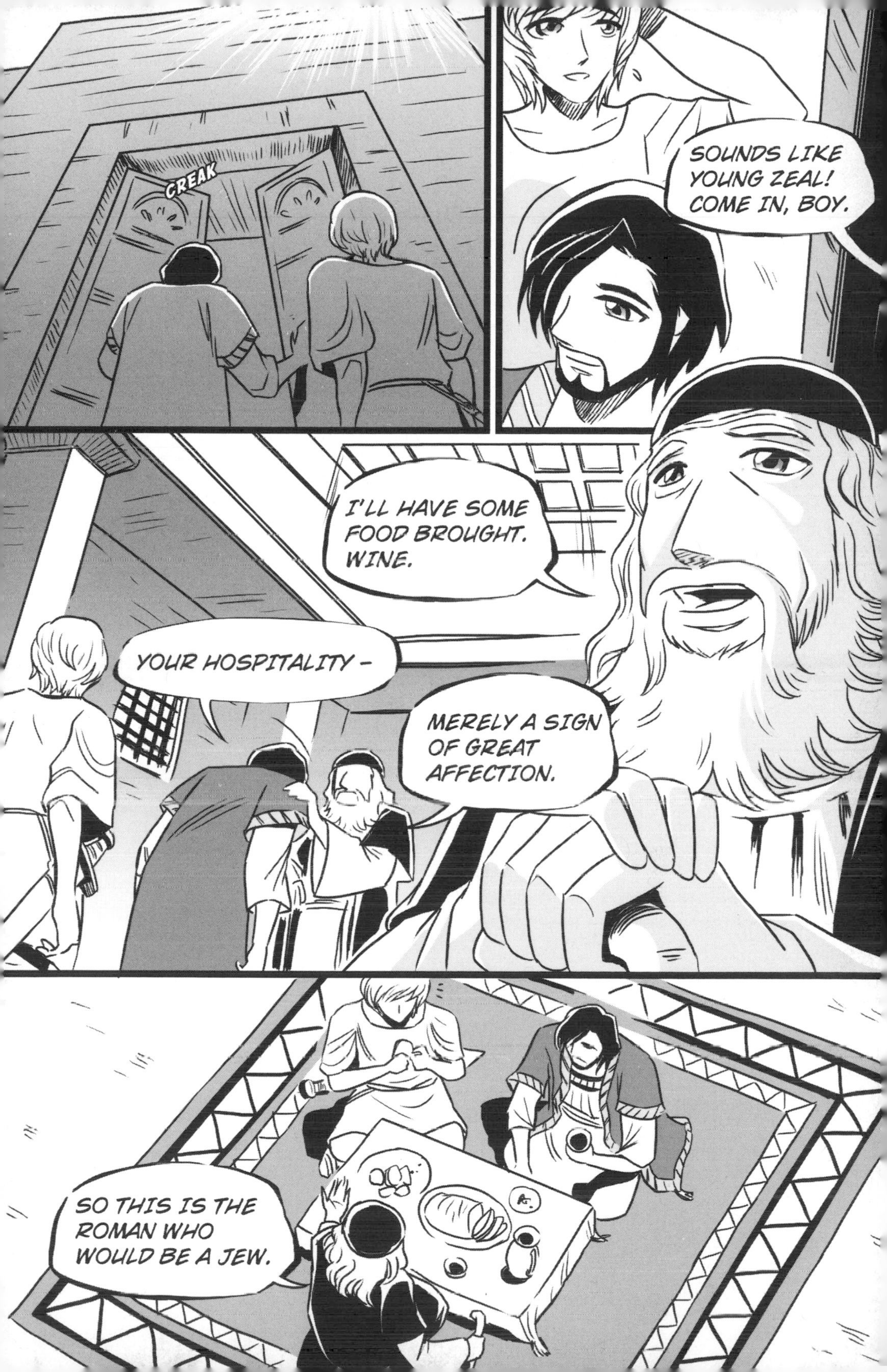
CREAK
SOUNDS LIKE YOUNG ZEAL! COME IN, BOY.
I'LL HAVE SOME FOOD BROUGHT. WINE.
YOUR HOSPITALITY –
MERELY A SIGN OF GREAT AFFECTION.
SO THIS IS THE ROMAN WHO WOULD BE A JEW.

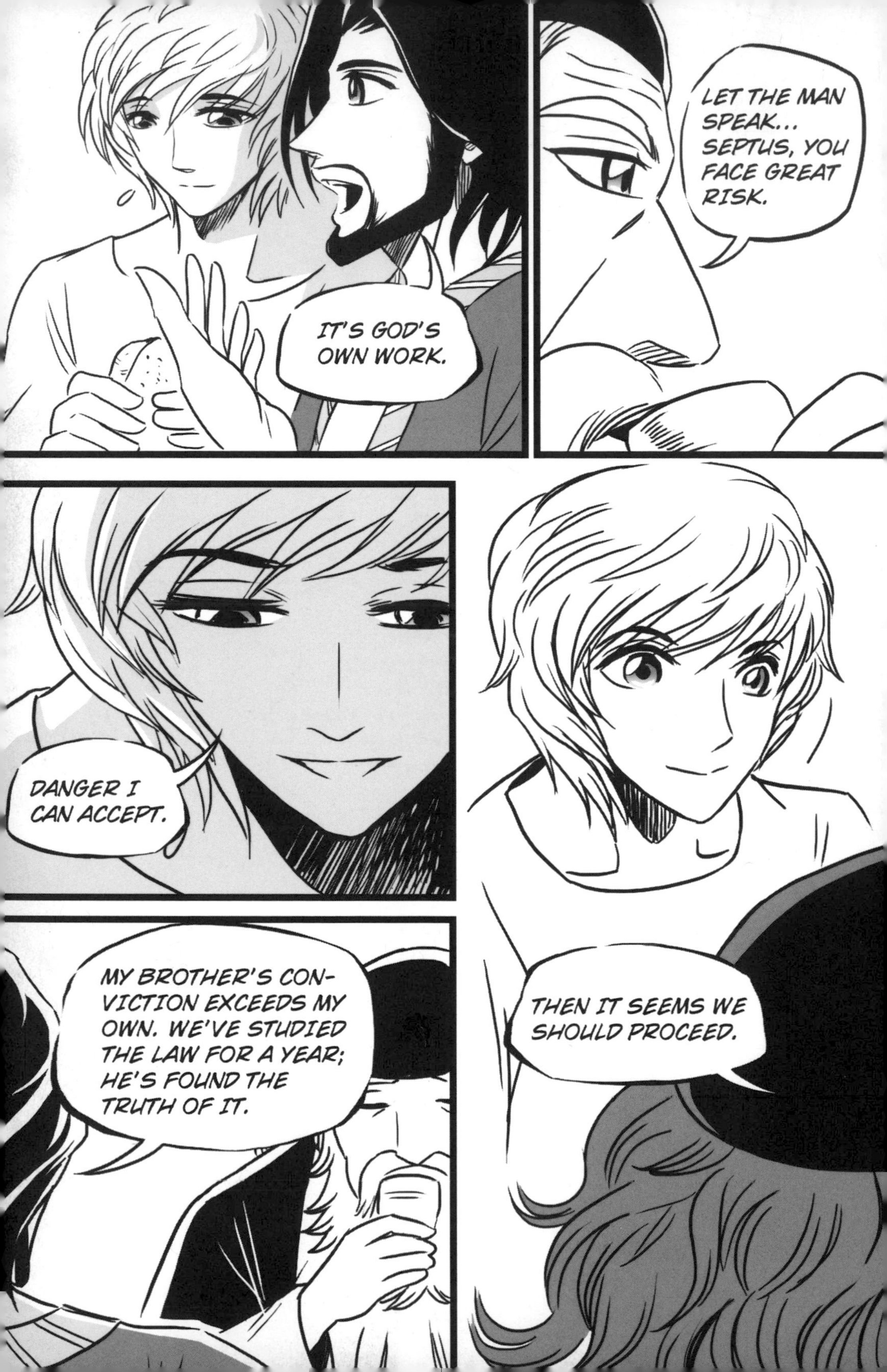
IT'S GOD'S OWN WORK.
LET THE MAN SPEAK... SEPTUS, YOU FACE GREAT RISK.
DANGER I CAN ACCEPT.
MY BROTHER'S CON-VICTION EXCEEDS MY OWN. WE'VE STUDIED THE LAW FOR A YEAR; HE'S FOUND THE TRUTH OF IT.
THEN IT SEEMS WE SHOULD PROCEED.

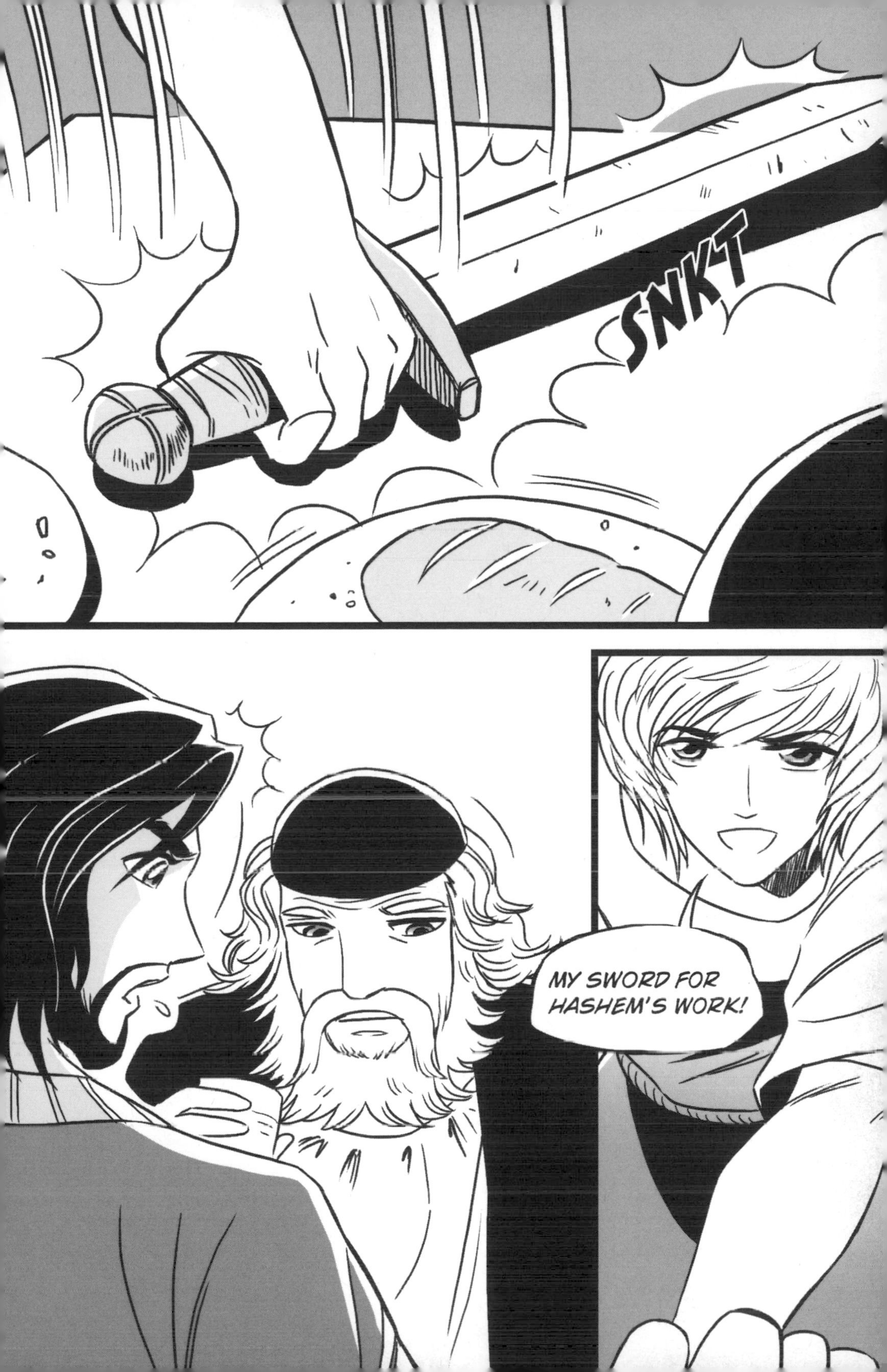
SNKT
MY SWORD FOR HASHEM'S WORK!

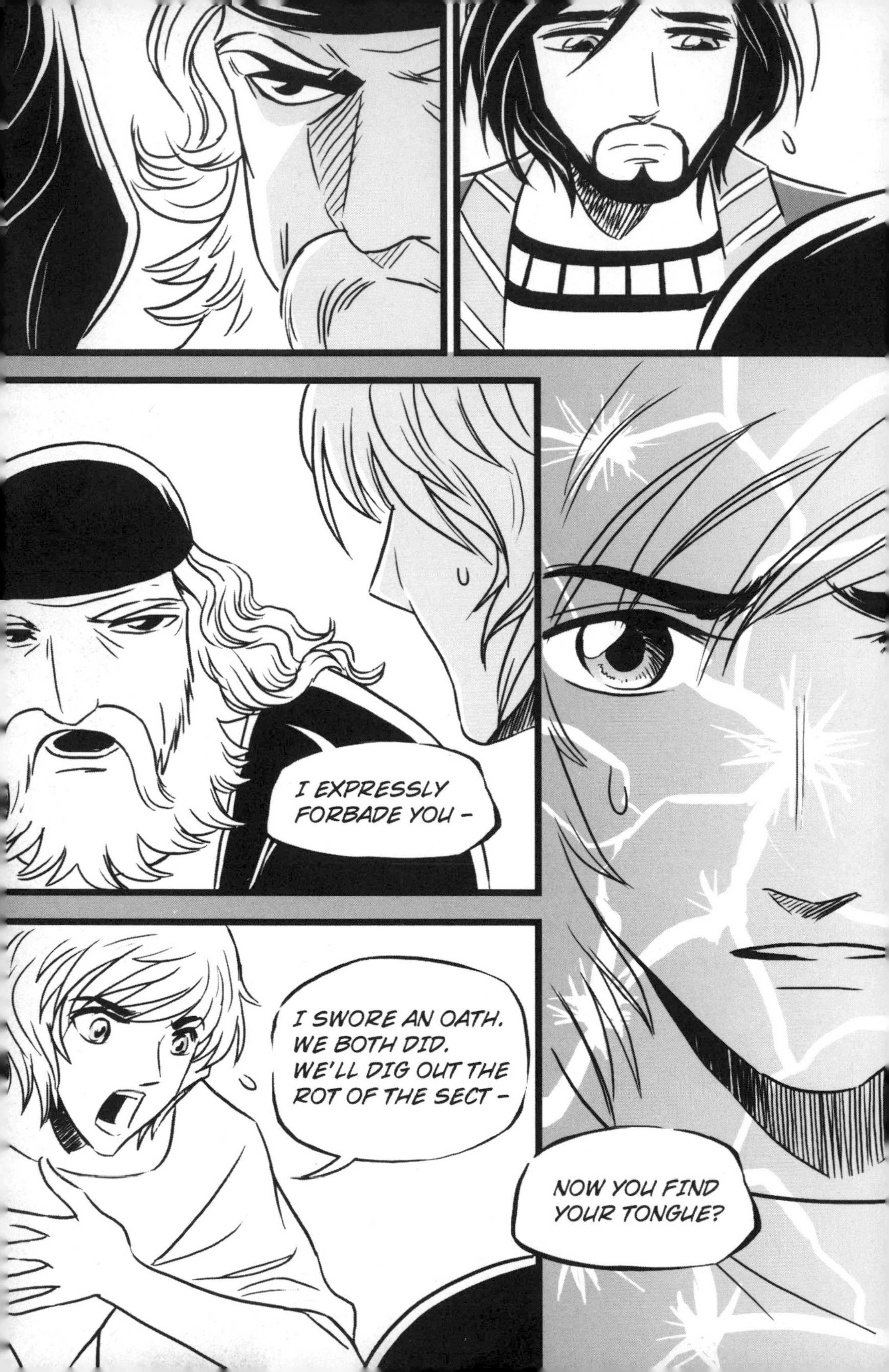
I EXPRESSLY FORBADE YOU -
I SWORE AN OATH. WE BOTH DID. WE'LL DIG OUT THE ROT OF THE SECT -
NOW YOU FIND YOUR TONGUE?

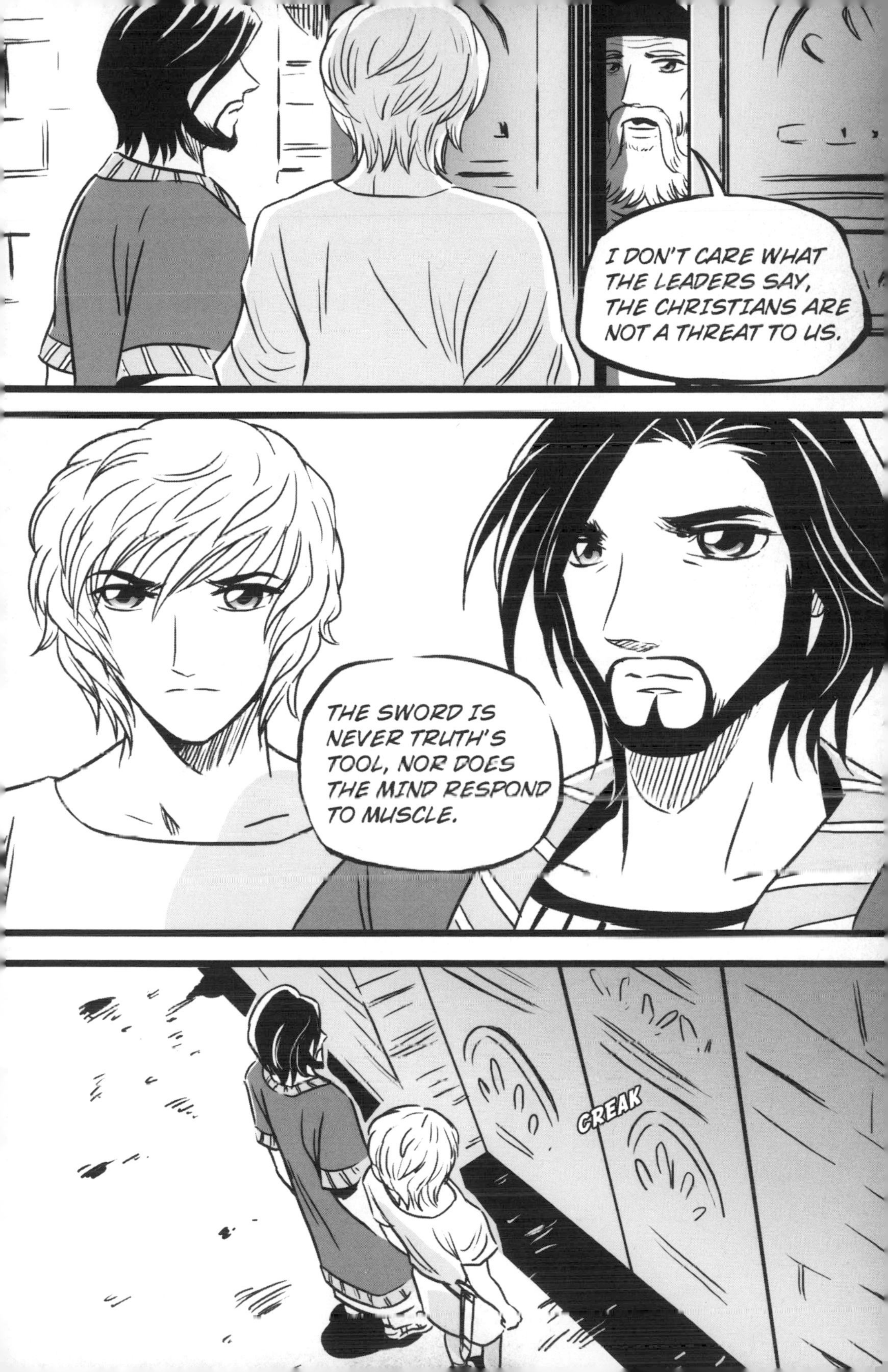
I DON'T CARE WHAT THE LEADERS SAY, THE CHRISTIANS ARE NOT A THREAT TO US.
THE SWORD IS NEVER TRUTH'S TOOL, NOR DOES THE MIND RESPOND TO MUSCLE.
CREAK

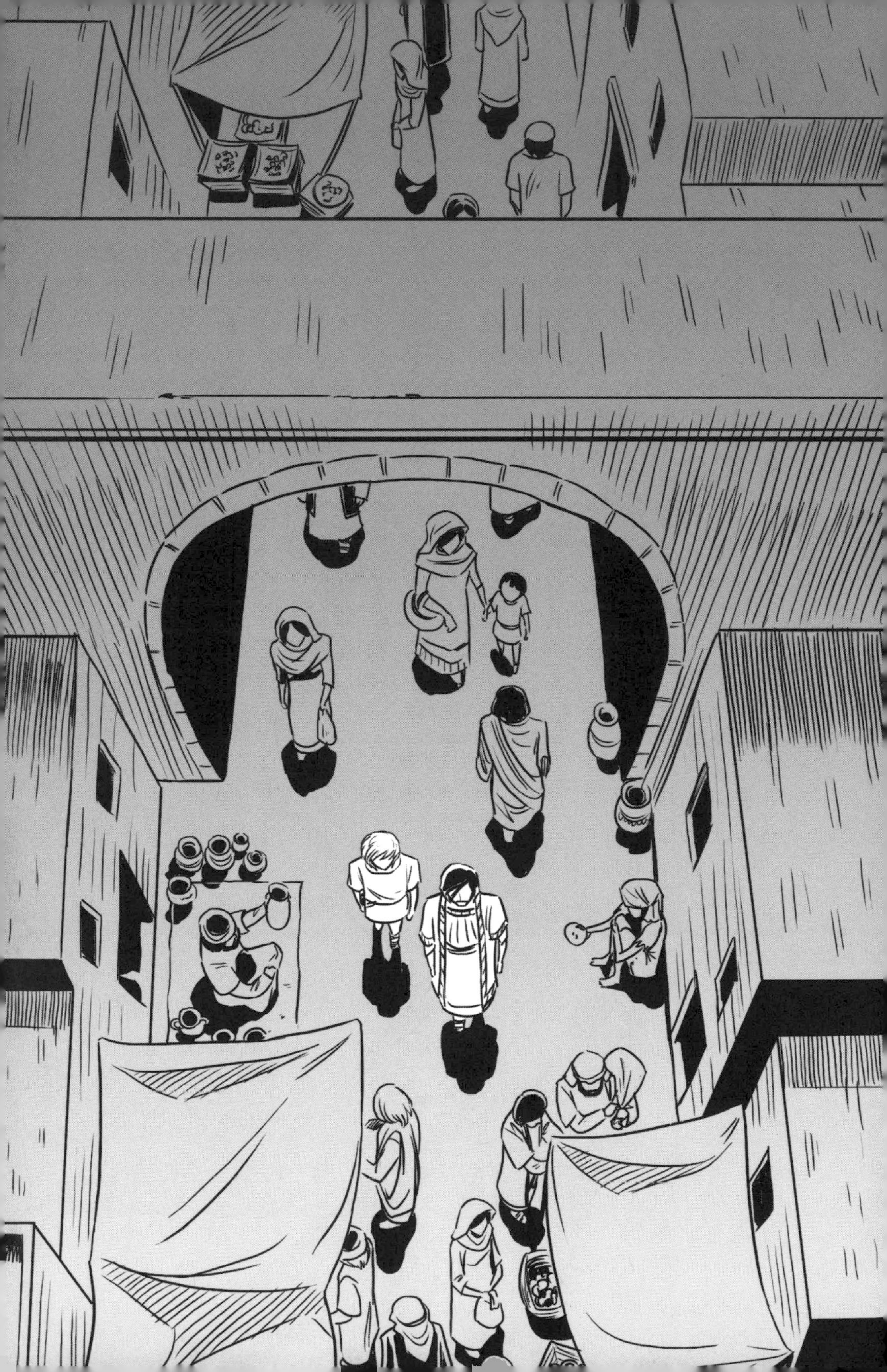

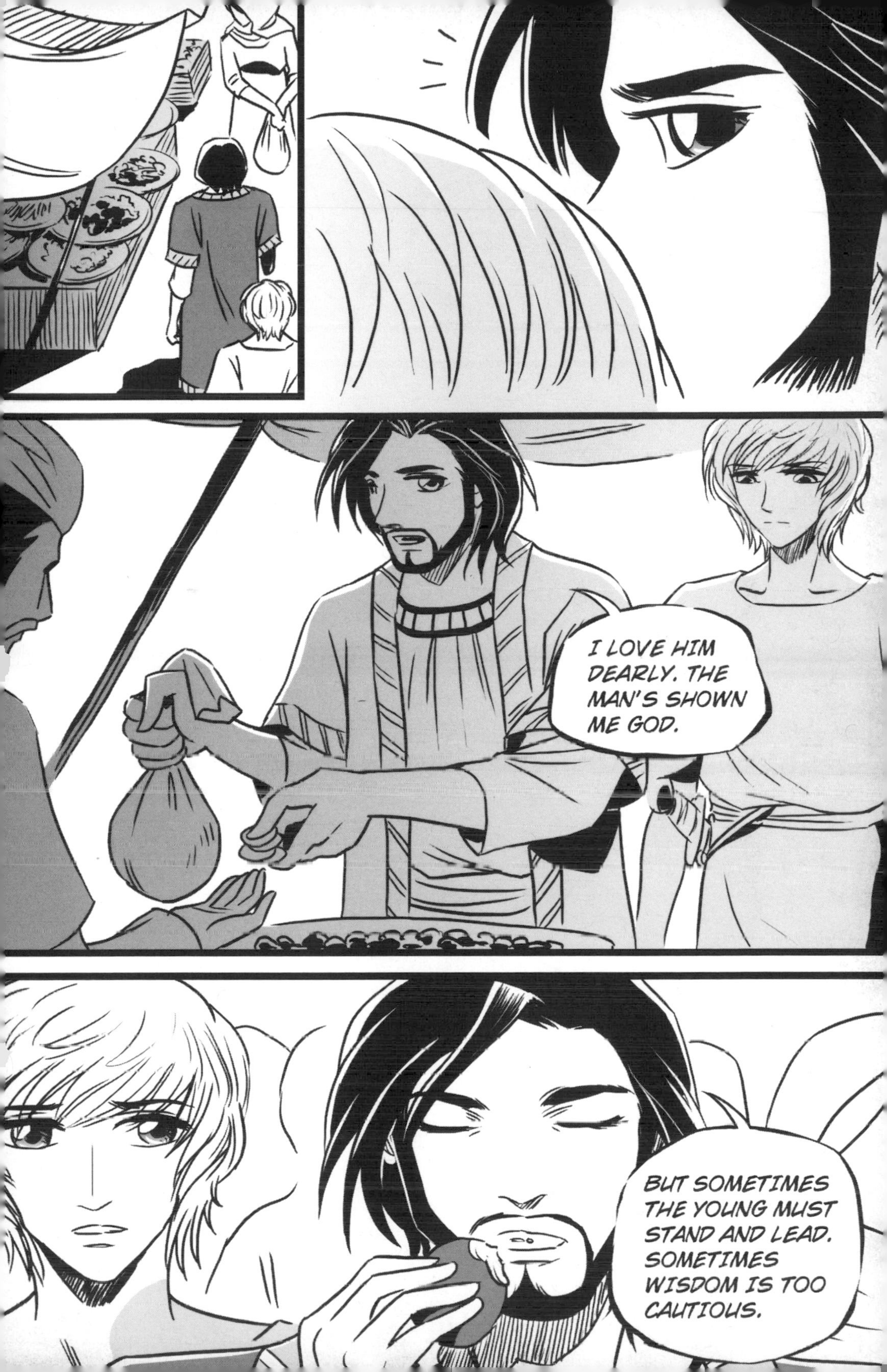
I LOVE HIM DEARLY. THE MAN'S SHOWN ME GOD.
BUT SOMETIMES THE YOUNG MUST STAND AND LEAD. SOMETIMES WISDOM IS TOO CAUTIOUS.

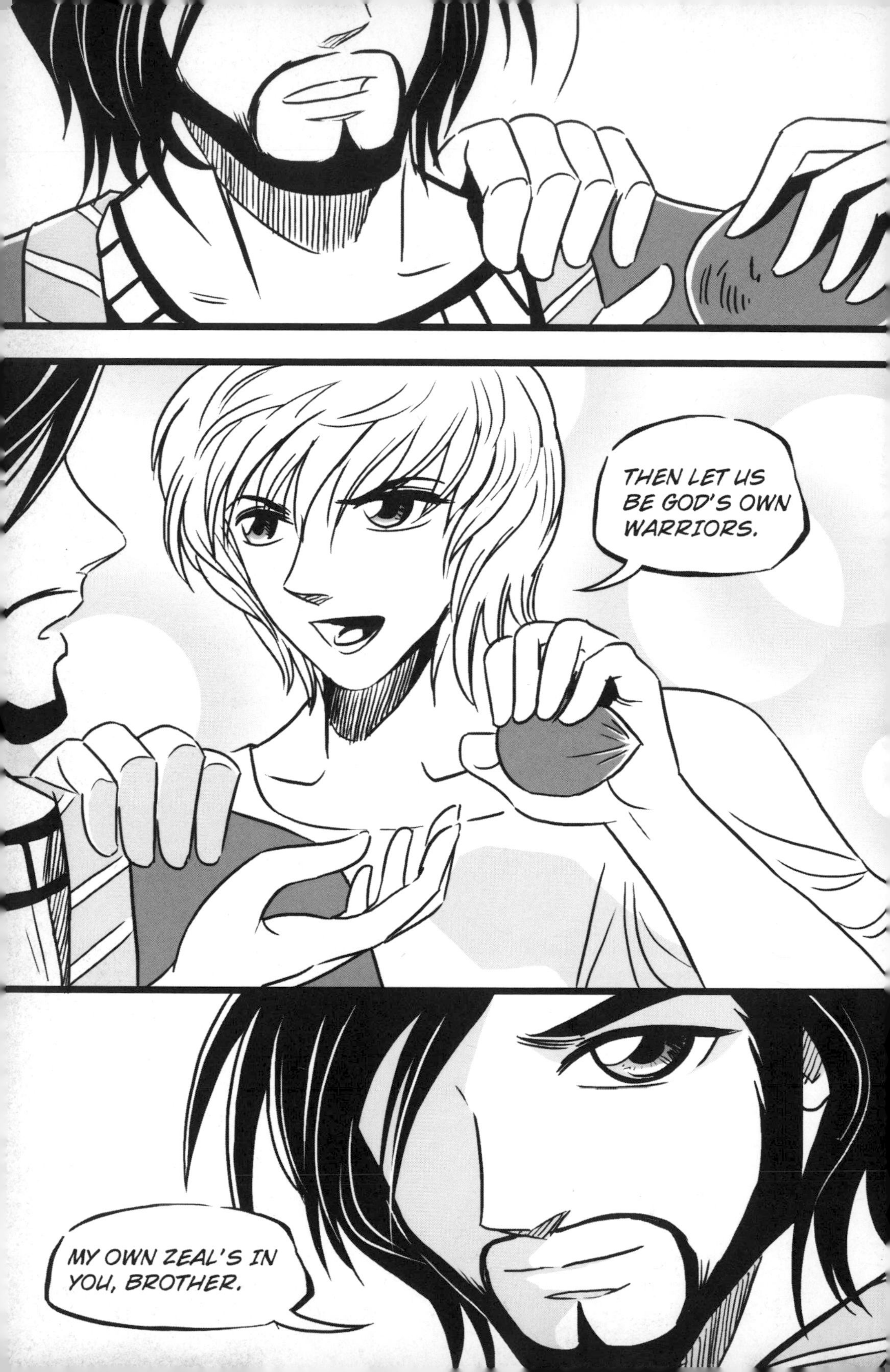
THEN LET US BE GOD'S OWN WARRIORS.
MY OWN ZEAL'S IN YOU, BROTHER.

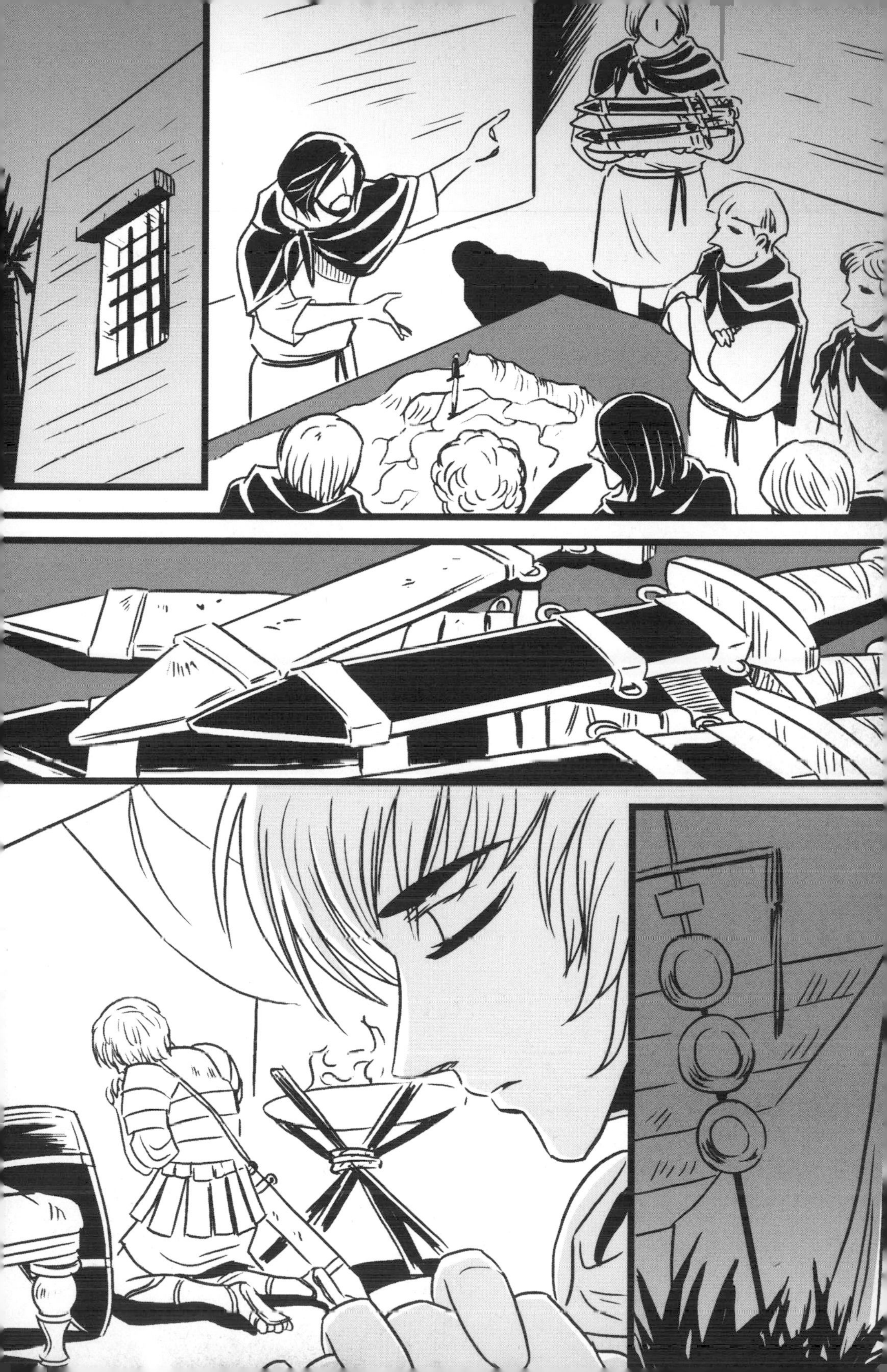

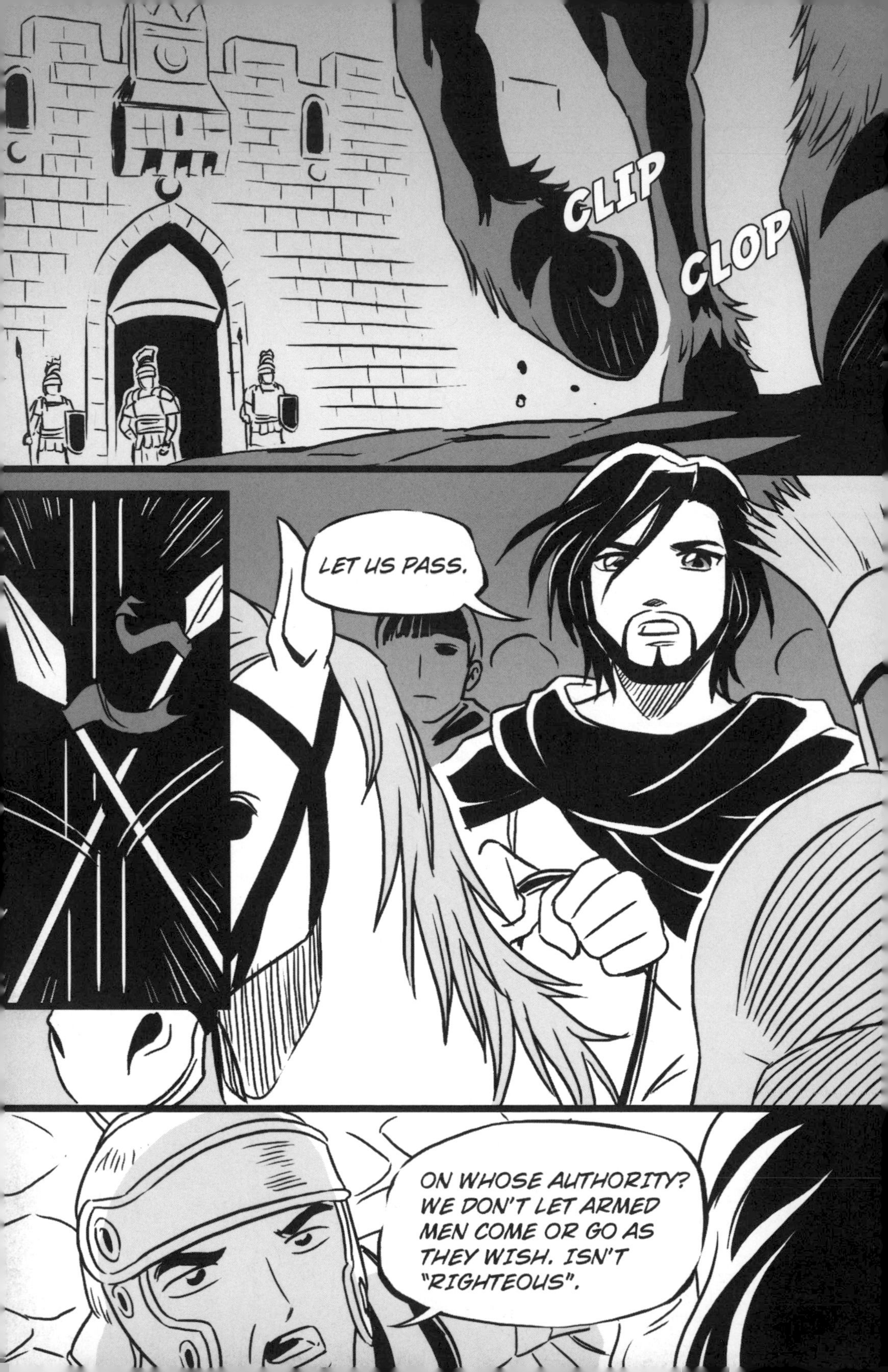
CLIP
CLOP
LET US PASS.
ON WHOSE AUTHORITY? WE DON'T LET ARMED MEN COME OR GO AS THEY WISH. ISN'T "RIGHTEOUS".

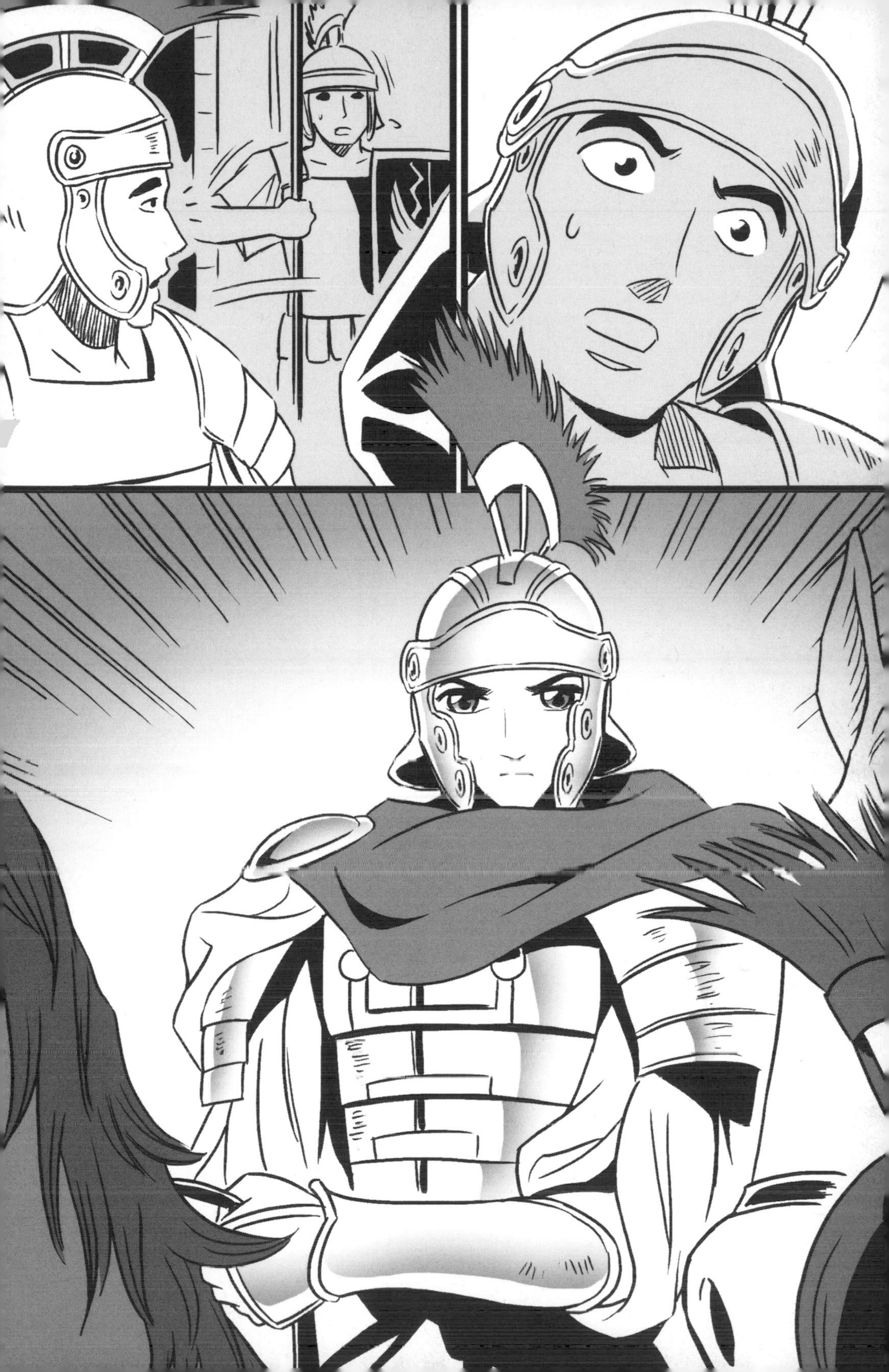

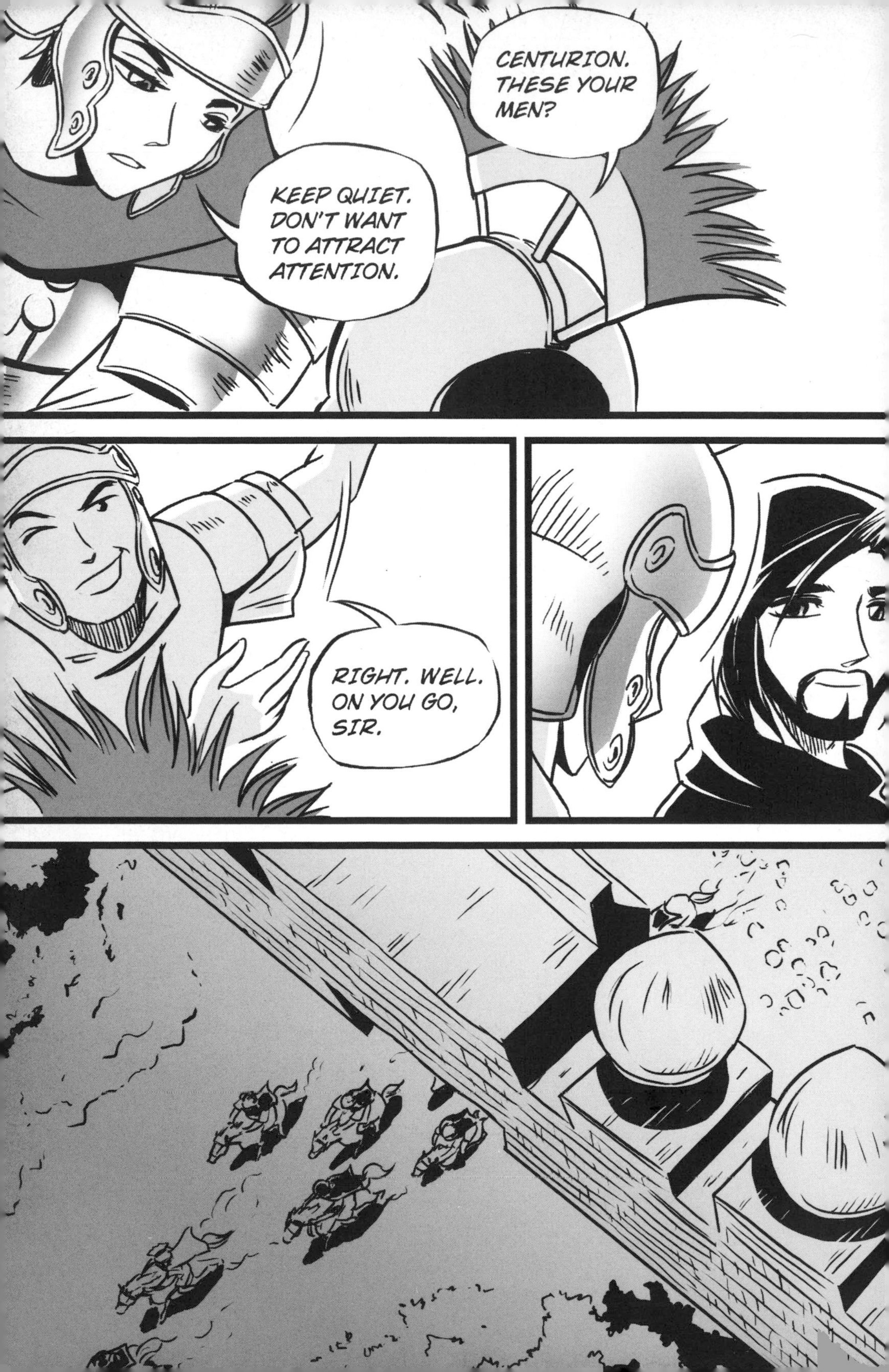
CENTURION. THESE YOUR MEN?
KEEP QUIET. DON'T WANT TO ATTRACT ATTENTION.
RIGHT. WELL. ON YOU GO, SIR.

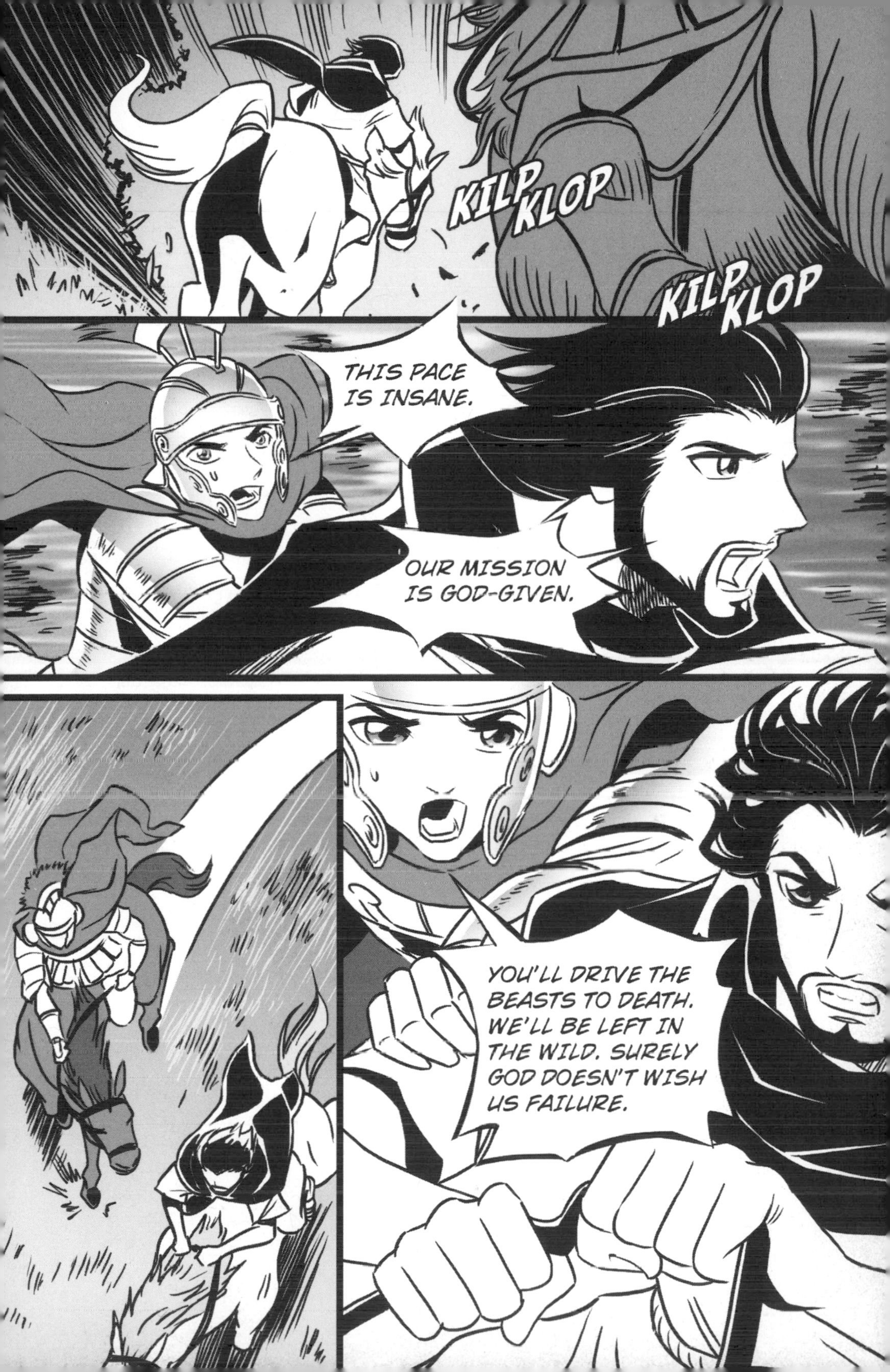

KILP KLOP
KILP KLOP
THIS PACE IS INSANE.
OUR MISSION IS GOD-GIVEN.
YOU'LL DRIVE THE BEASTS TO DEATH. WE'LL BE LEFT IN THE WILD. SURELY GOD DOESN'T WISH US FAILURE.

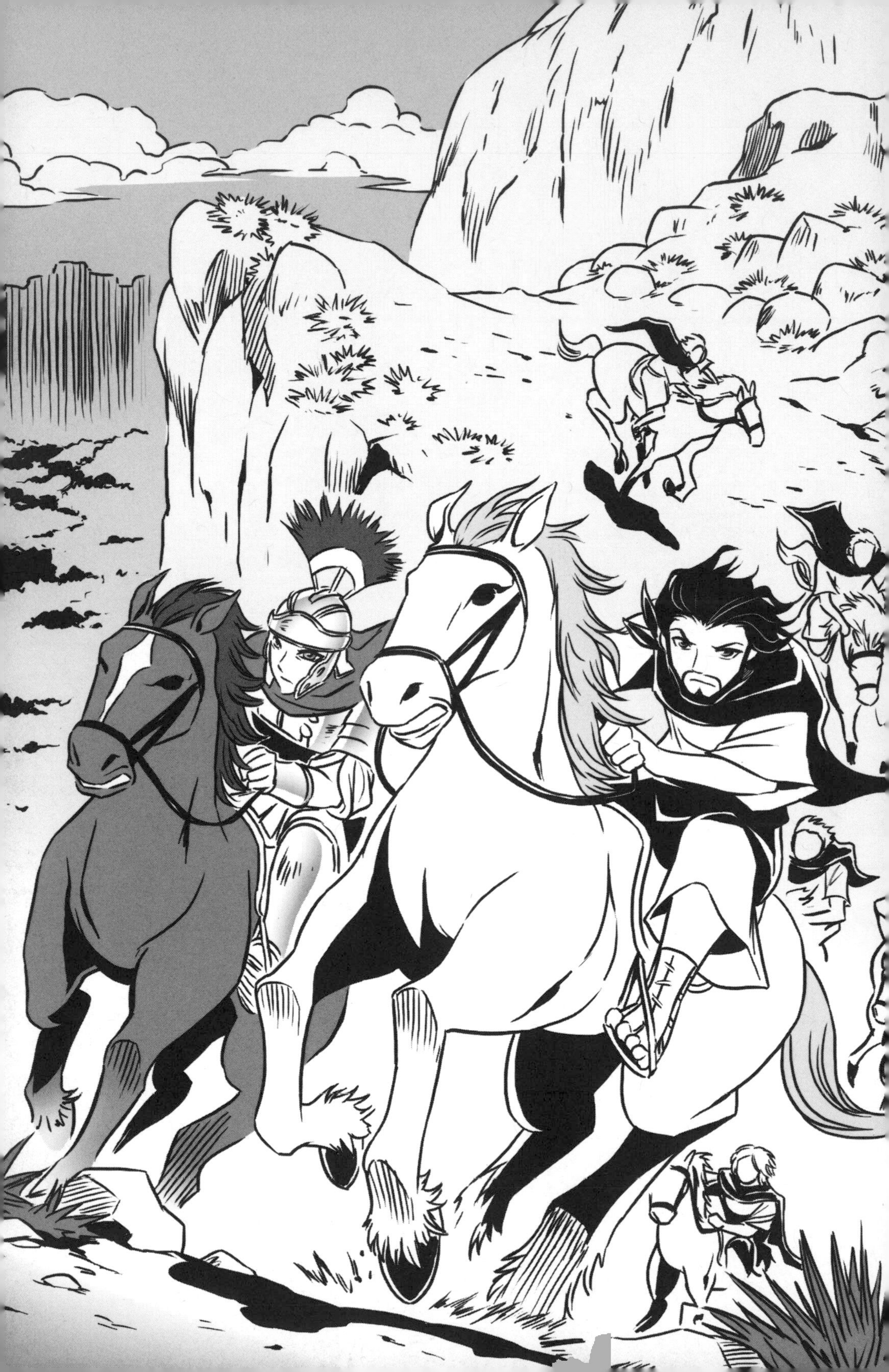

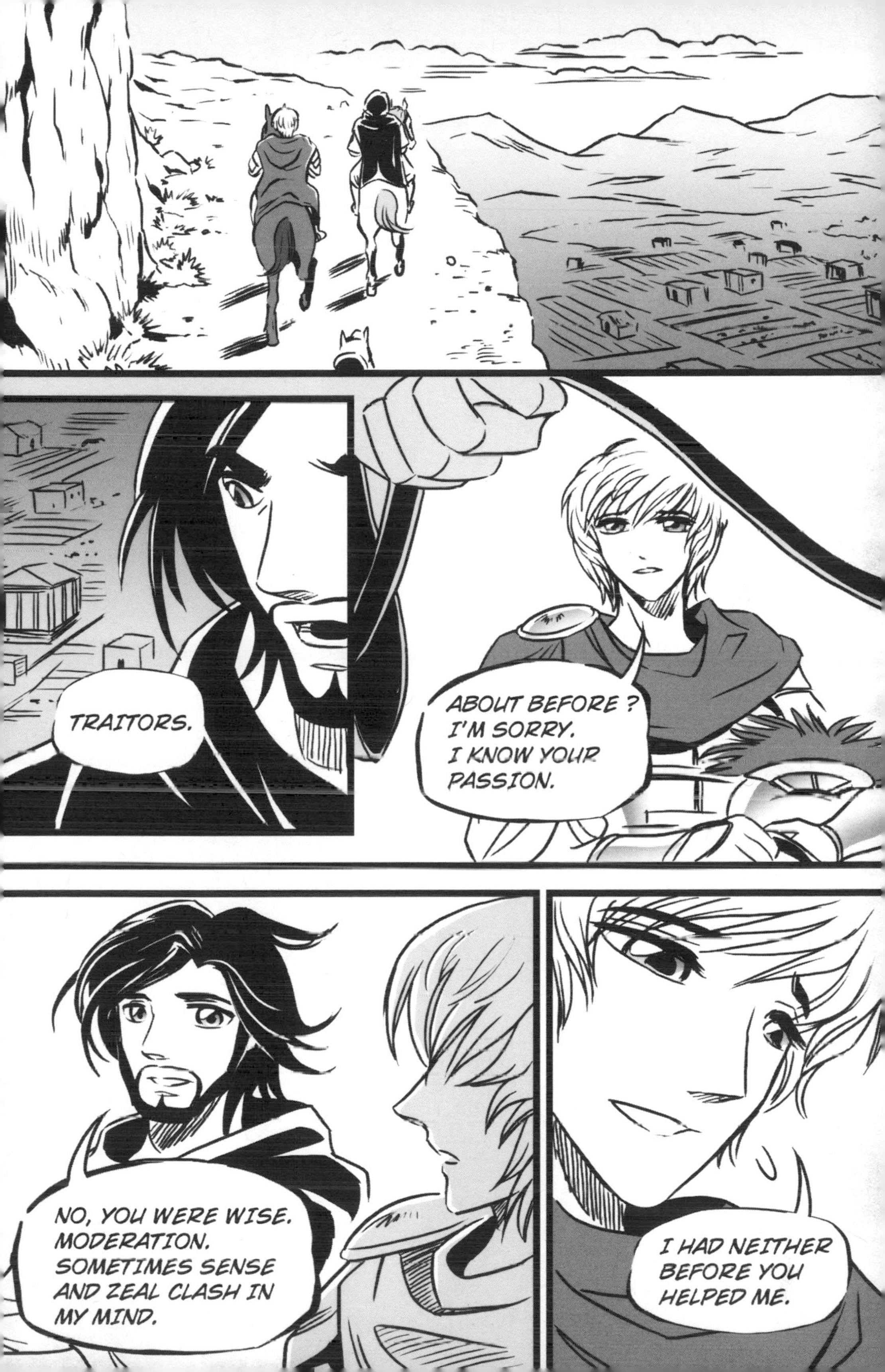
TRAITORS.
ABOUT BEFORE ? I'M SORRY. I KNOW YOUR PASSION.
NO, YOU WERE WISE. MODERATION. SOMETIMES SENSE AND ZEAL CLASH IN MY MIND.
I HAD NEITHER BEFORE YOU HELPED ME.

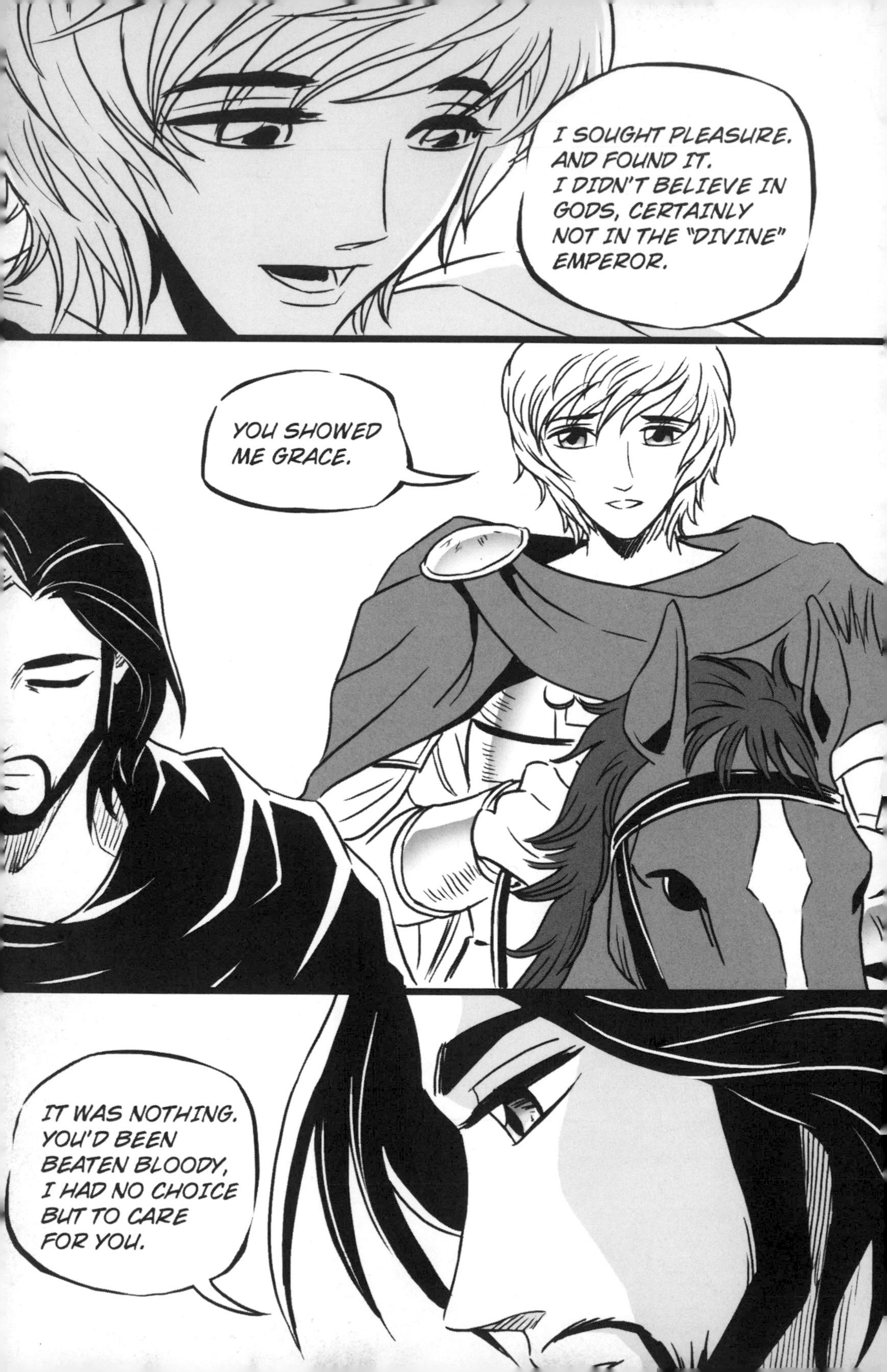
I SOUGHT PLEASURE. AND FOUND IT. I DIDN'T BELIEVE IN GODS, CERTAINLY NOT IN THE "DIVINE" EMPEROR.
YOU SHOWED ME GRACE.
IT WAS NOTHING. YOU'D BEEN BEATEN BLOODY, I HAD NO CHOICE BUT TO CARE FOR YOU.

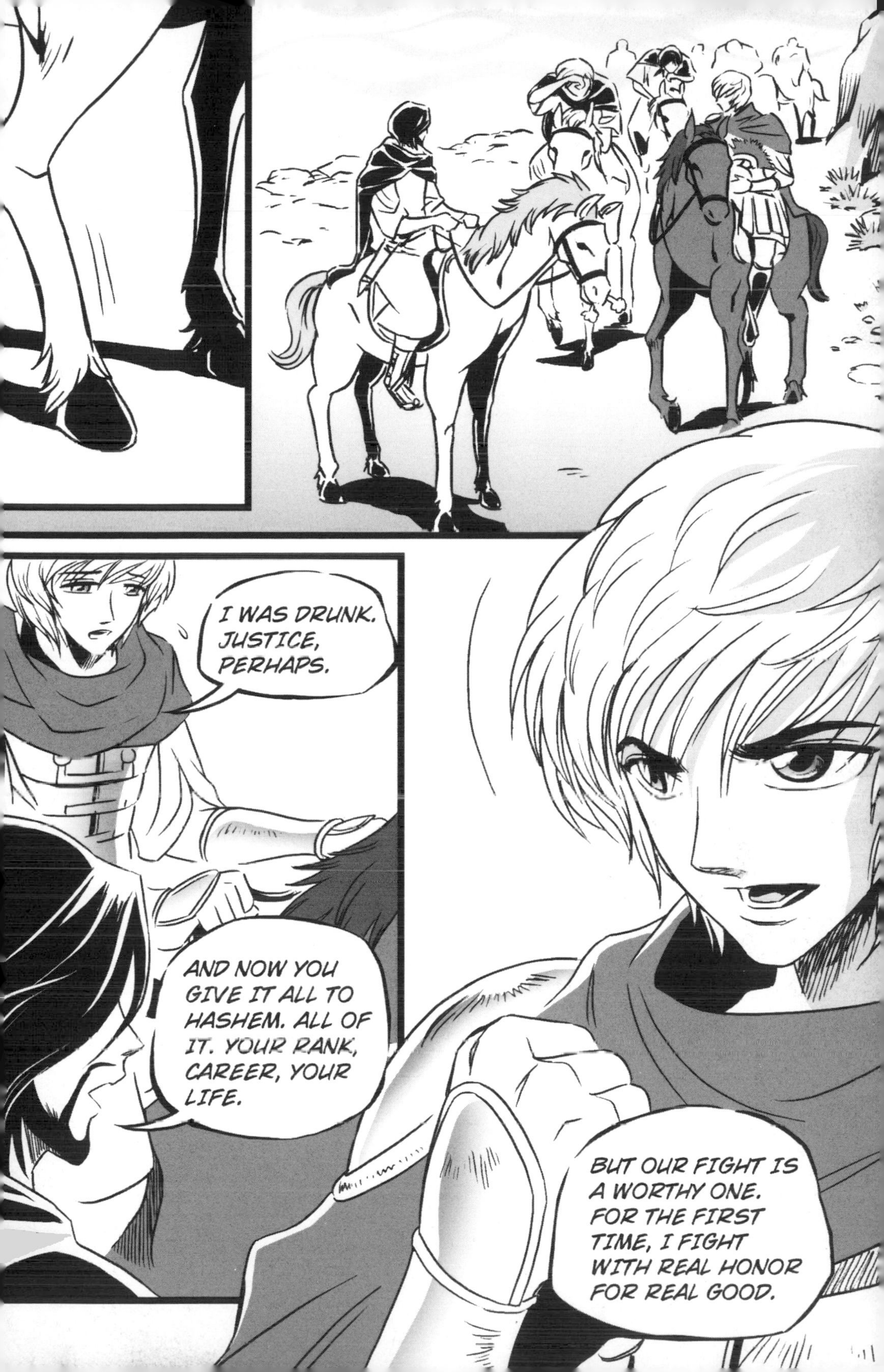
I WAS DRUNK. JUSTICE, PERHAPS.
AND NOW YOU GIVE IT ALL TO HASHEM. ALL OF IT. YOUR RANK, CAREER, YOUR LIFE.
BUT OUR FIGHT IS A WORTHY ONE. FOR THE FIRST TIME, I FIGHT WITH REAL HONOR FOR REAL GOOD.

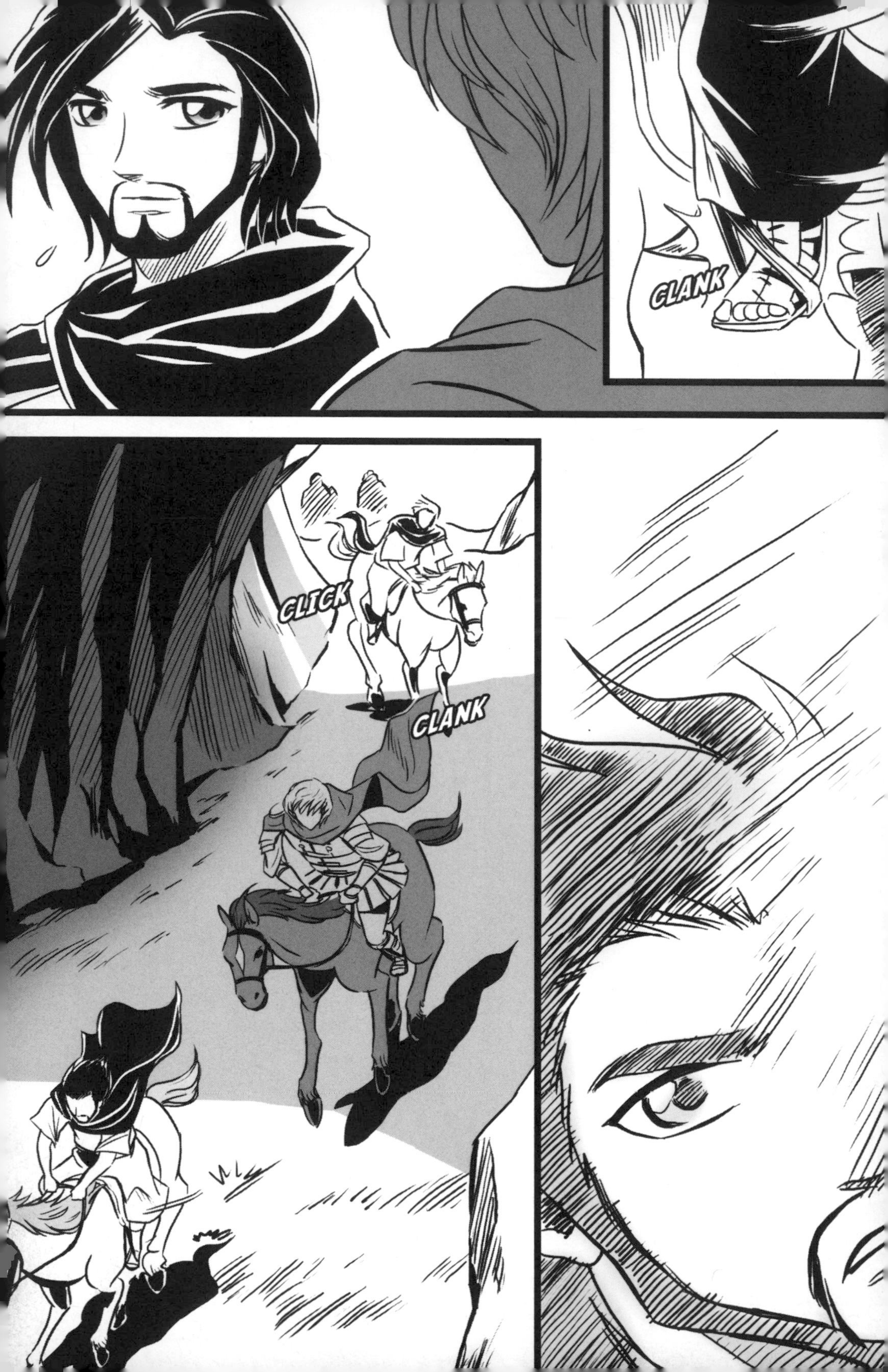
CLANK
CLICK
CLANK

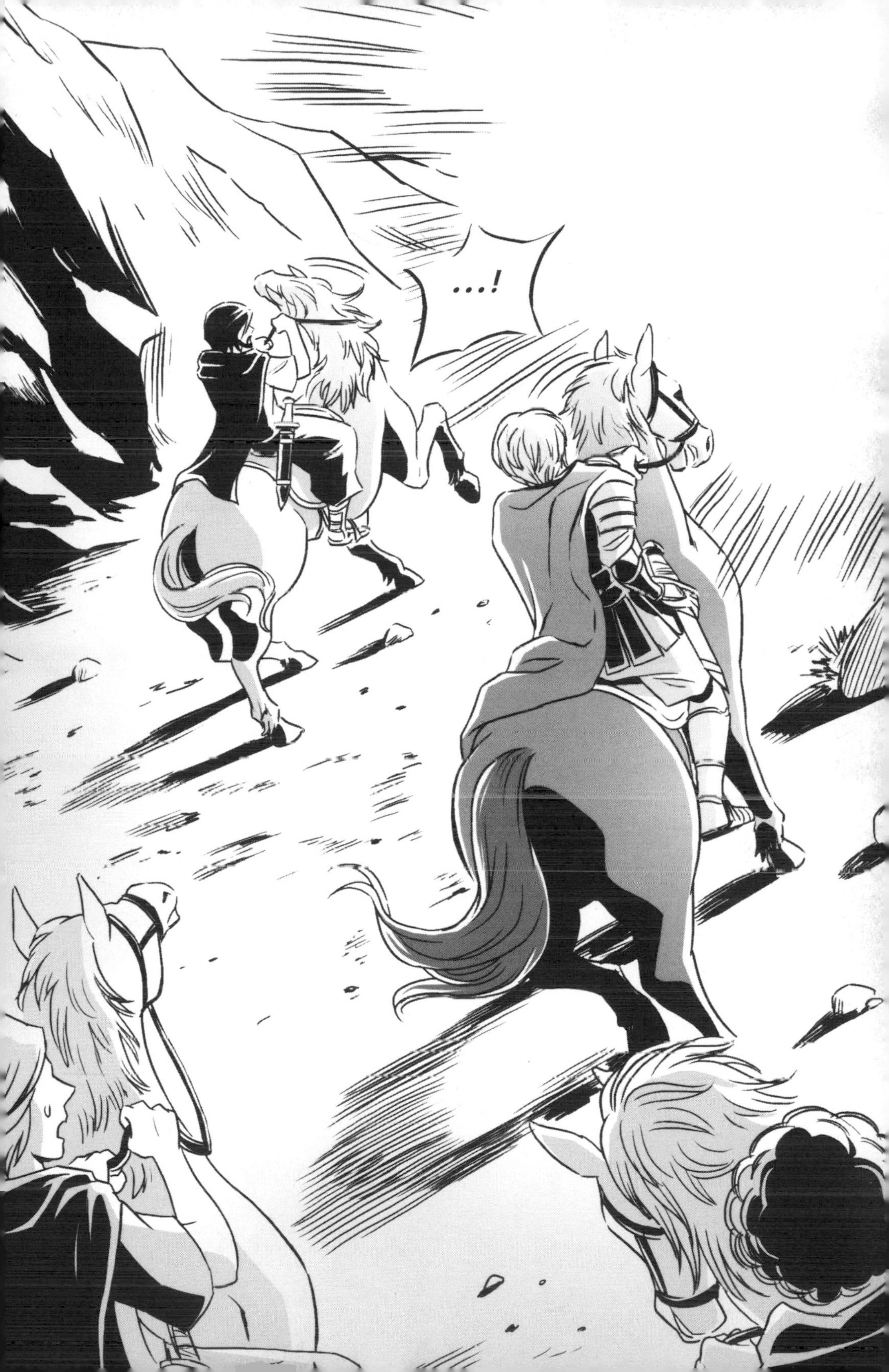
...!

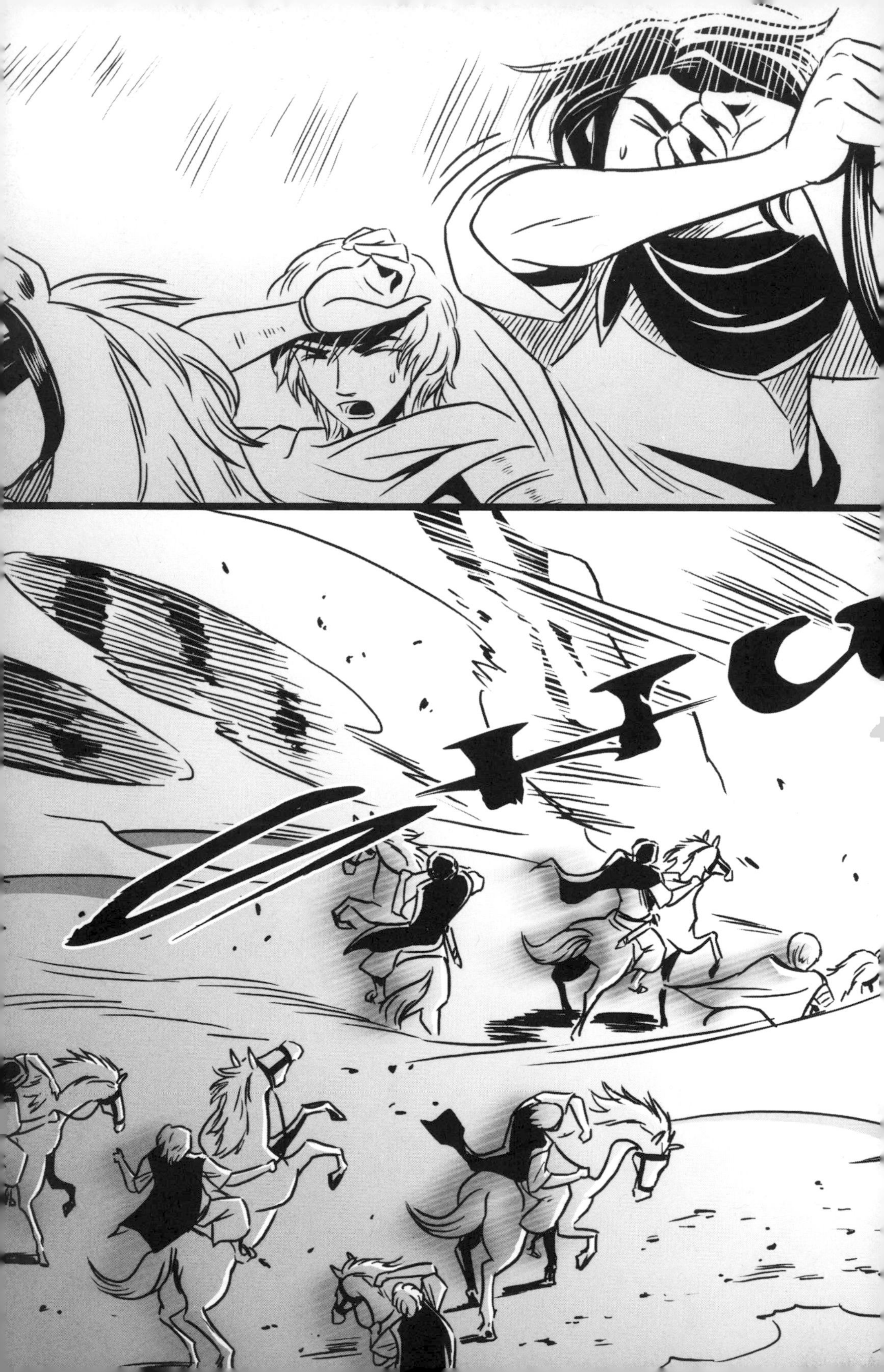

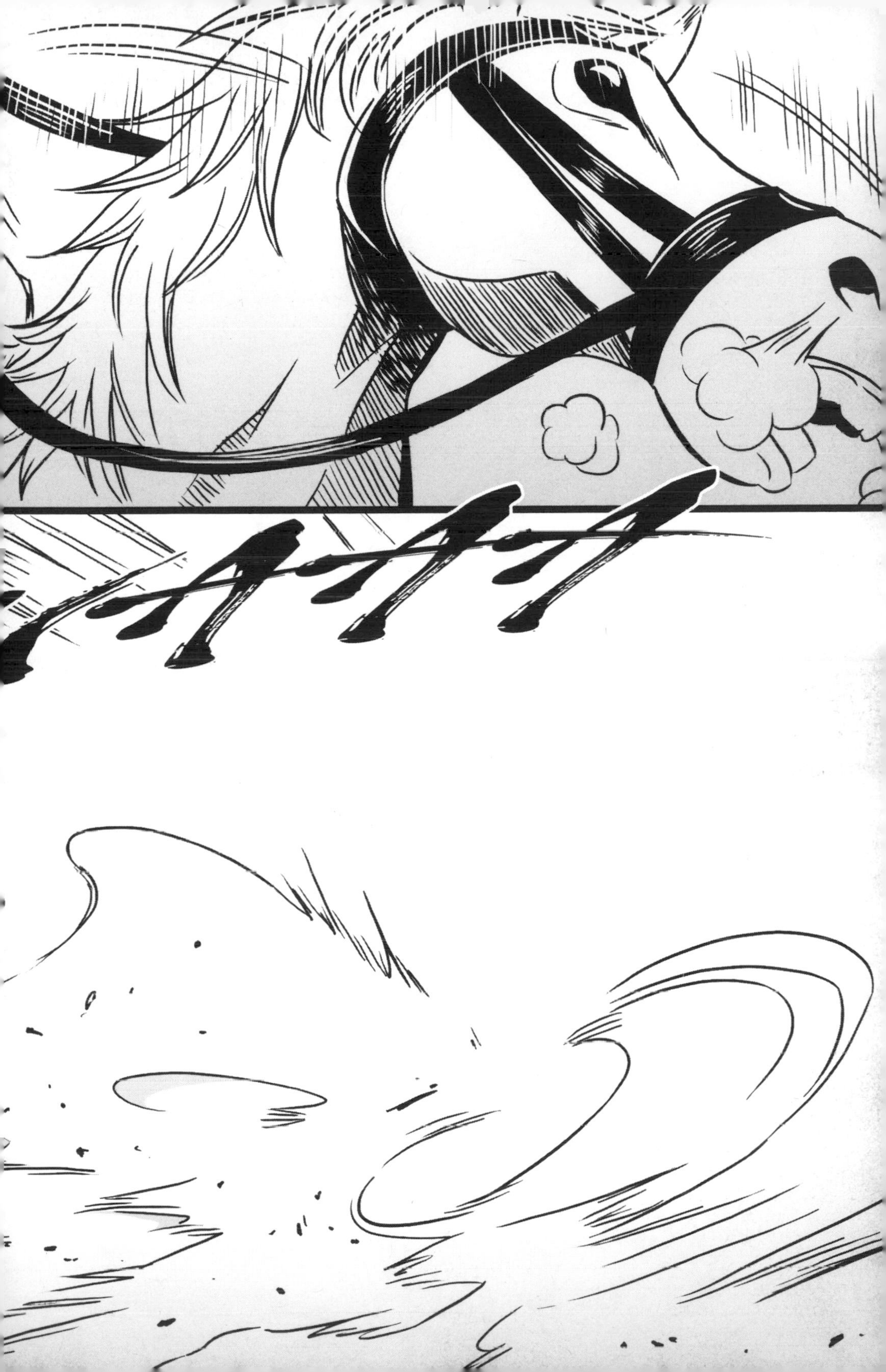

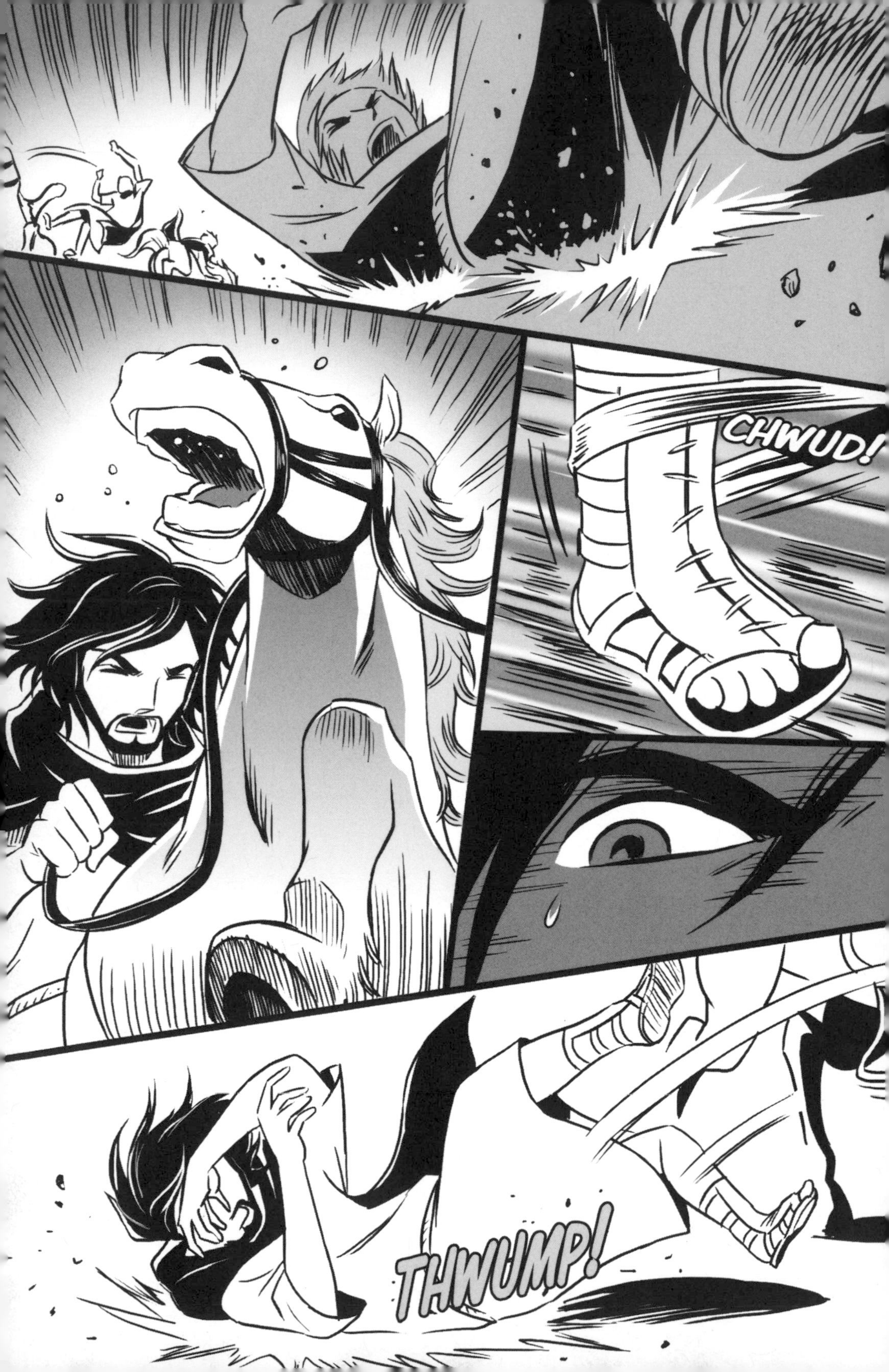
CHWUD!
THWUMP!

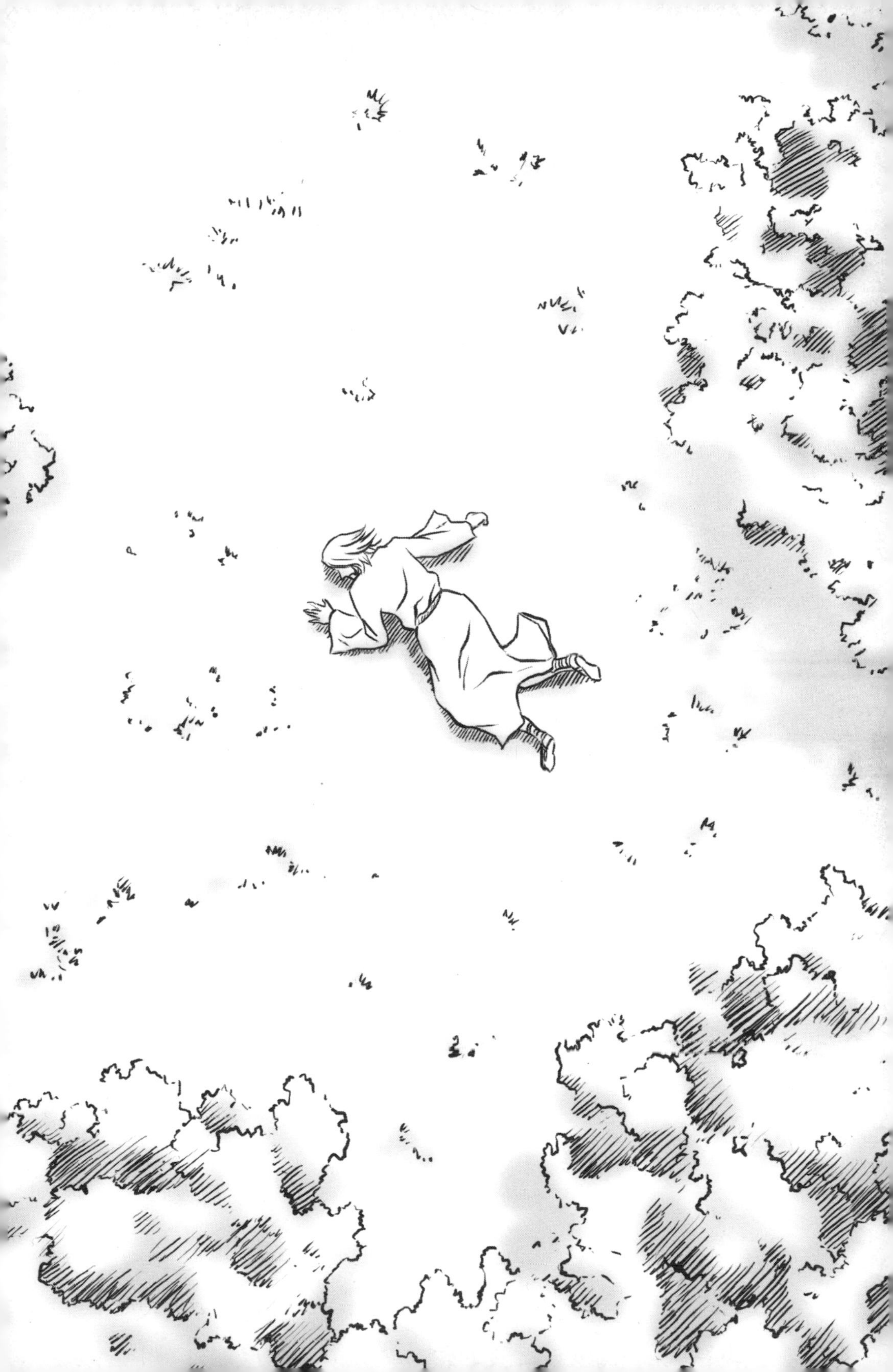

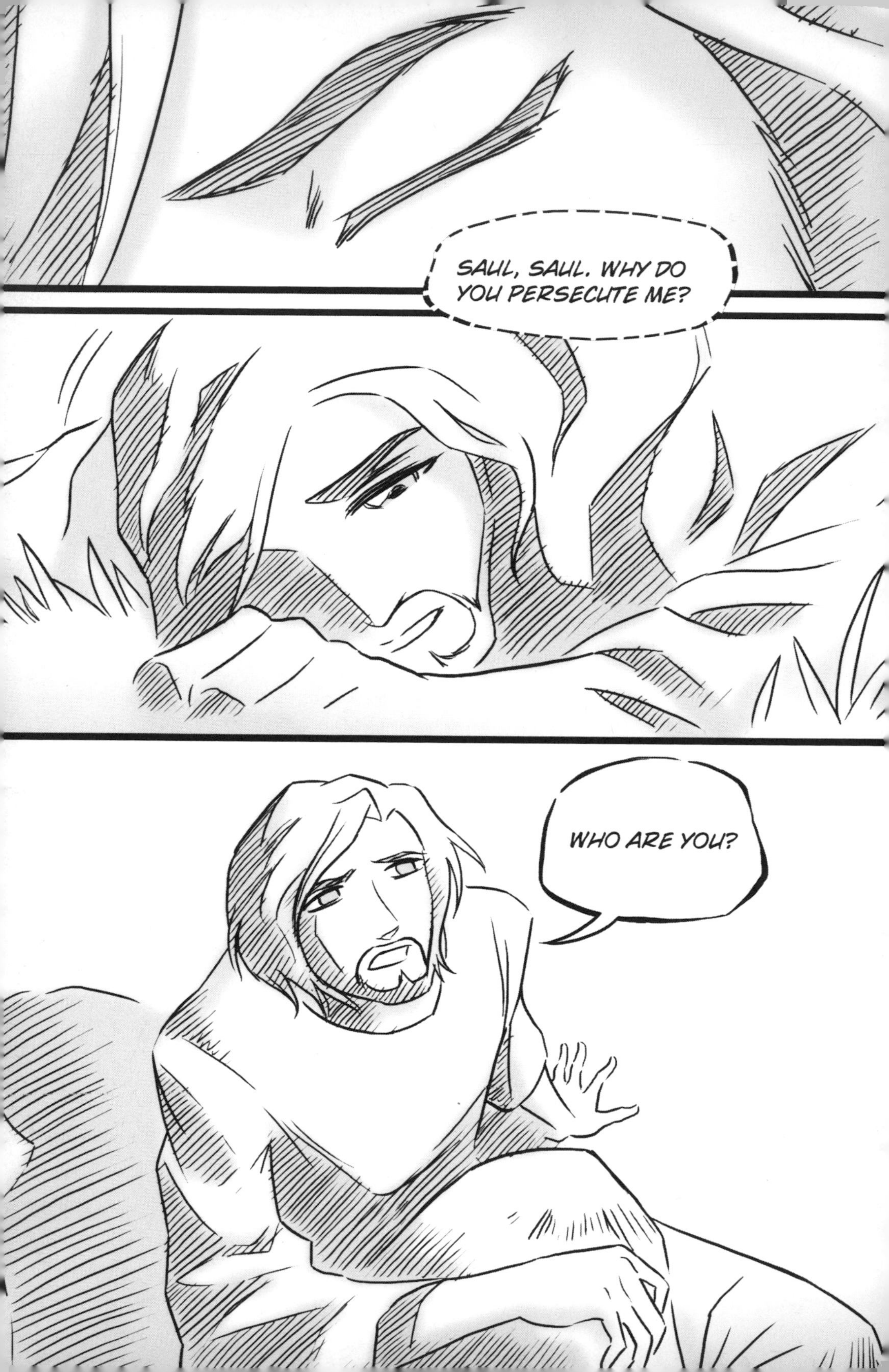
SAUL, SAUL. WHY DO YOU PERSECUTE ME?
WHO ARE YOU?

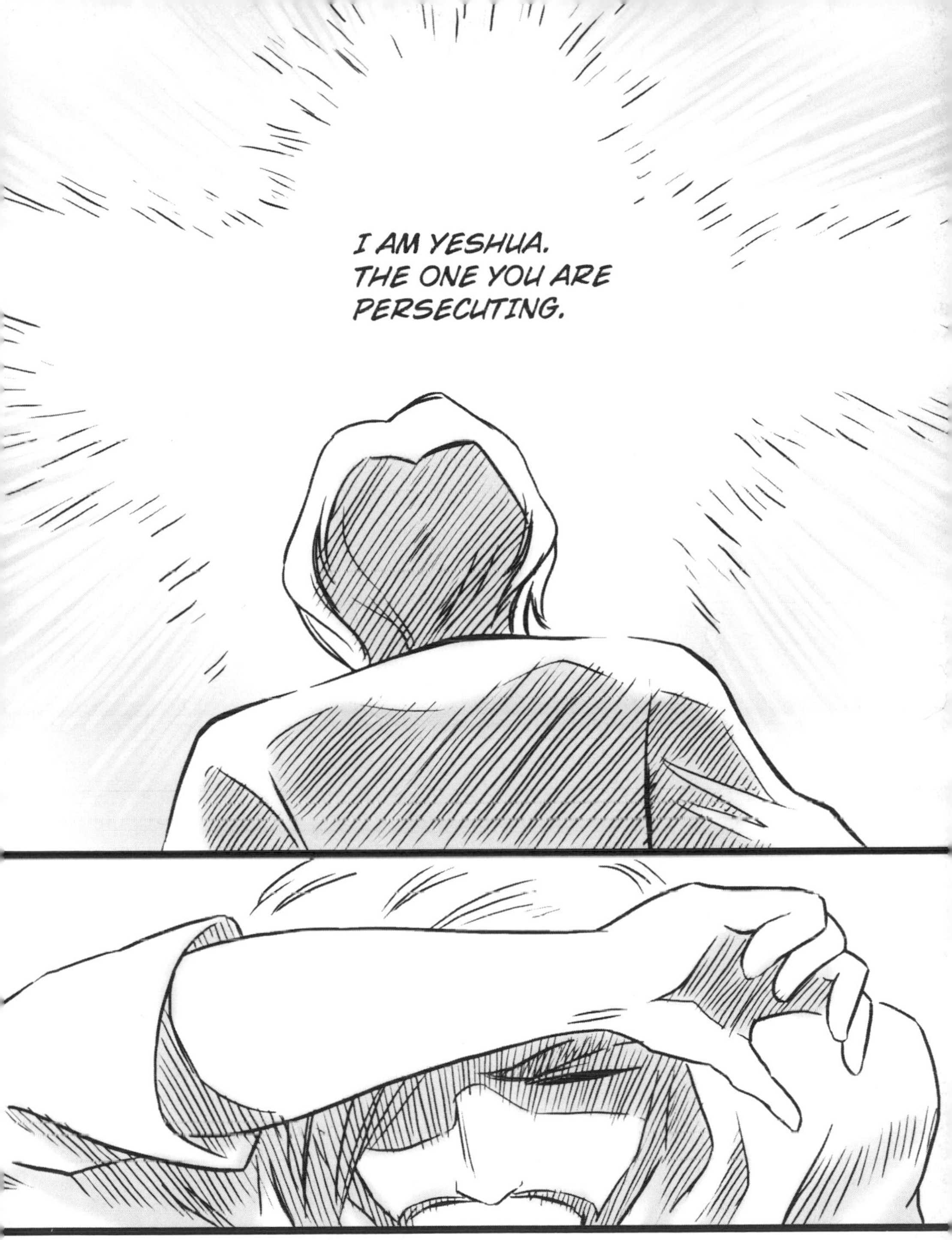
I AM YESHUA.
THE ONE YOU ARE
PERSECUTING.

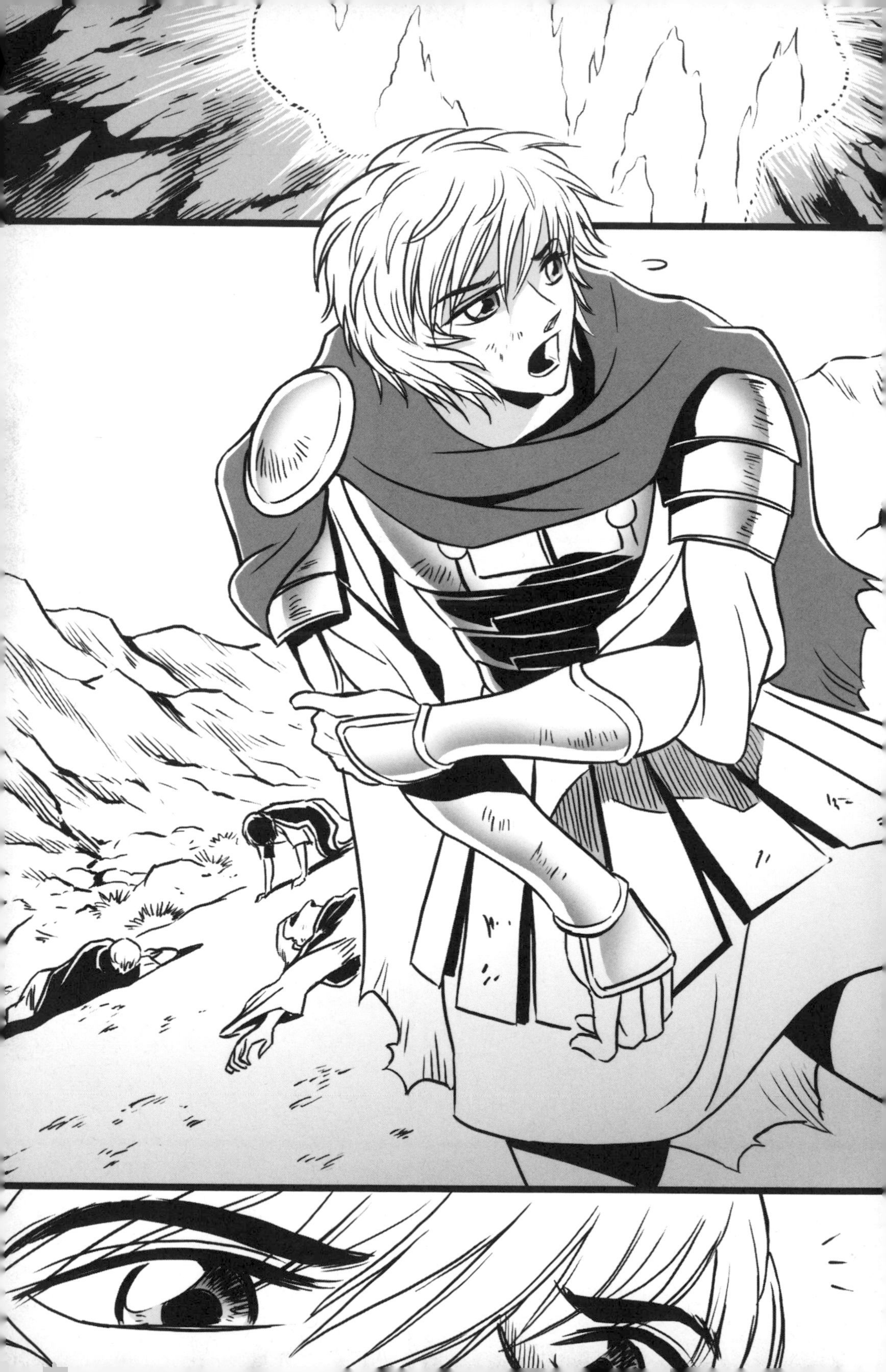

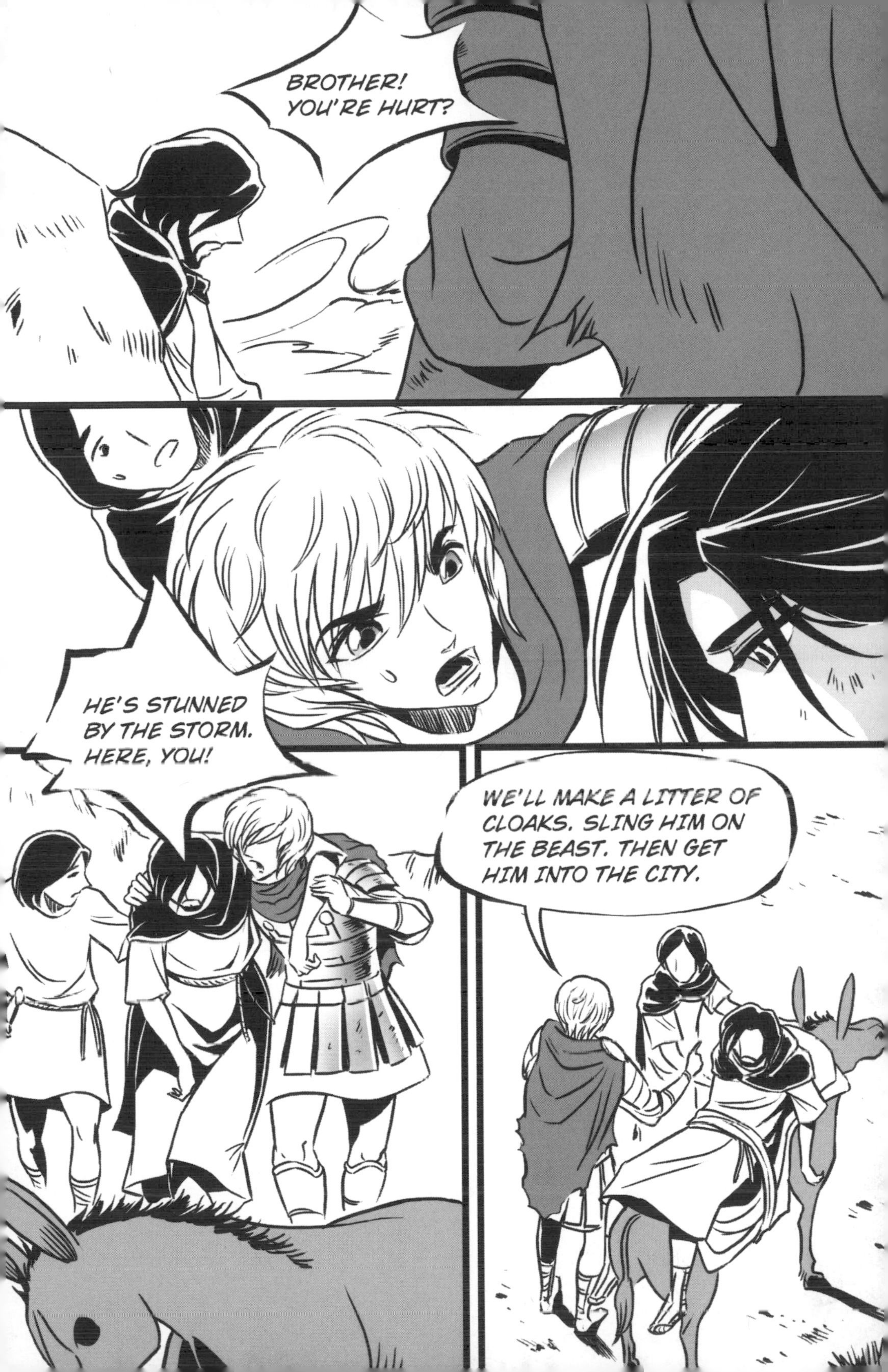
BROTHER! YOU'RE HURT?
HE'S STUNNED BY THE STORM. HERE, YOU!
WE'LL MAKE A LITTER OF CLOAKS. SLING HIM ON THE BEAST. THEN GET HIM INTO THE CITY.

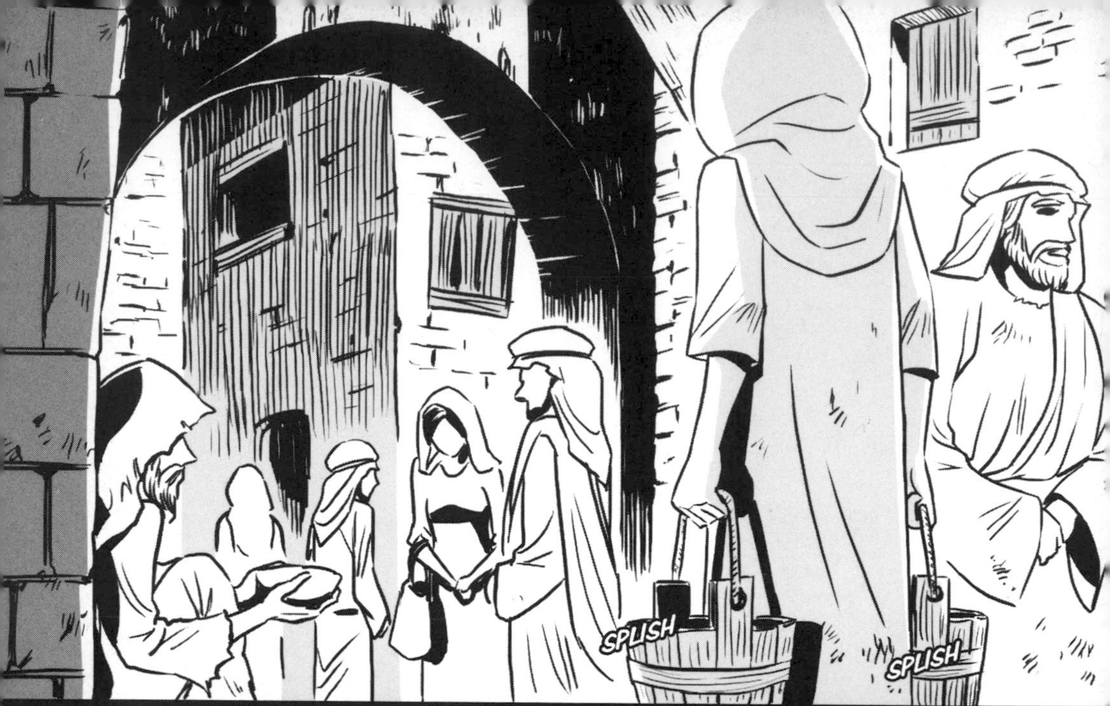
SPLISH
SPLISH

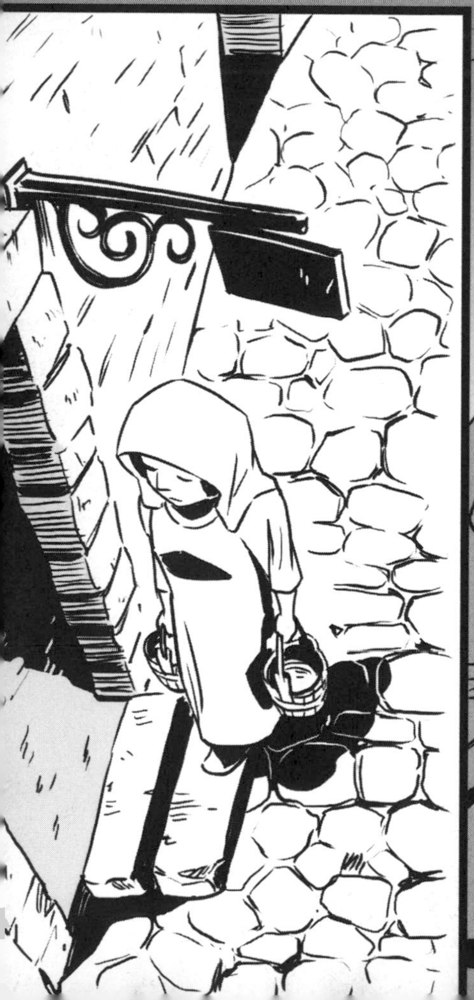

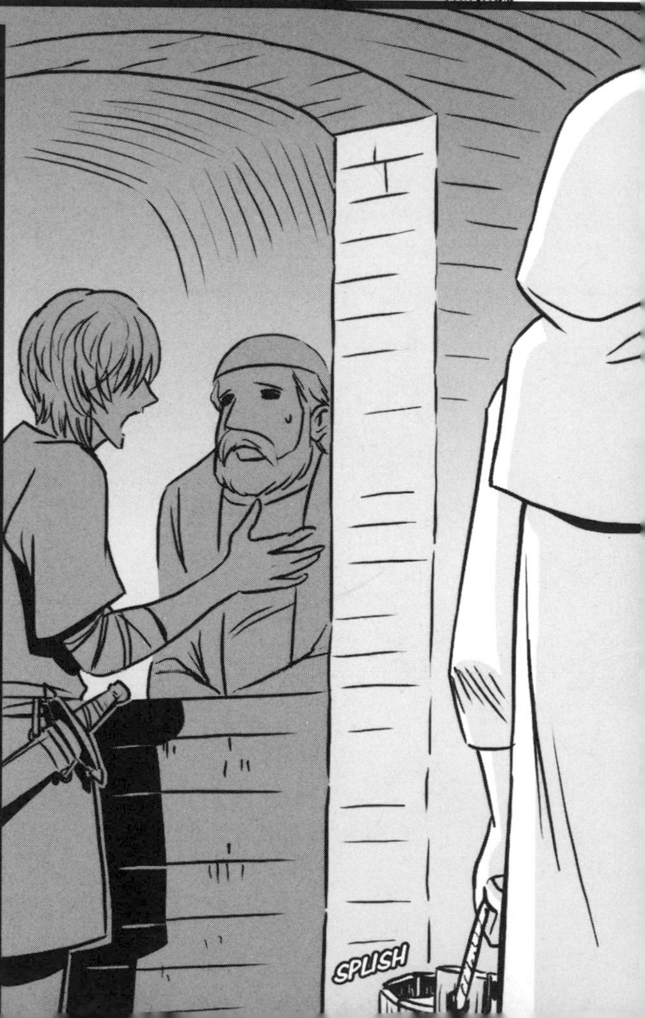
SPLISH

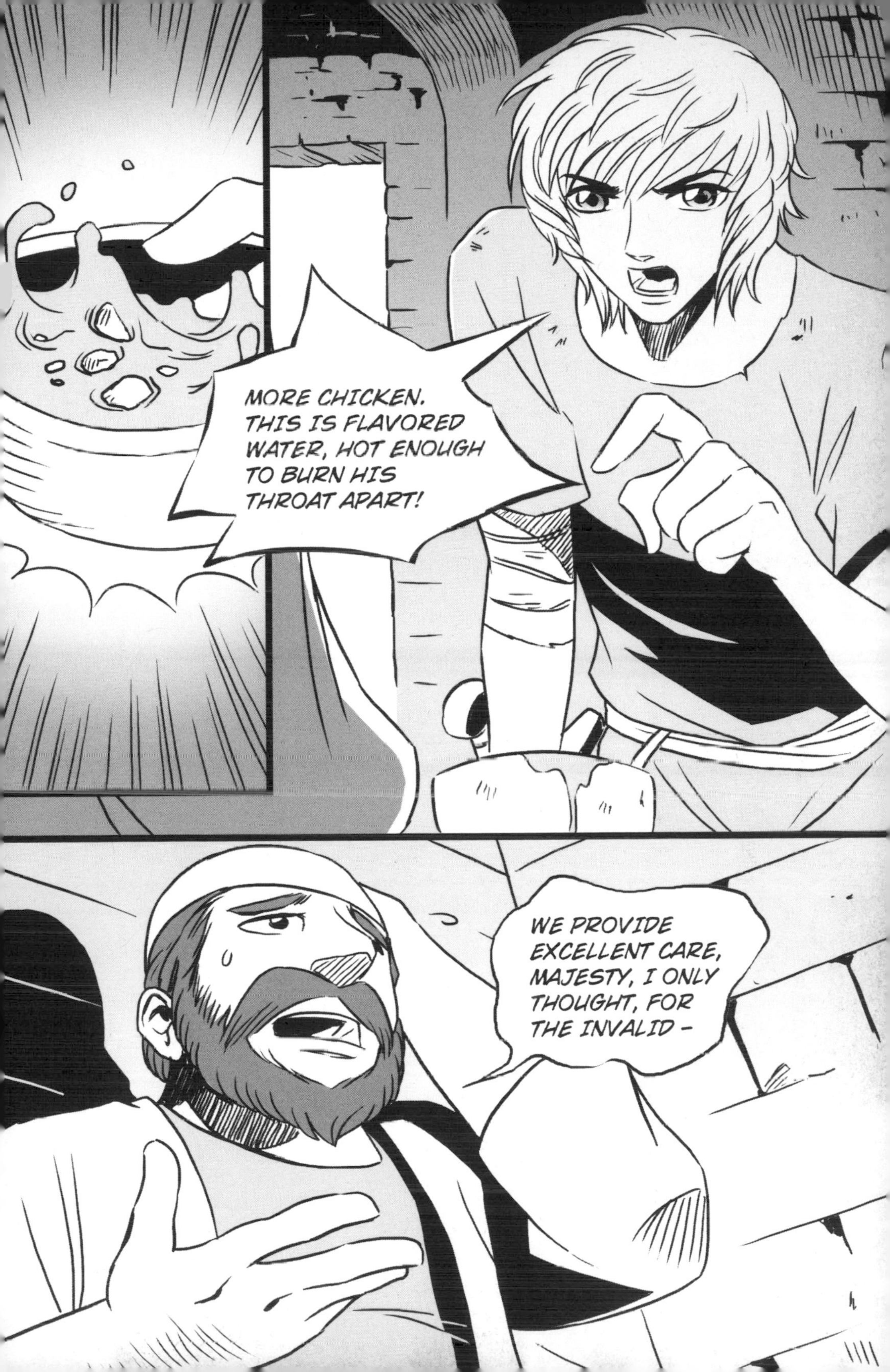
MORE CHICKEN. THIS IS FLAVORED WATER, HOT ENOUGH TO BURN HIS THROAT APART!
WE PROVIDE EXCELLENT CARE, MAJESTY, I ONLY THOUGHT, FOR THE INVALID -

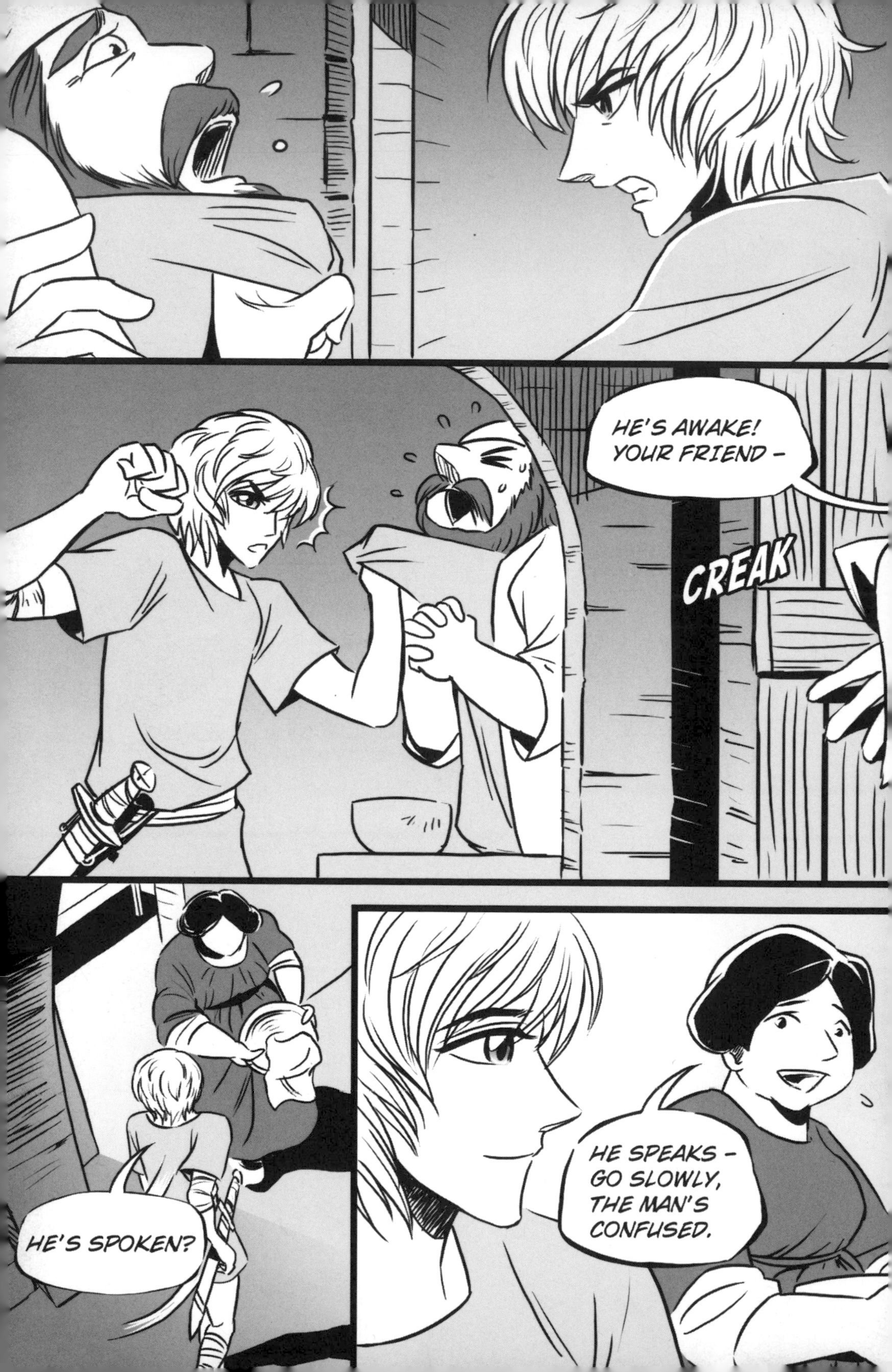
HE'S AWAKE! YOUR FRIEND -
CREAK
HE'S SPOKEN?
HE SPEAKS - GO SLOWLY, THE MAN'S CONFUSED.

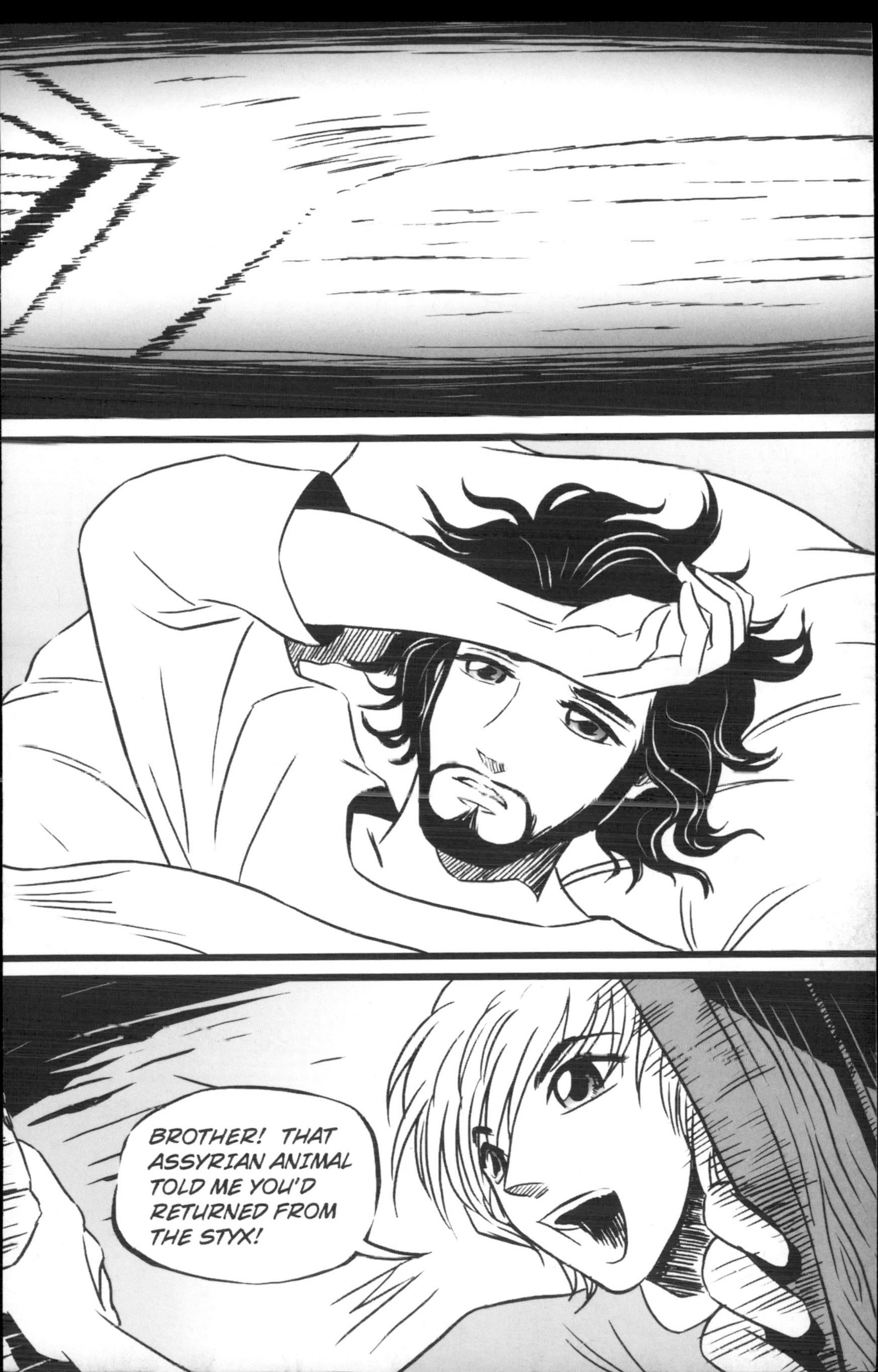
BROTHER! THAT ASSYRIAN ANIMAL TOLD ME YOU'D RETURNED FROM THE STYX!

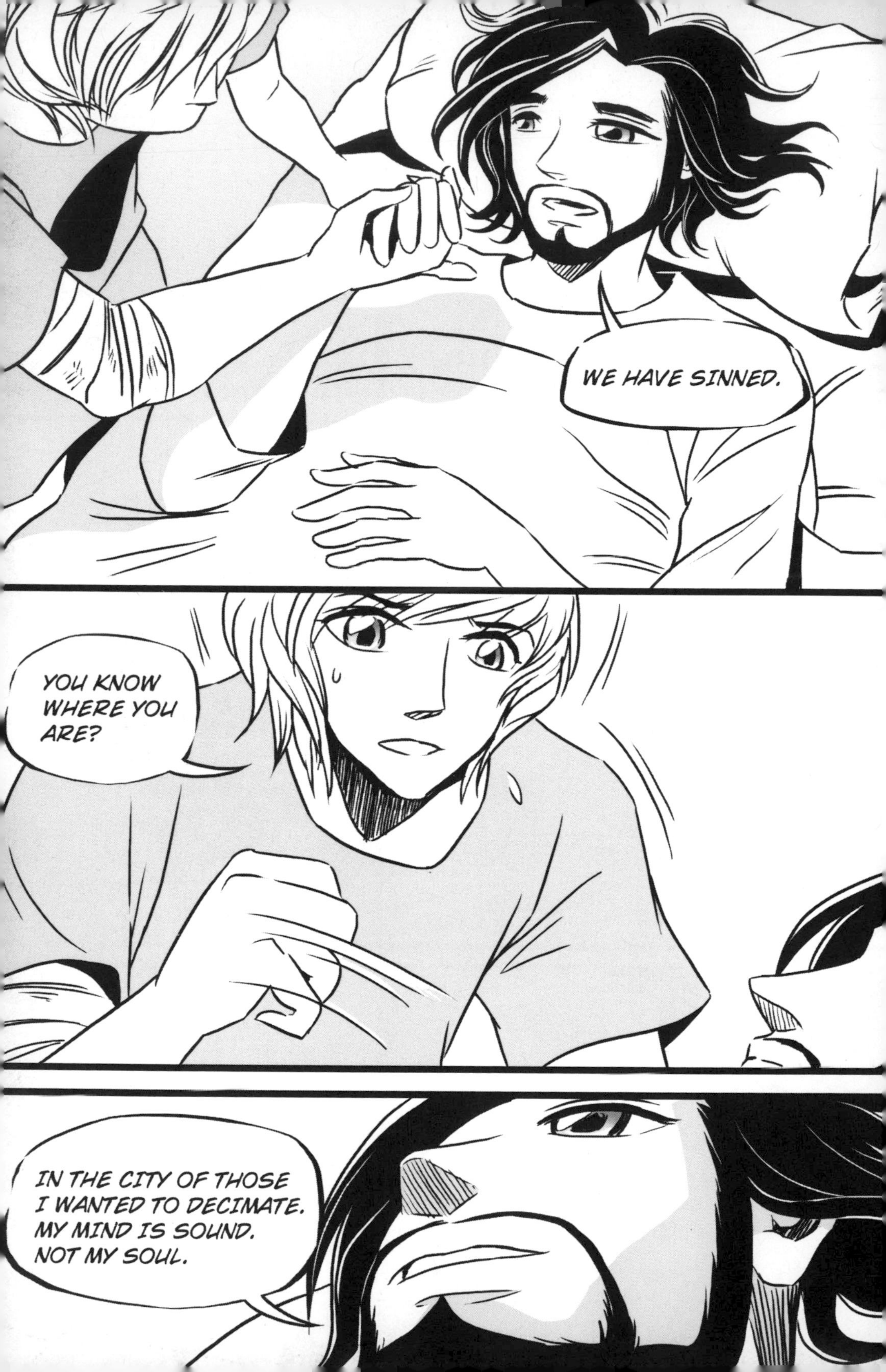
WE HAVE SINNED.
YOU KNOW WHERE YOU ARE?
IN THE CITY OF THOSE I WANTED TO DECIMATE. MY MIND IS SOUND. NOT MY SOUL.

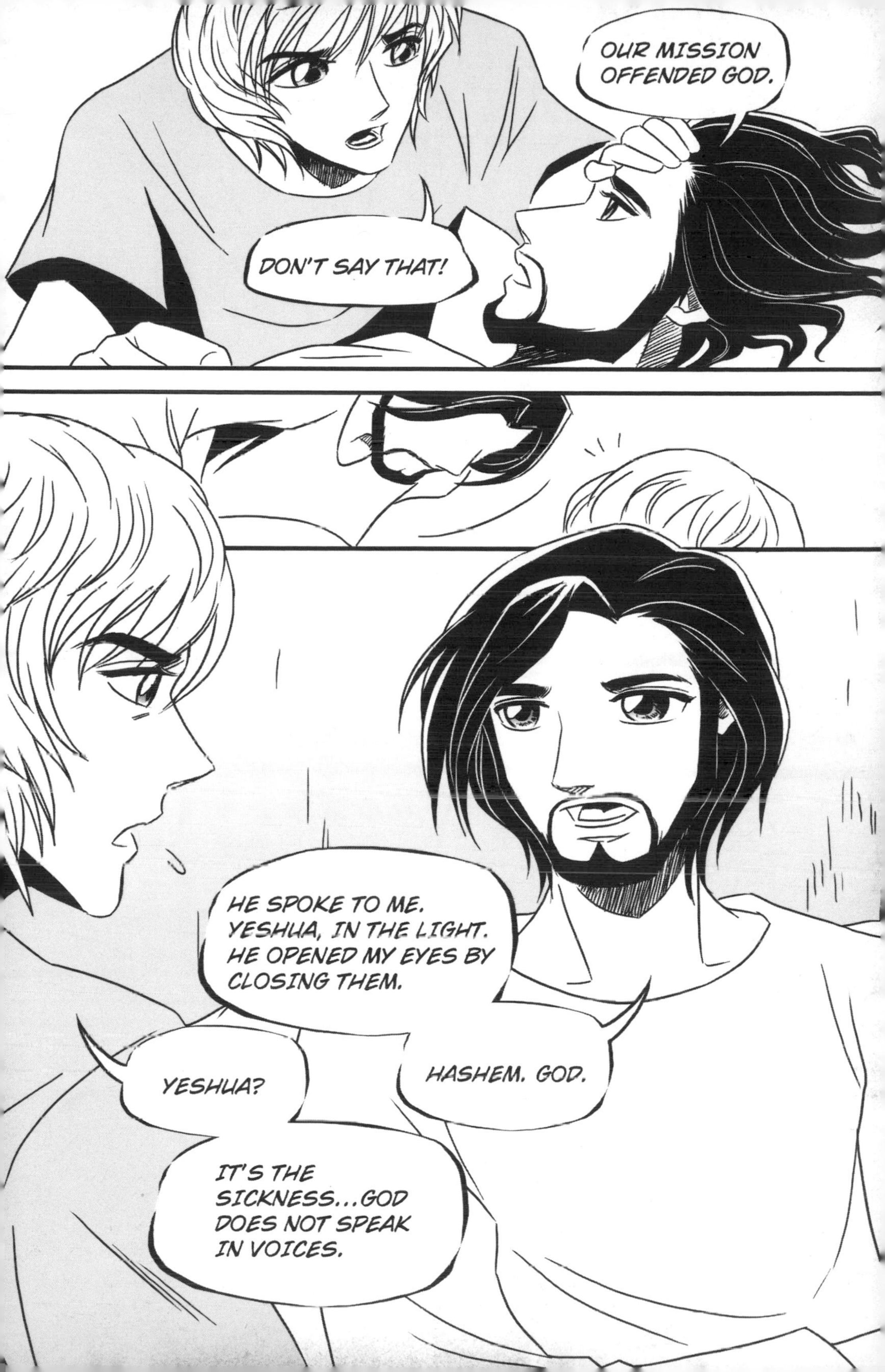
OUR MISSION OFFENDED GOD.
DON'T SAY THAT!
HE SPOKE TO ME. YESHUA, IN THE LIGHT. HE OPENED MY EYES BY CLOSING THEM.
YESHUA?
HASHEM. GOD.
IT'S THE SICKNESS...GOD DOES NOT SPEAK IN VOICES.

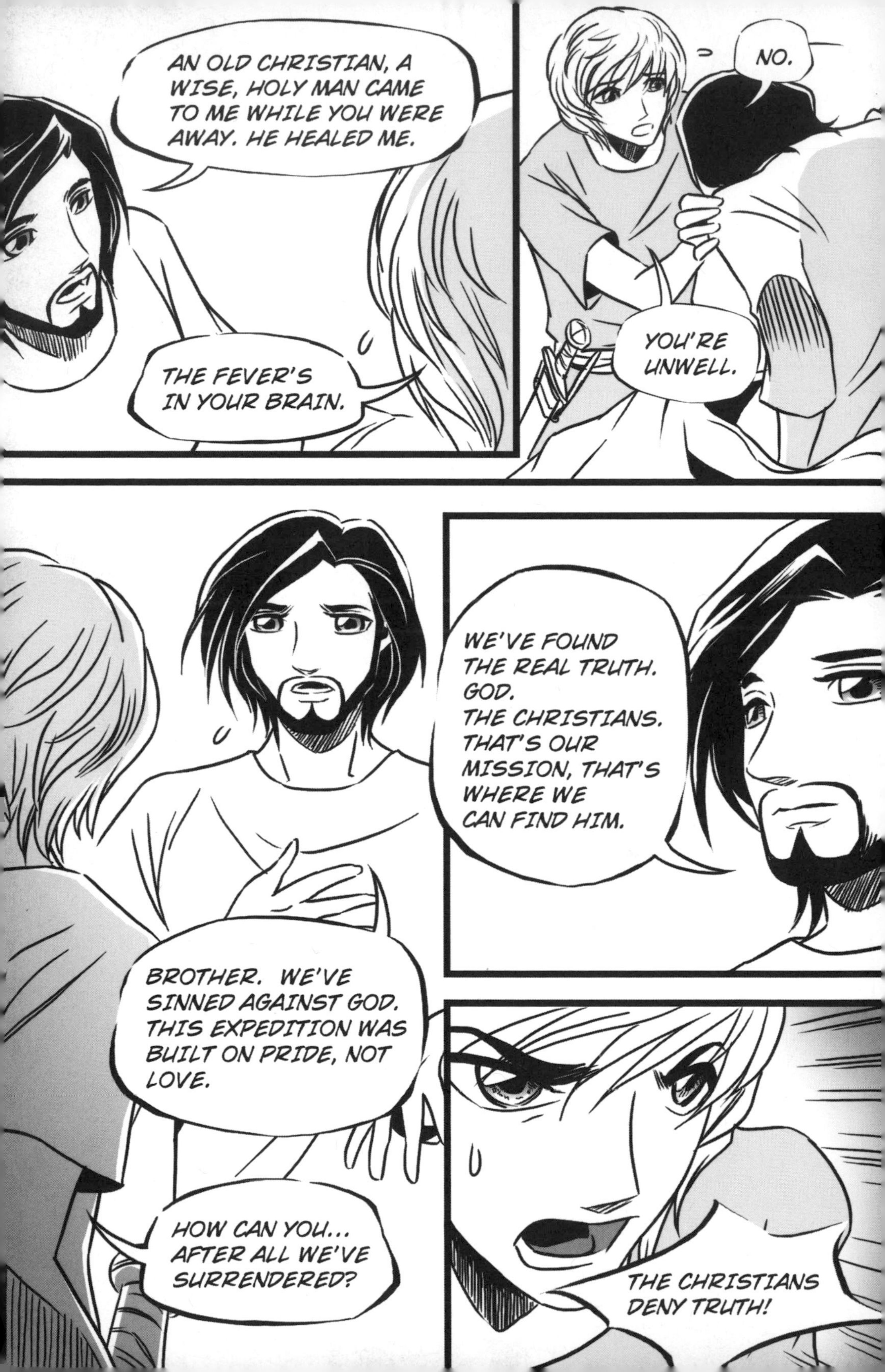
AN OLD CHRISTIAN, A WISE, HOLY MAN CAME TO ME WHILE YOU WERE AWAY. HE HEALED ME.
THE FEVER'S IN YOUR BRAIN.
NO.
YOU'RE UNWELL.
WE'VE FOUND THE REAL TRUTH. GOD. THE CHRISTIANS. THAT'S OUR MISSION, THAT'S WHERE WE CAN FIND HIM.
BROTHER. WE'VE SINNED AGAINST GOD. THIS EXPEDITION WAS BUILT ON PRIDE, NOT LOVE.
HOW CAN YOU... AFTER ALL WE'VE SURRENDERED?
THE CHRISTIANS DENY TRUTH!

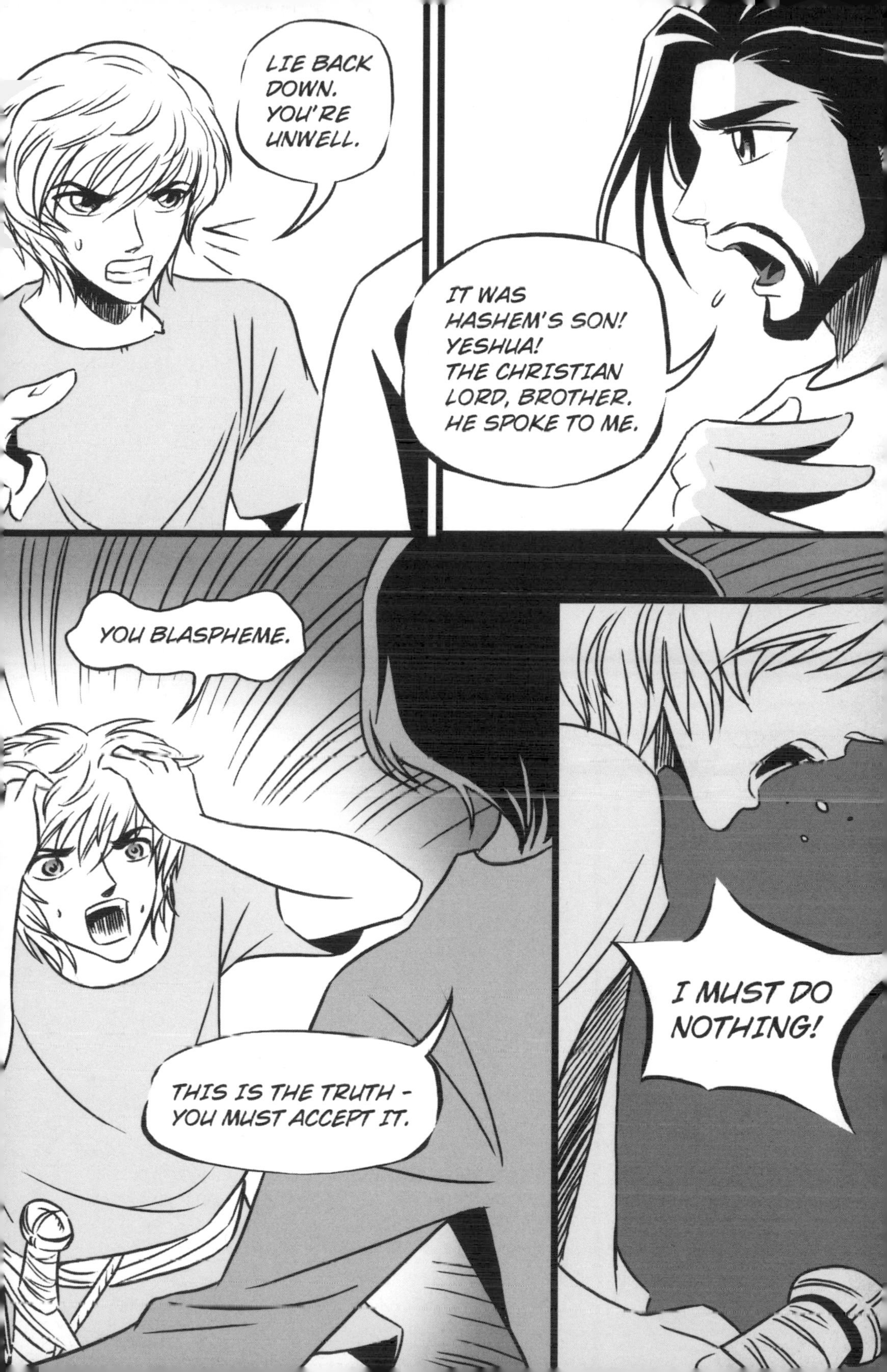
LIE BACK DOWN. YOU'RE UNWELL.
IT WAS HASHEM'S SON! YESHUA! THE CHRISTIAN LORD, BROTHER. HE SPOKE TO ME.
YOU BLASPHEME.
THIS IS THE TRUTH - YOU MUST ACCEPT IT.
I MUST DO NOTHING!

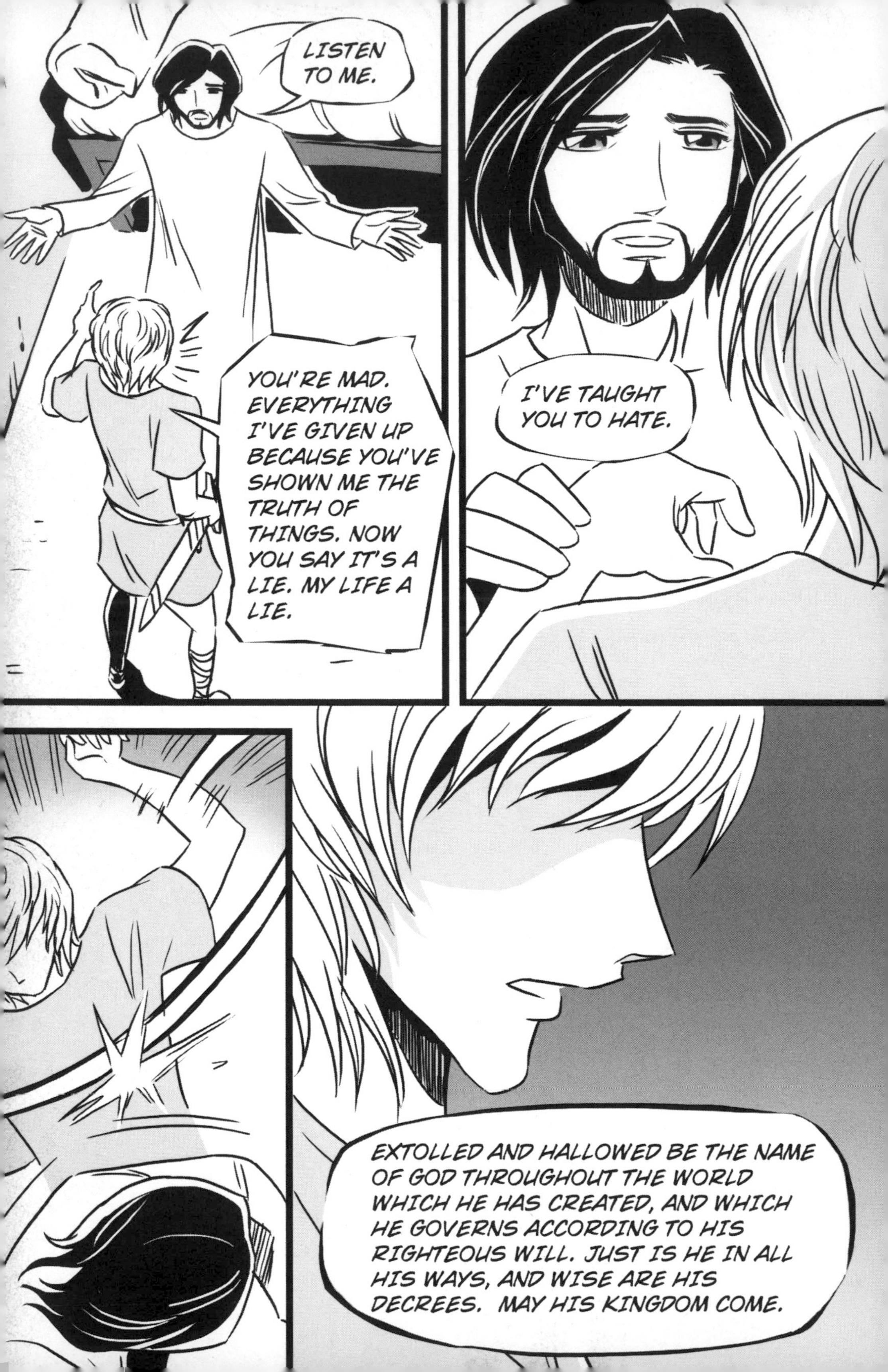
LISTEN TO ME.
YOU'RE MAD. EVERYTHING I'VE GIVEN UP BECAUSE YOU'VE SHOWN ME THE TRUTH OF THINGS. NOW YOU SAY IT'S A LIE. MY LIFE A LIE.
I'VE TAUGHT YOU TO HATE.
EXTOLLED AND HALLOWED BE THE NAME OF GOD THROUGHOUT THE WORLD WHICH HE HAS CREATED, AND WHICH HE GOVERNS ACCORDING TO HIS RIGHTEOUS WILL. JUST IS HE IN ALL HIS WAYS, AND WISE ARE HIS DECREES. MAY HIS KINGDOM COME.

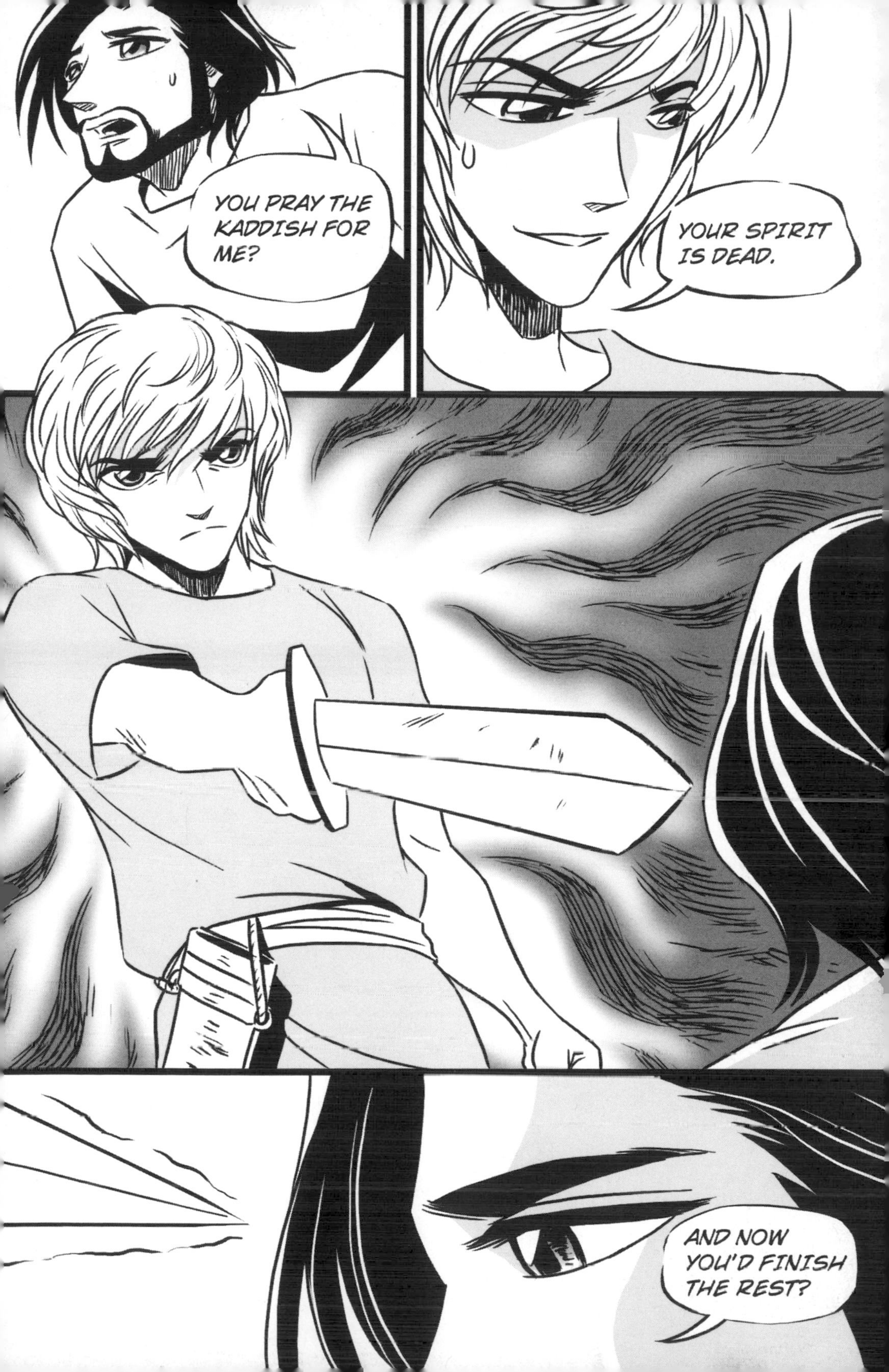
YOU PRAY THE KADDISH FOR ME?
YOUR SPIRIT IS DEAD.
AND NOW YOU'D FINISH THE REST?

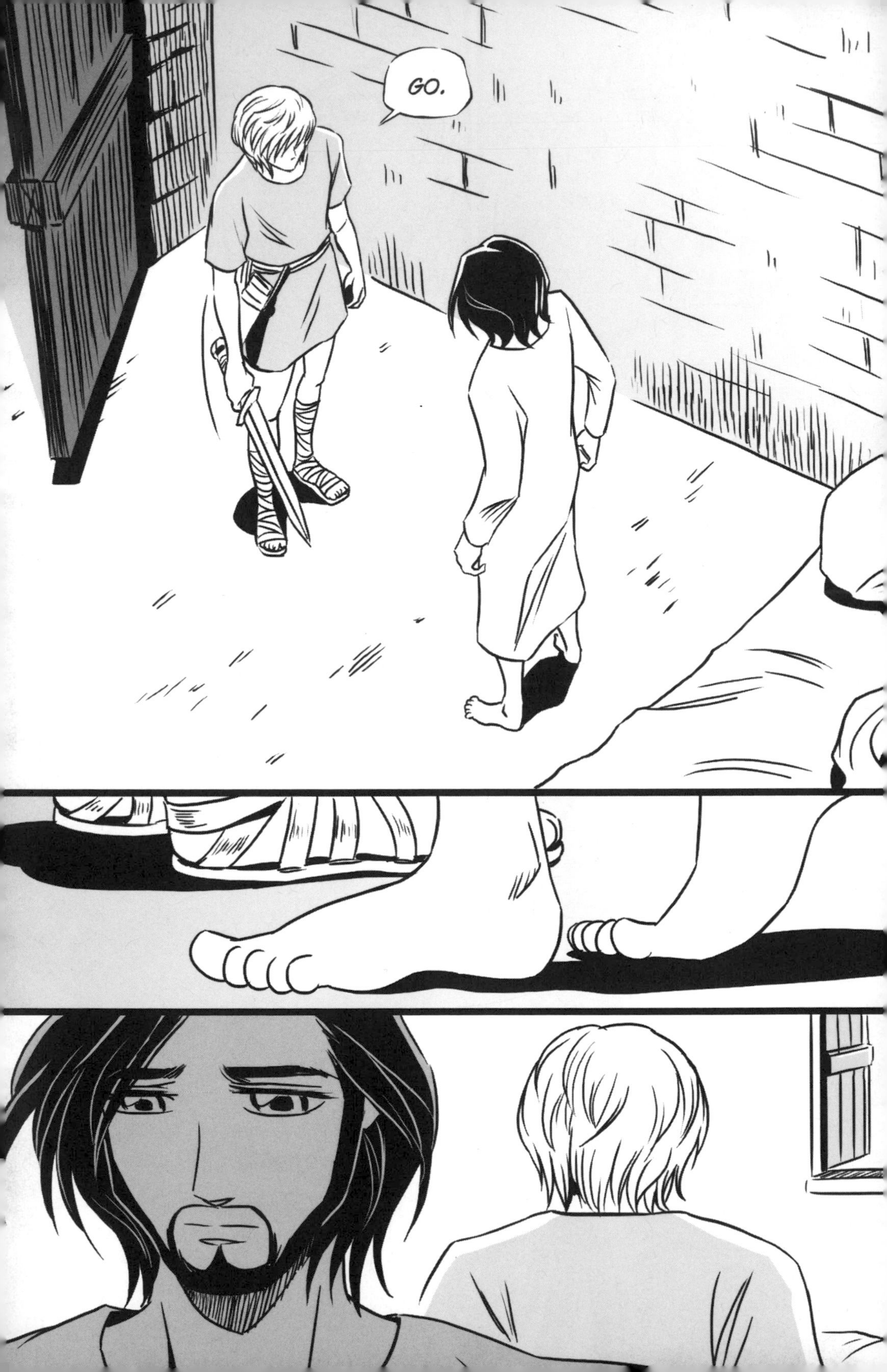
GO.

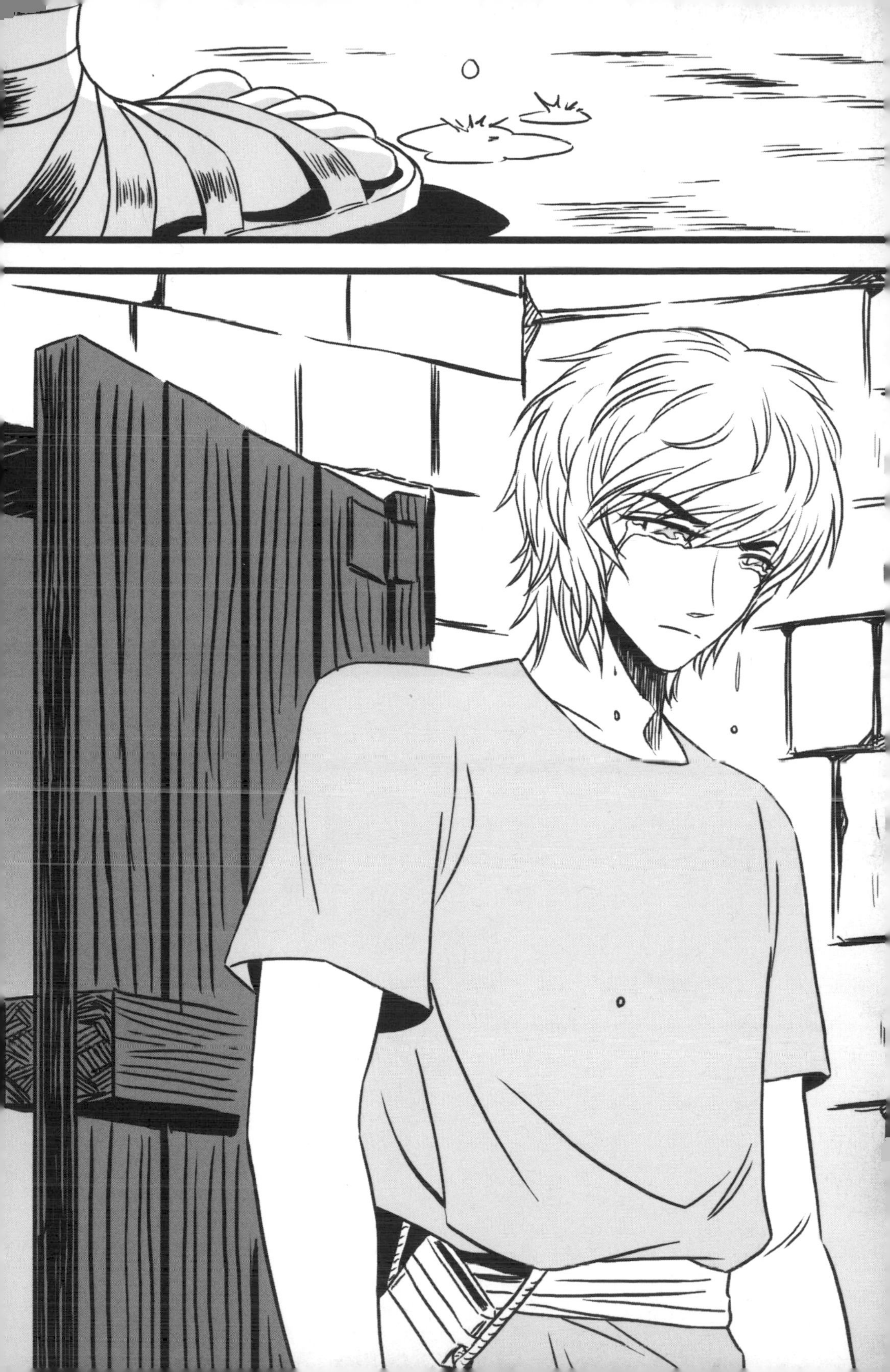

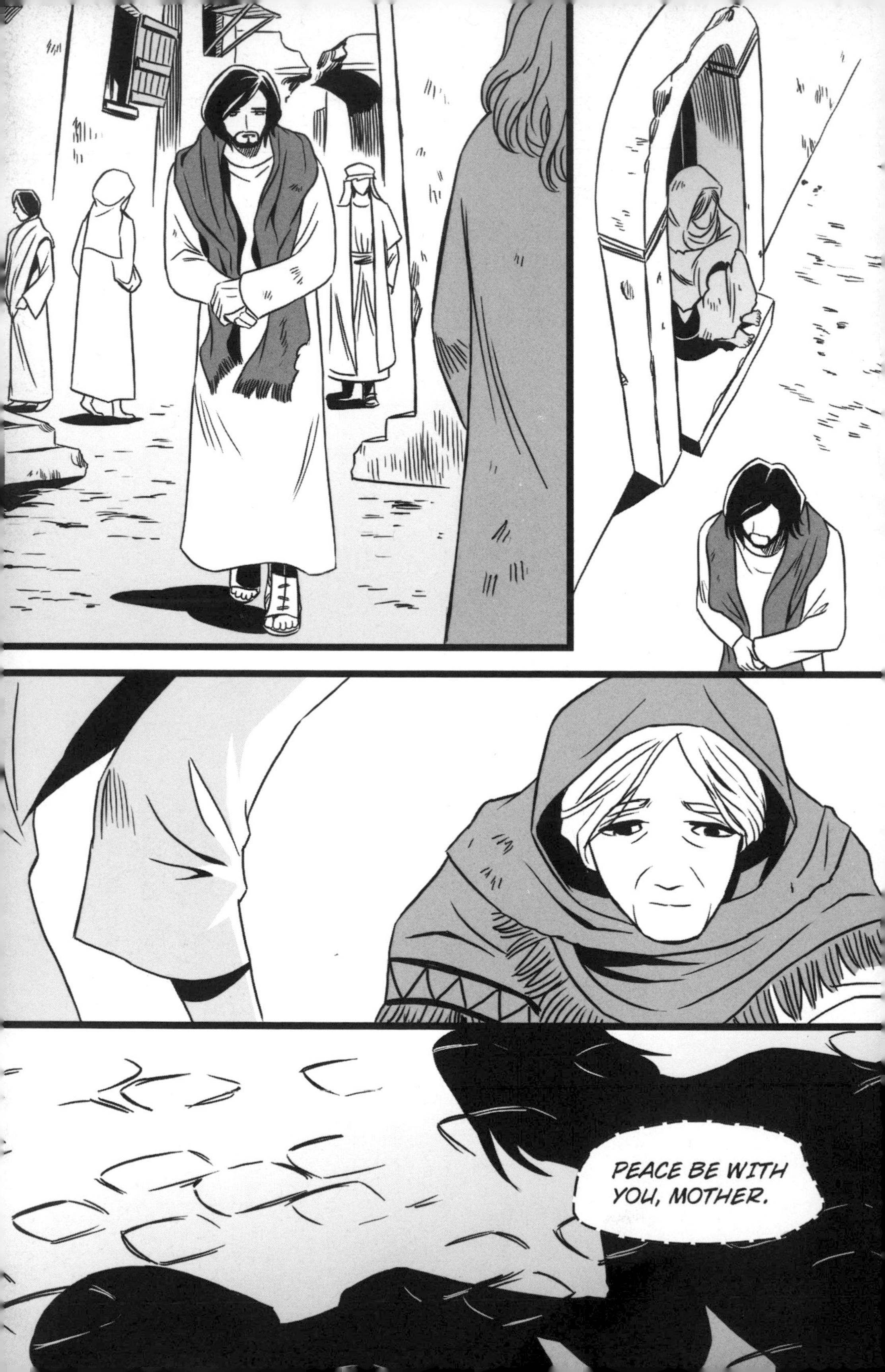
PEACE BE WITH YOU, MOTHER.

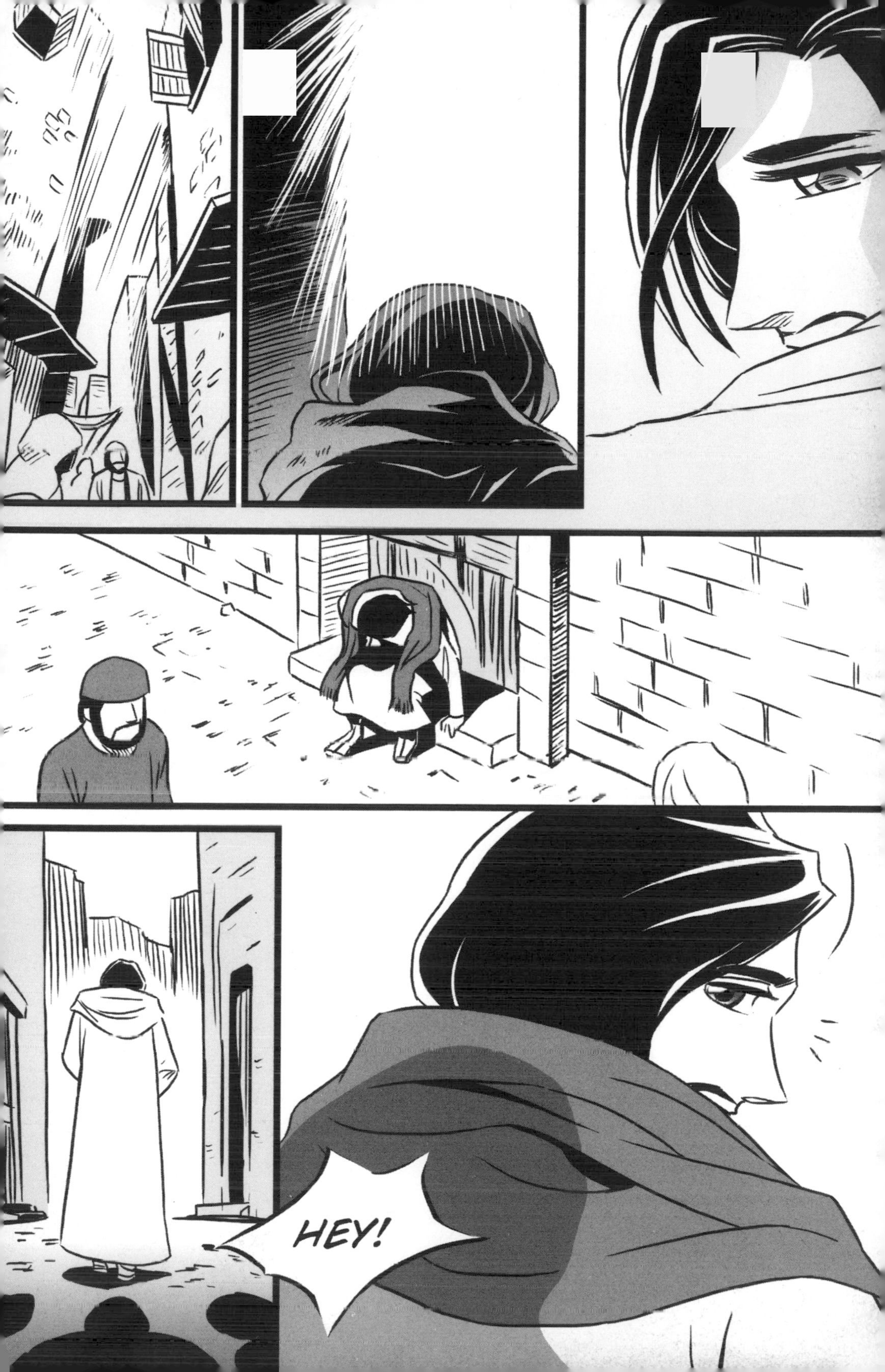
HEY!

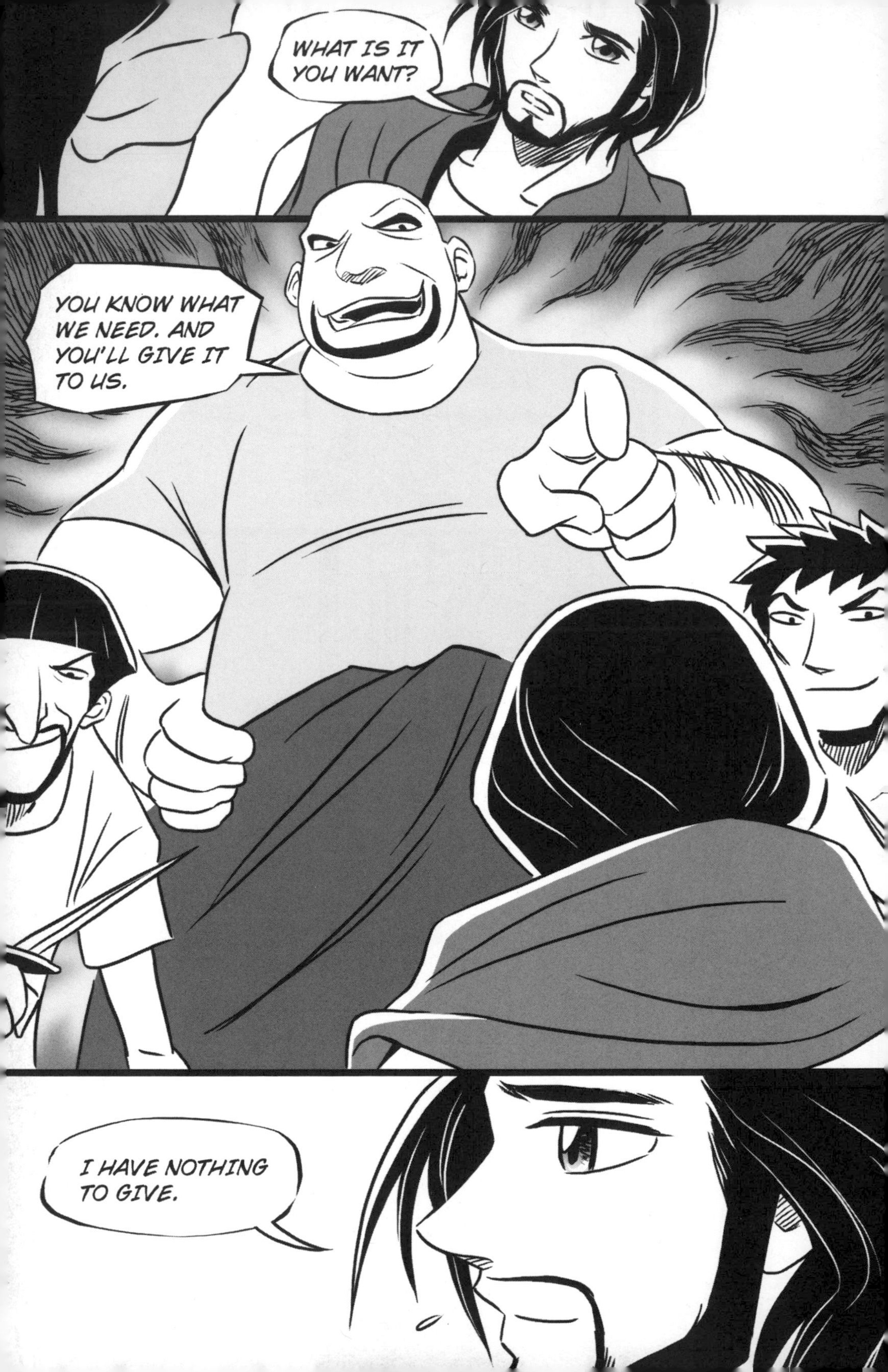
WHAT IS IT YOU WANT?
YOU KNOW WHAT WE NEED. AND YOU'LL GIVE IT TO US.
I HAVE NOTHING TO GIVE.

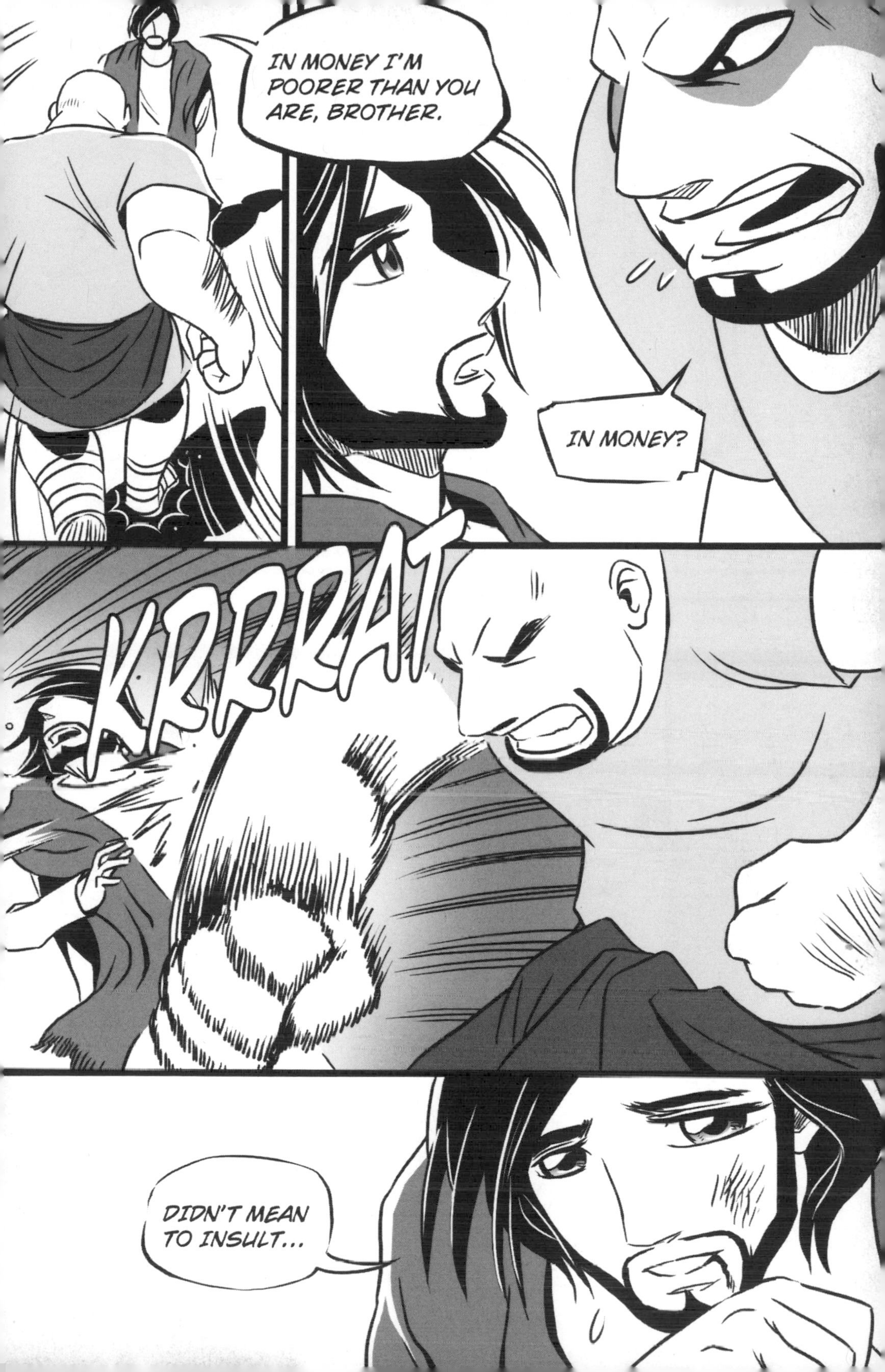
IN MONEY I'M POORER THAN YOU ARE, BROTHER.
IN MONEY?
KRRRAT
DIDN'T MEAN TO INSULT...

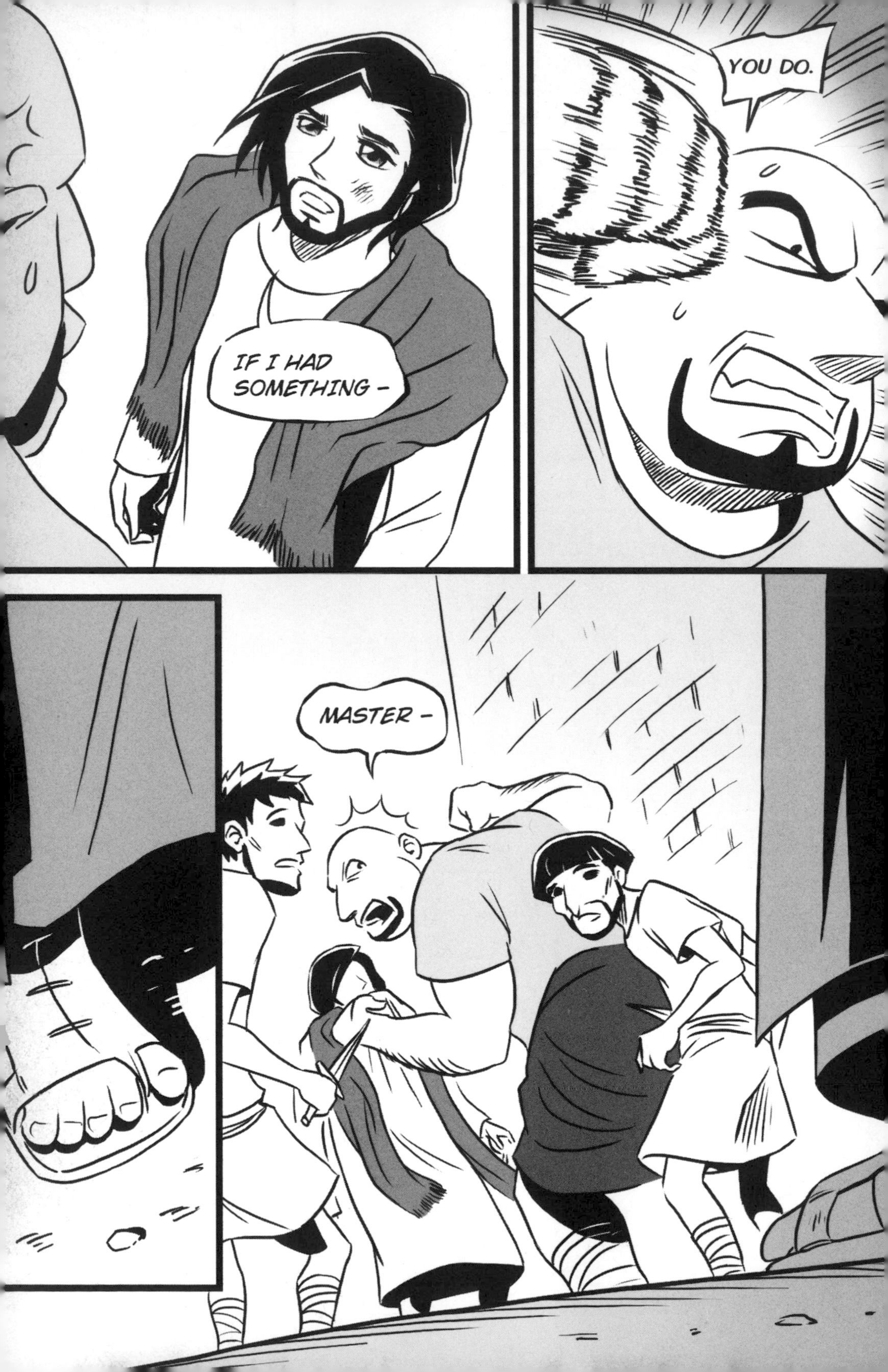
IF I HAD SOMETHING -
YOU DO.
MASTER -

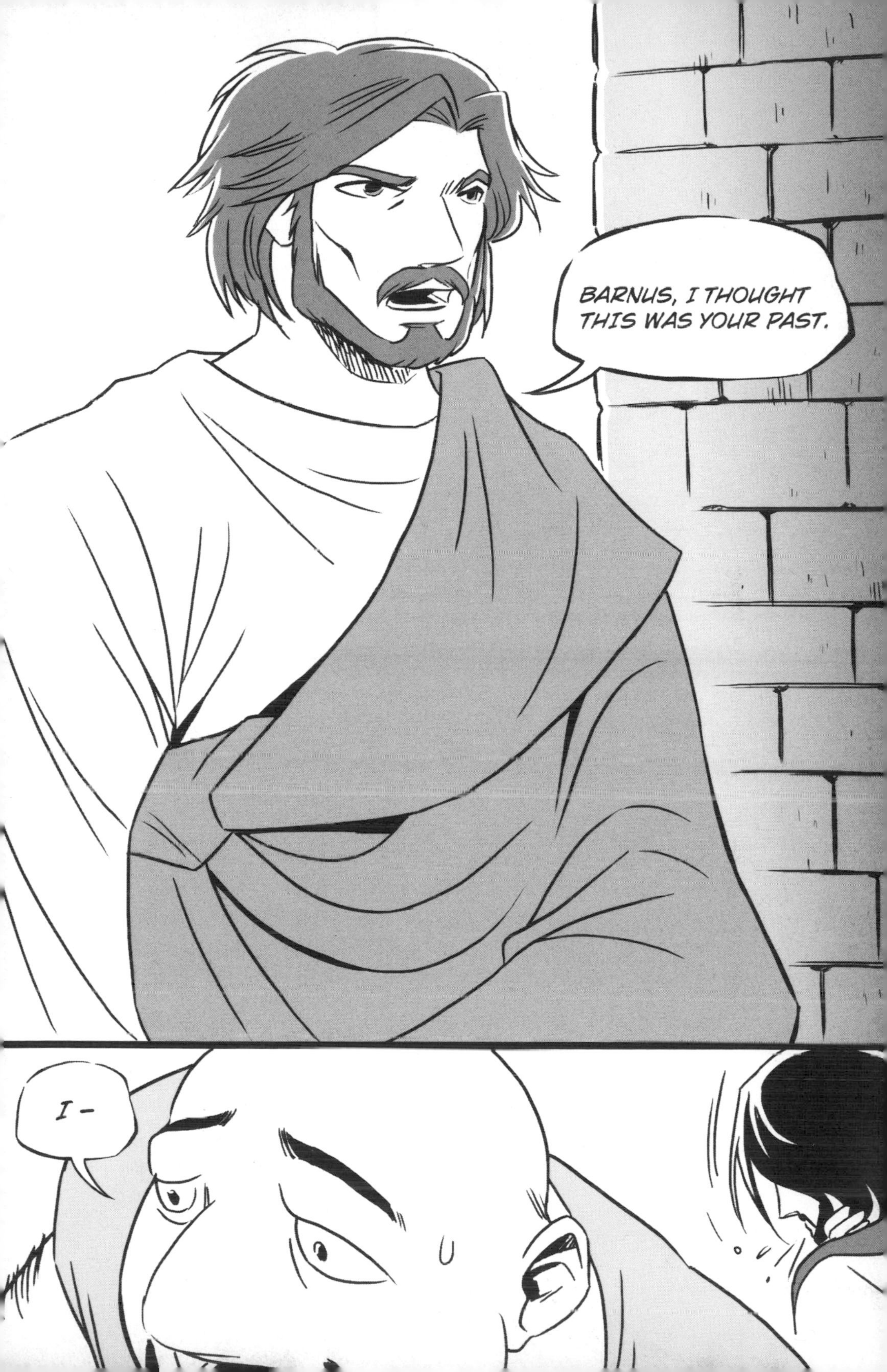
BARNUS, I THOUGHT THIS WAS YOUR PAST.
I -

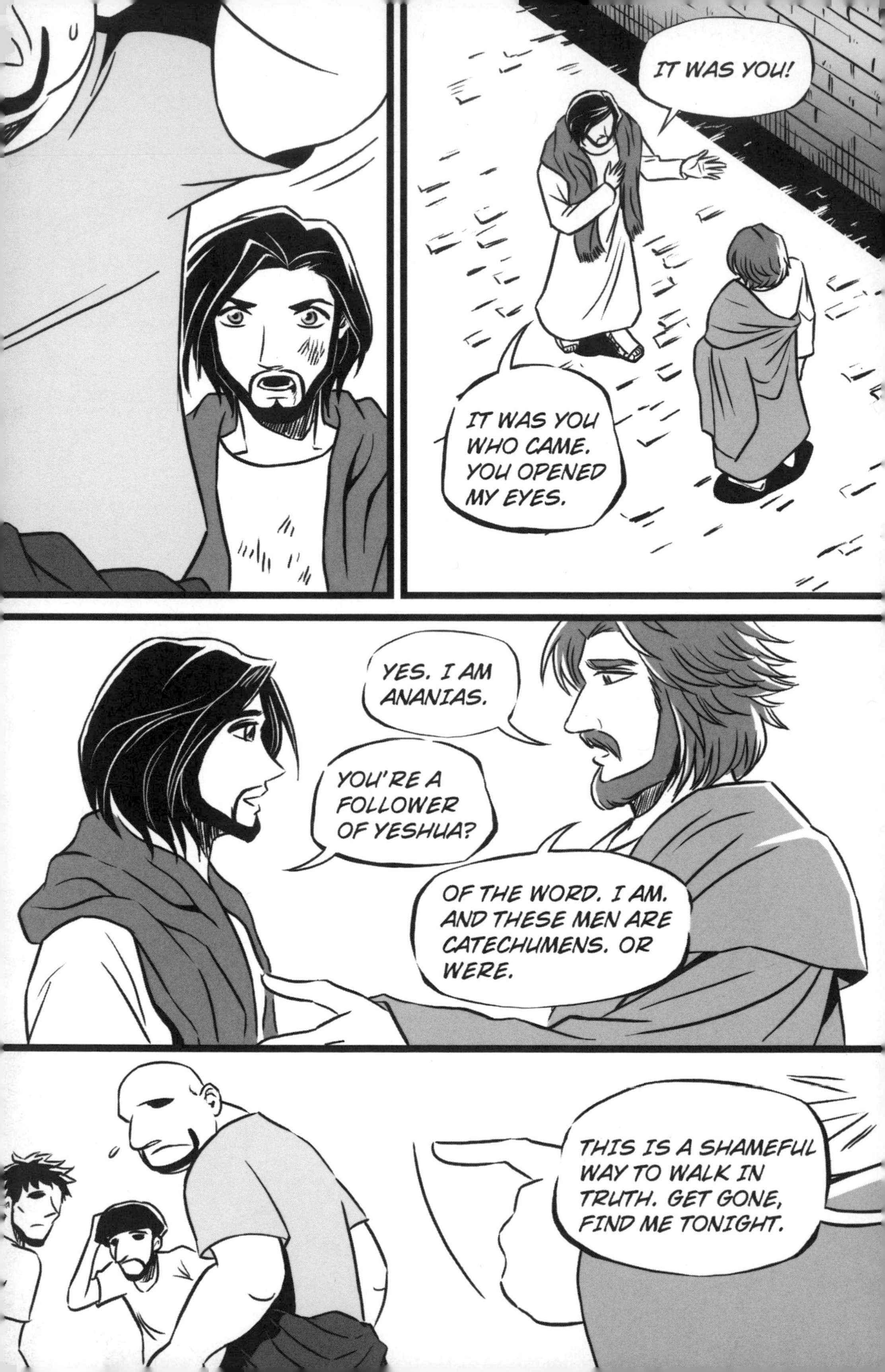
IT WAS YOU!
IT WAS YOU WHO CAME. YOU OPENED MY EYES.
YES. I AM ANANIAS.
YOU'RE A FOLLOWER OF YESHUA?
OF THE WORD. I AM. AND THESE MEN ARE CATECHUMENS. OR WERE.
THIS IS A SHAMEFUL WAY TO WALK IN TRUTH. GET GONE, FIND ME TONIGHT.

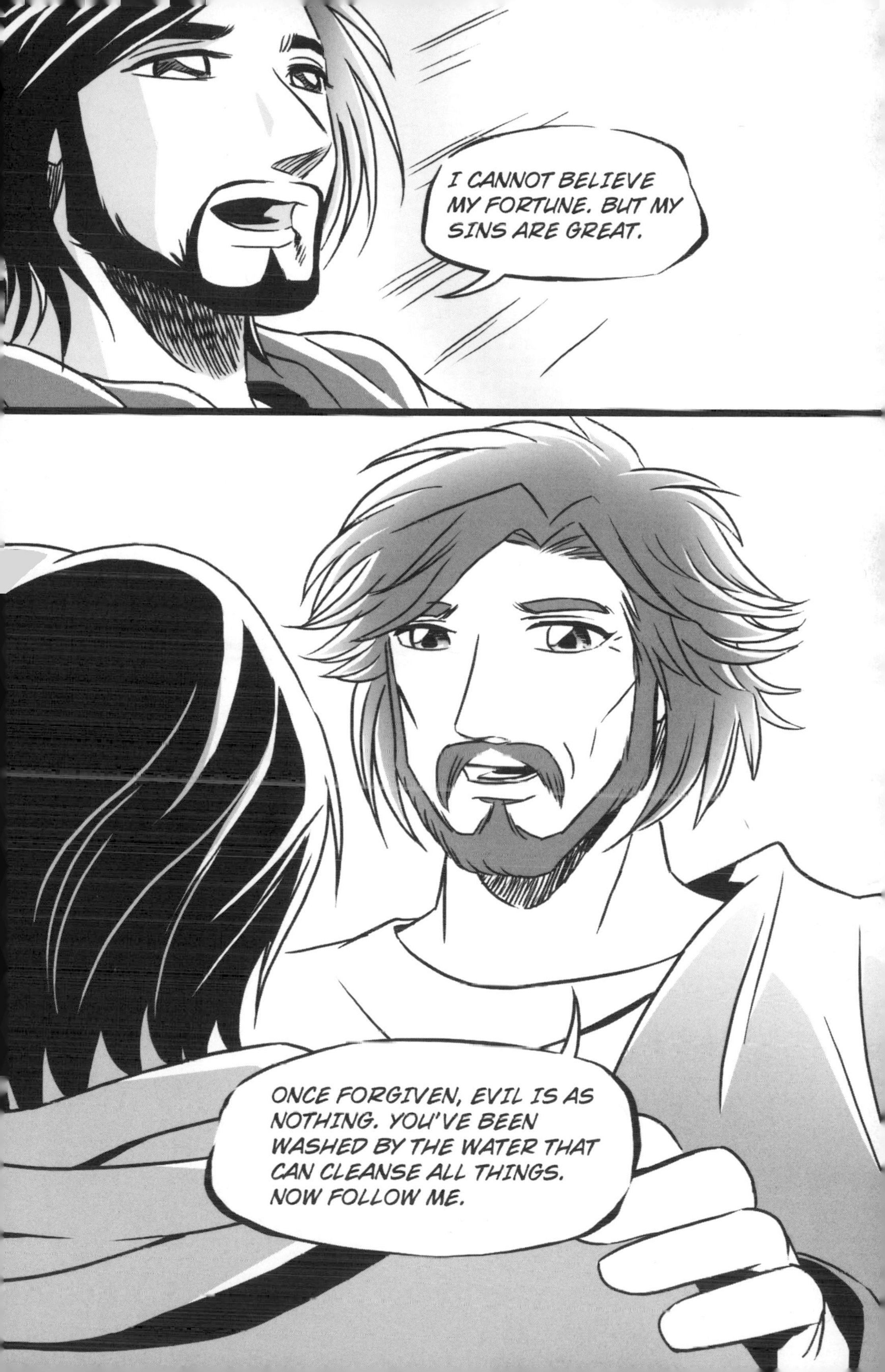
I CANNOT BELIEVE MY FORTUNE. BUT MY SINS ARE GREAT.
ONCE FORGIVEN, EVIL IS AS NOTHING. YOU'VE BEEN WASHED BY THE WATER THAT CAN CLEANSE ALL THINGS. NOW FOLLOW ME.

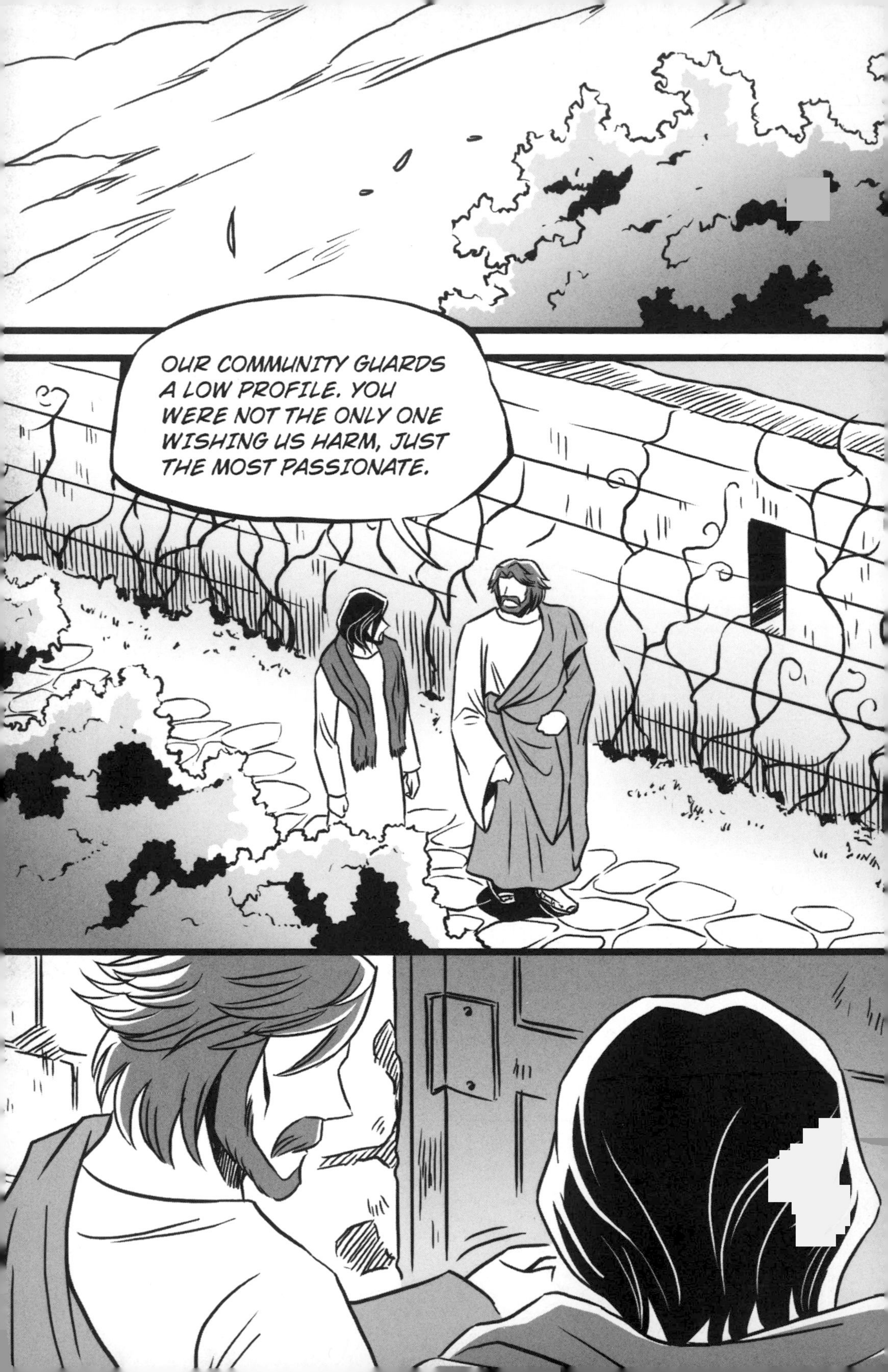
OUR COMMUNITY GUARDS A LOW PROFILE. YOU WERE NOT THE ONLY ONE WISHING US HARM, JUST THE MOST PASSIONATE.

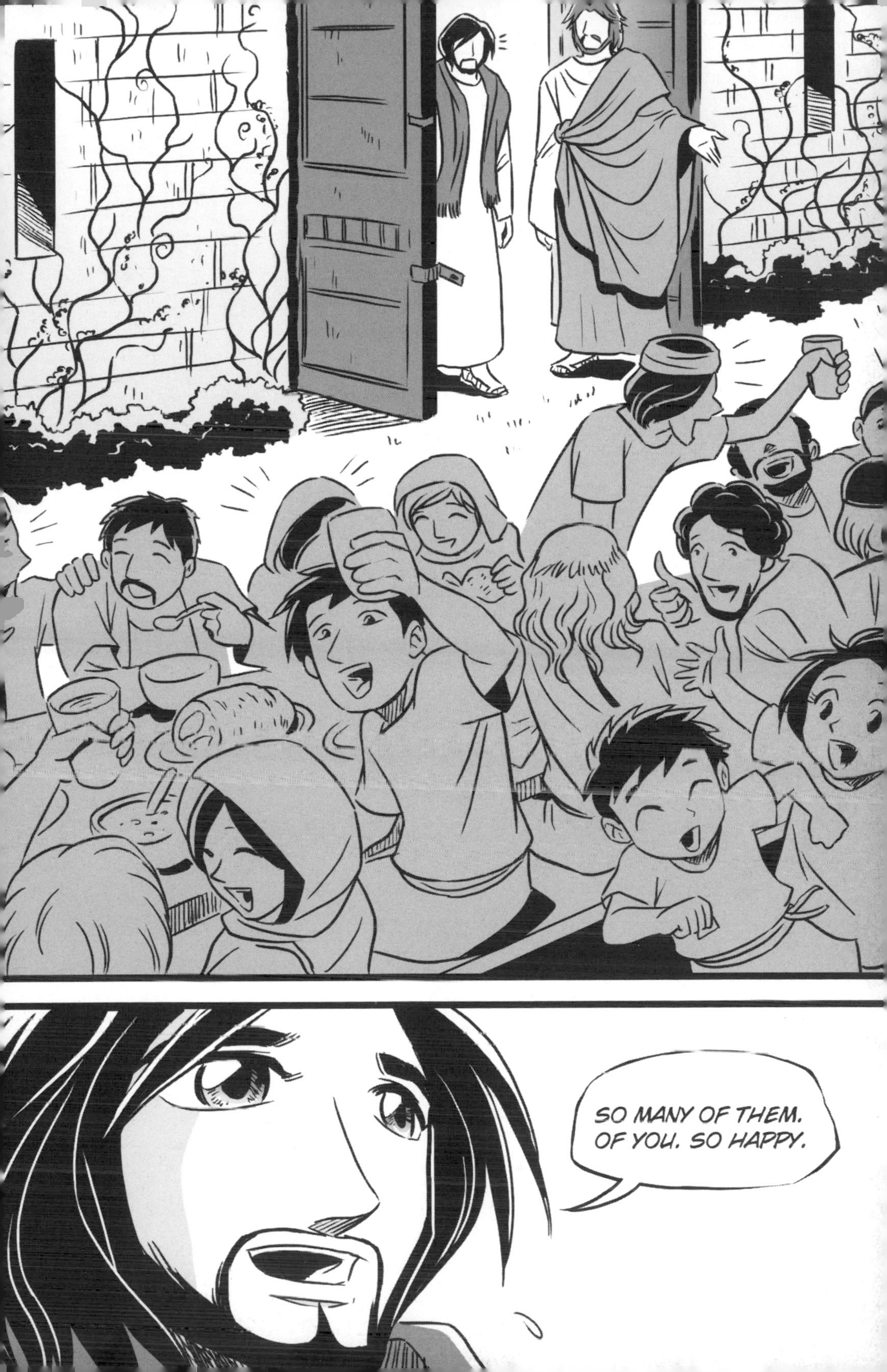
SO MANY OF THEM.
OF YOU. SO HAPPY.

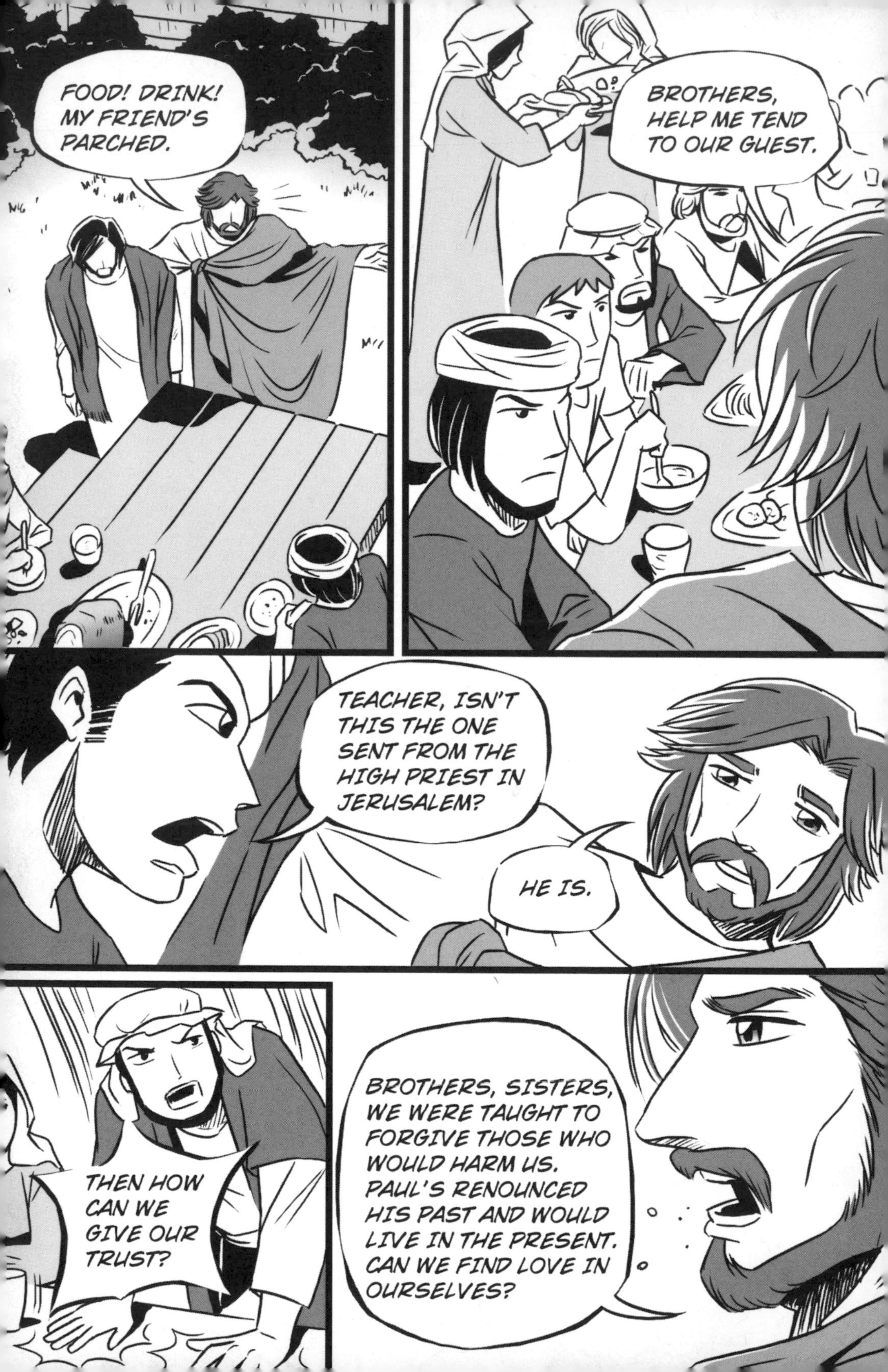
FOOD! DRINK! MY FRIEND'S PARCHED.
BROTHERS, HELP ME TEND TO OUR GUEST.
TEACHER, ISN'T THIS THE ONE SENT FROM THE HIGH PRIEST IN JERUSALEM?
HE IS.
THEN HOW CAN WE GIVE OUR TRUST?
BROTHERS, SISTERS, WE WERE TAUGHT TO FORGIVE THOSE WHO WOULD HARM US. PAUL'S RENOUNCED HIS PAST AND WOULD LIVE IN THE PRESENT. CAN WE FIND LOVE IN OURSELVES?

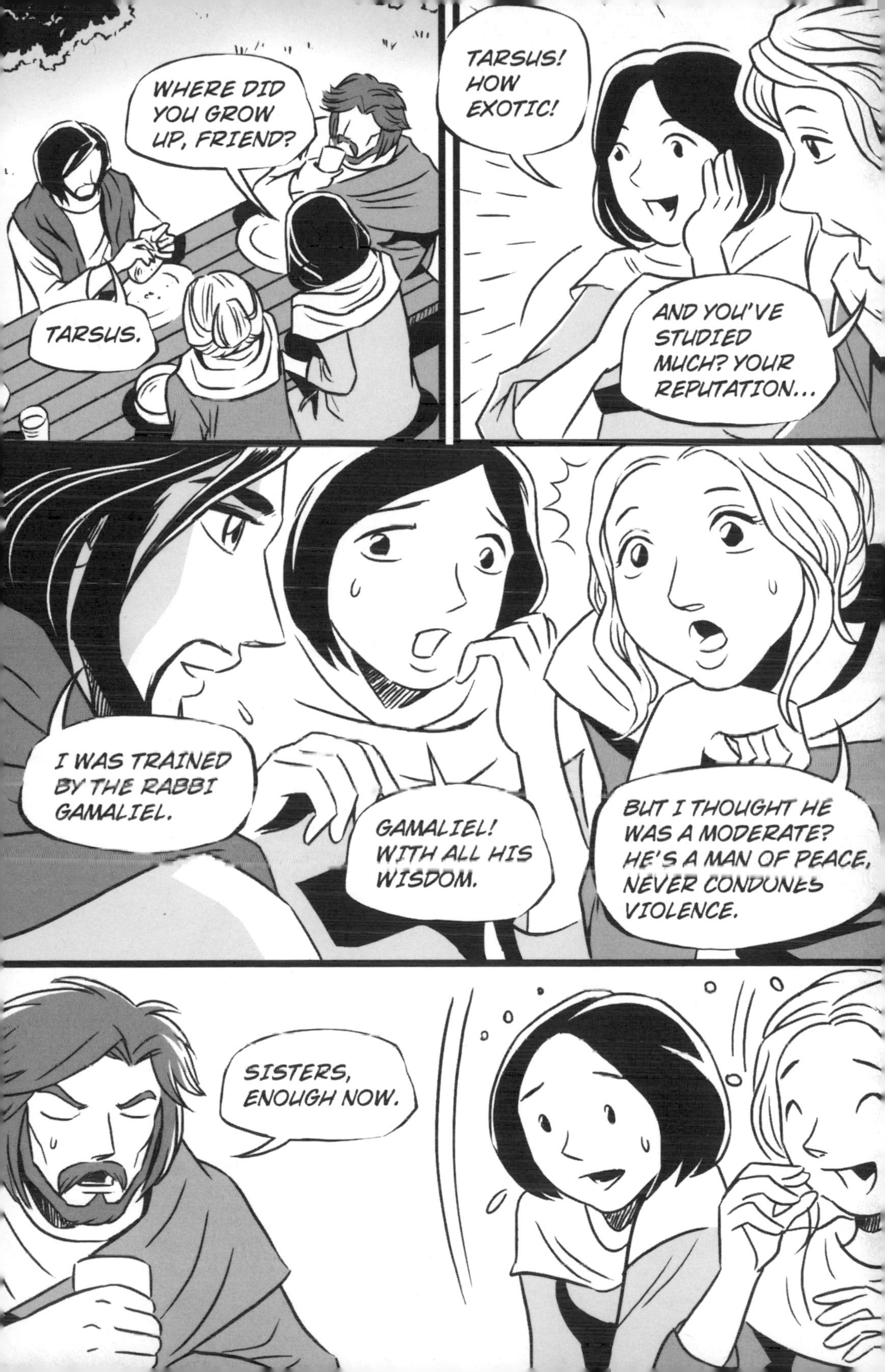
WHERE DID YOU GROW UP, FRIEND?
TARSUS.
TARSUS! HOW EXOTIC!
AND YOU'VE STUDIED MUCH? YOUR REPUTATION...
I WAS TRAINED BY THE RABBI GAMALIEL.
GAMALIEL! WITH ALL HIS WISDOM.
BUT I THOUGHT HE WAS A MODERATE? HE'S A MAN OF PEACE, NEVER CONDONES VIOLENCE.
SISTERS, ENOUGH NOW.

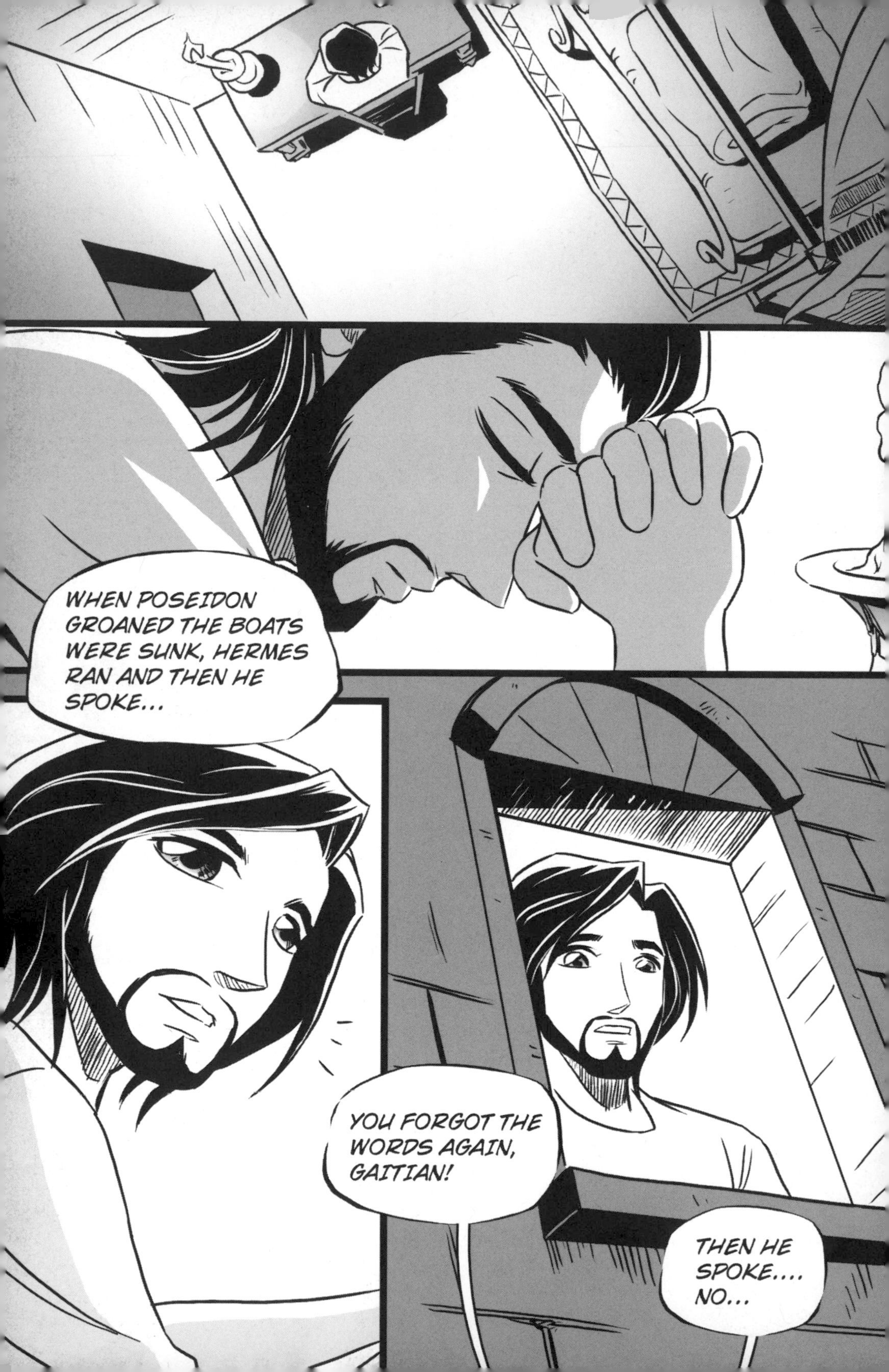
WHEN POSEIDON GROANED THE BOATS WERE SUNK, HERMES RAN AND THEN HE SPOKE...
YOU FORGOT THE WORDS AGAIN, GAITIAN!
THEN HE SPOKE.... NO...

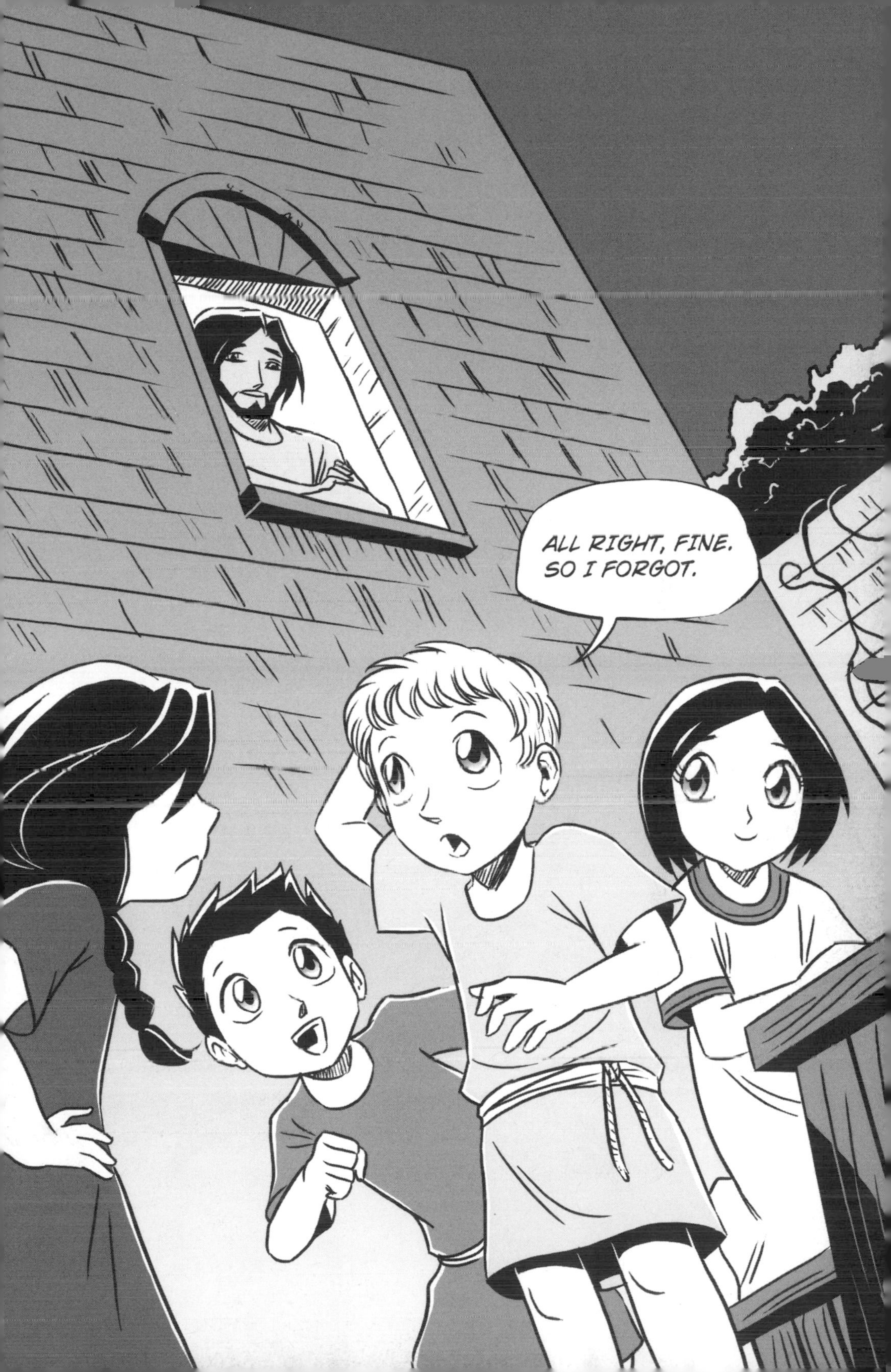
ALL RIGHT, FINE. SO I FORGOT.

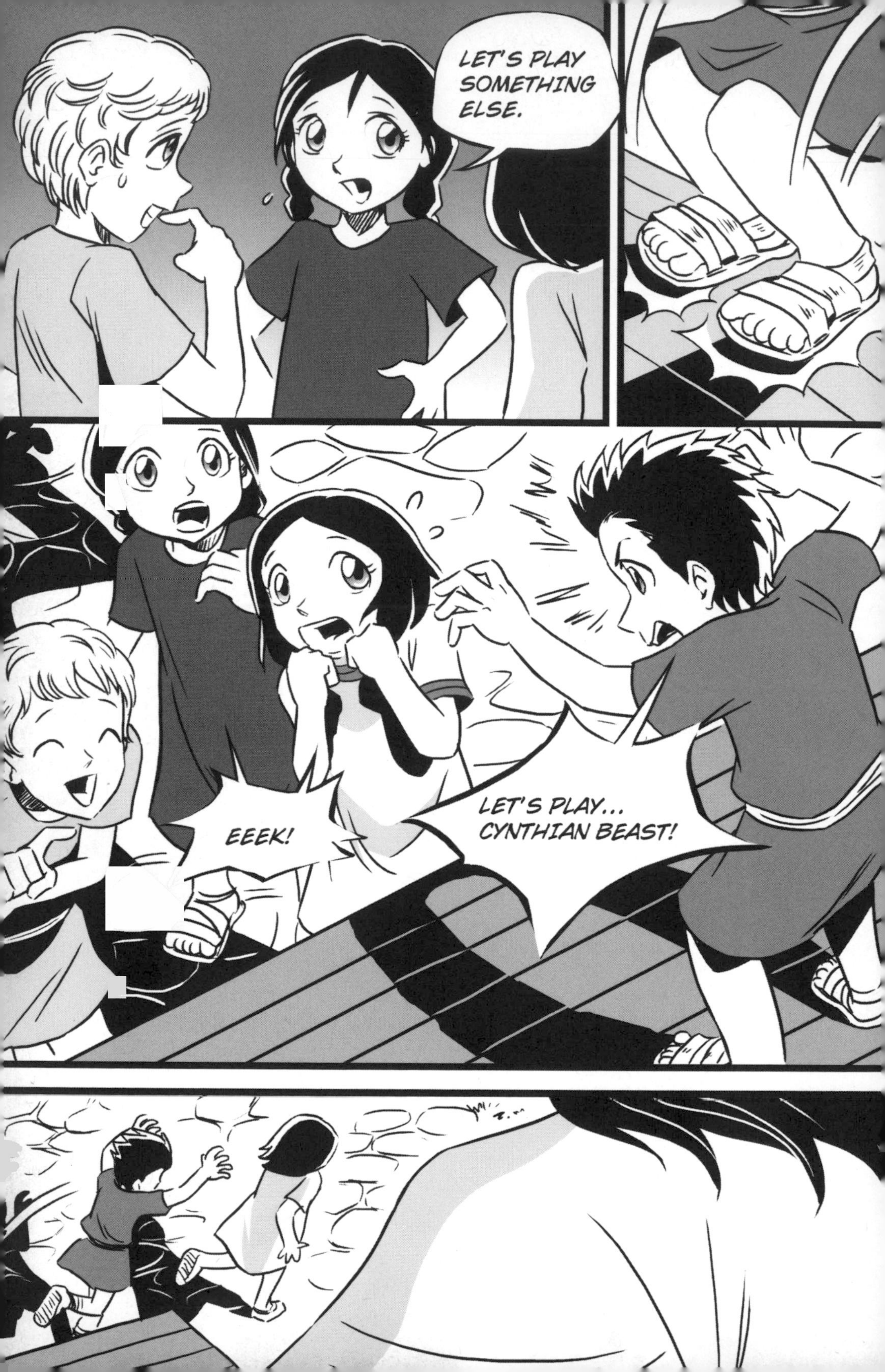
LET'S PLAY SOMETHING ELSE.
EEEK!
LET'S PLAY... CYNTHIAN BEAST!

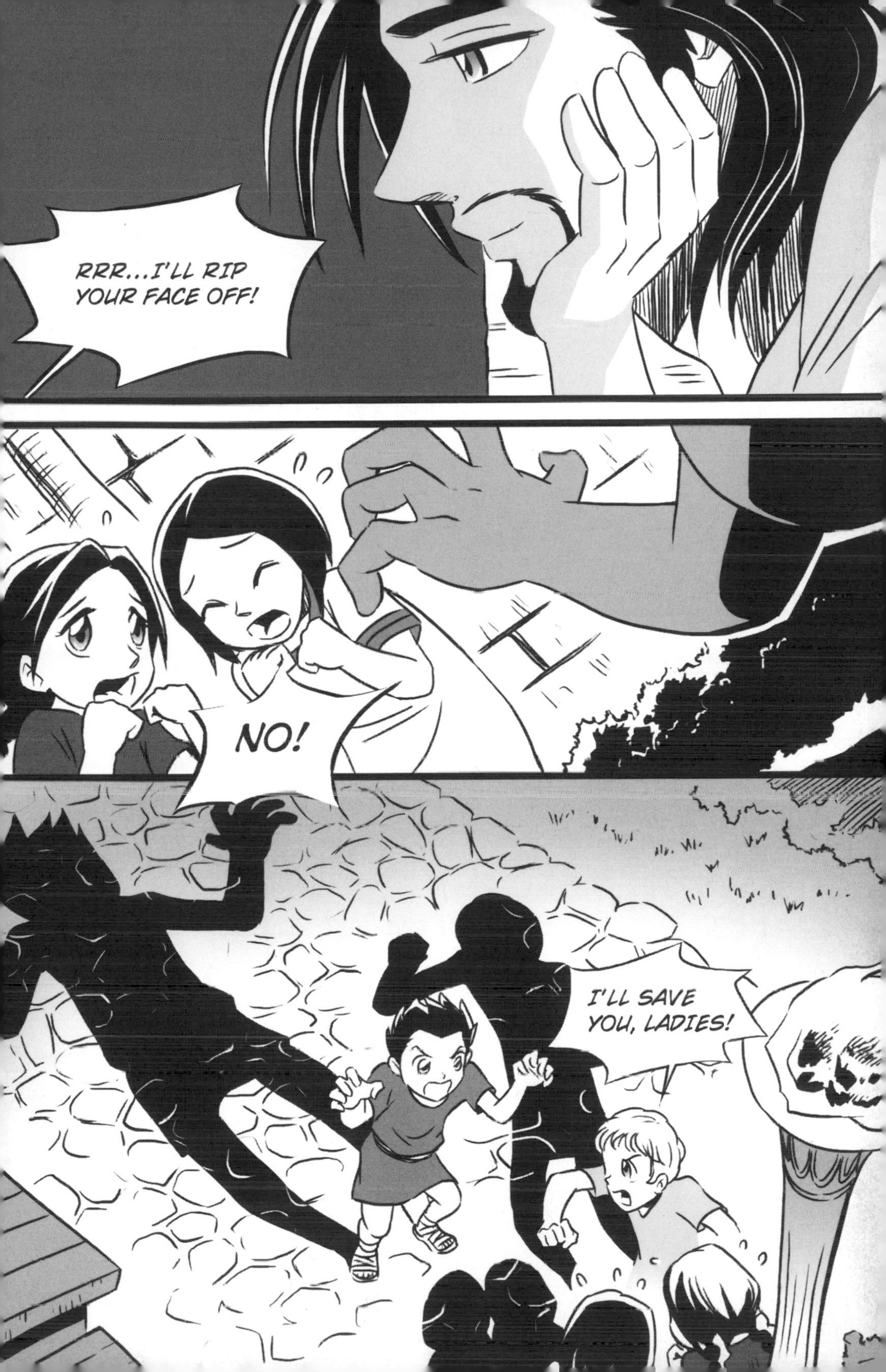
RRR...I'LL RIP YOUR FACE OFF!
NO!
I'LL SAVE YOU, LADIES!

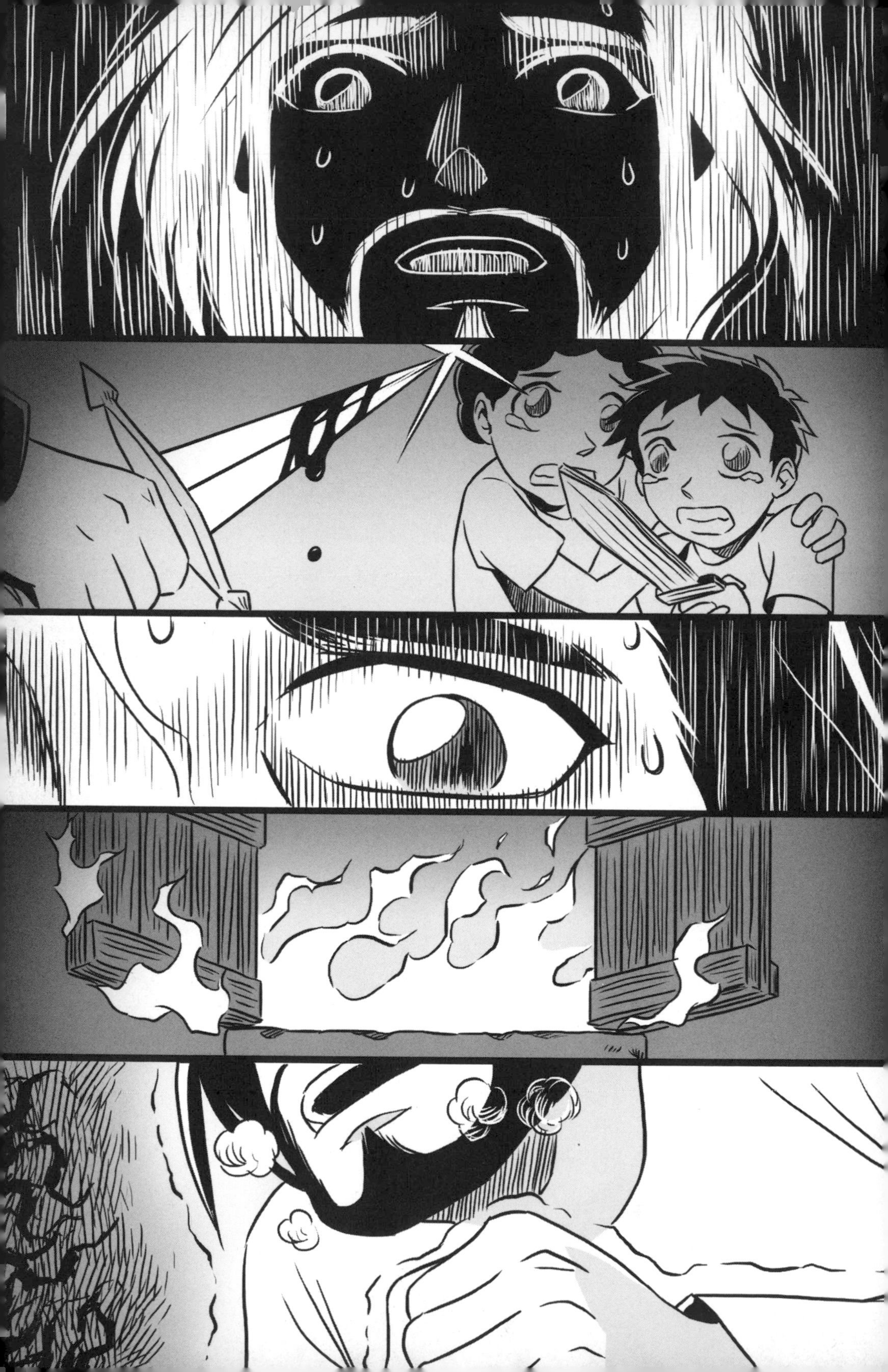

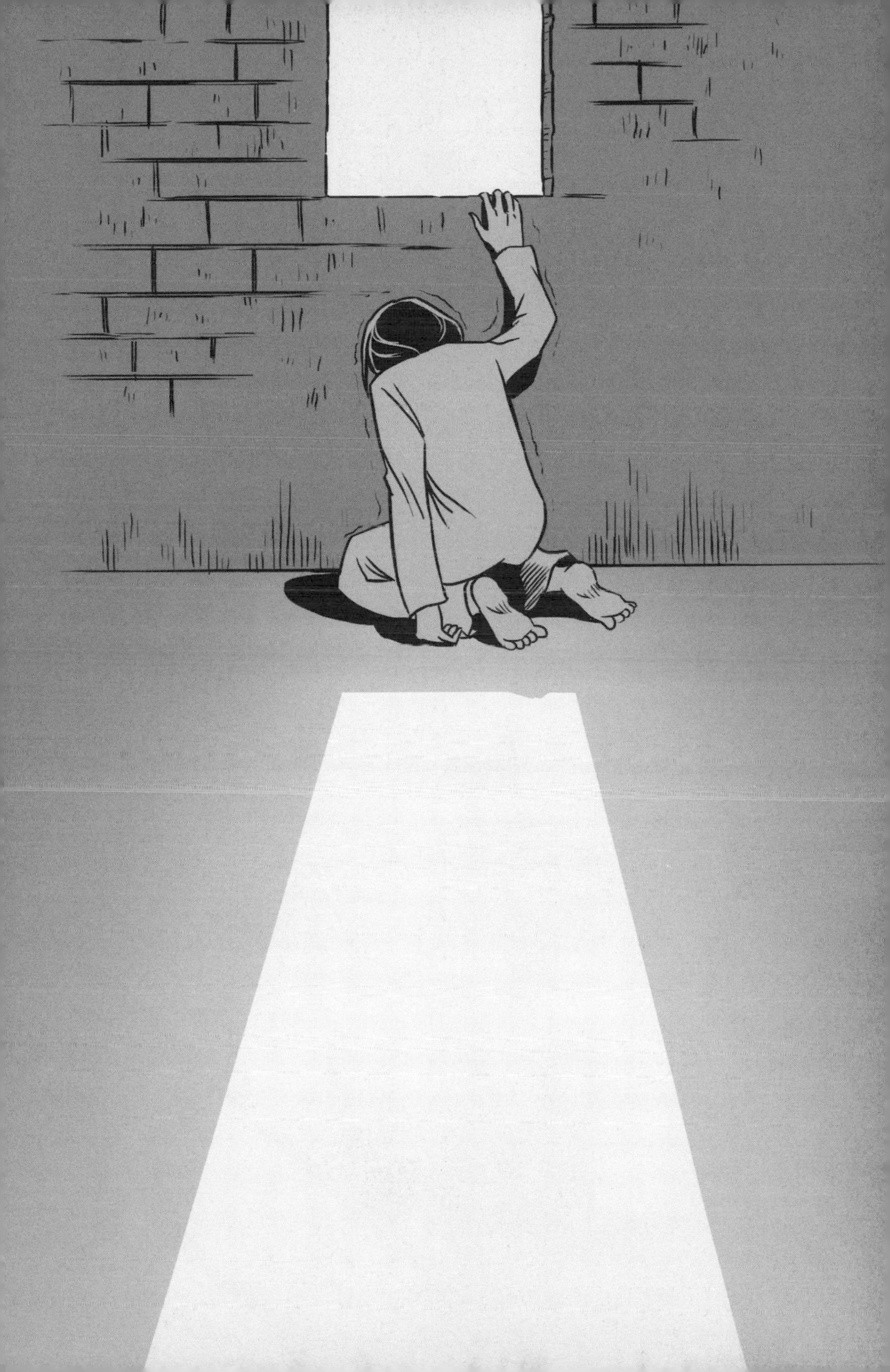

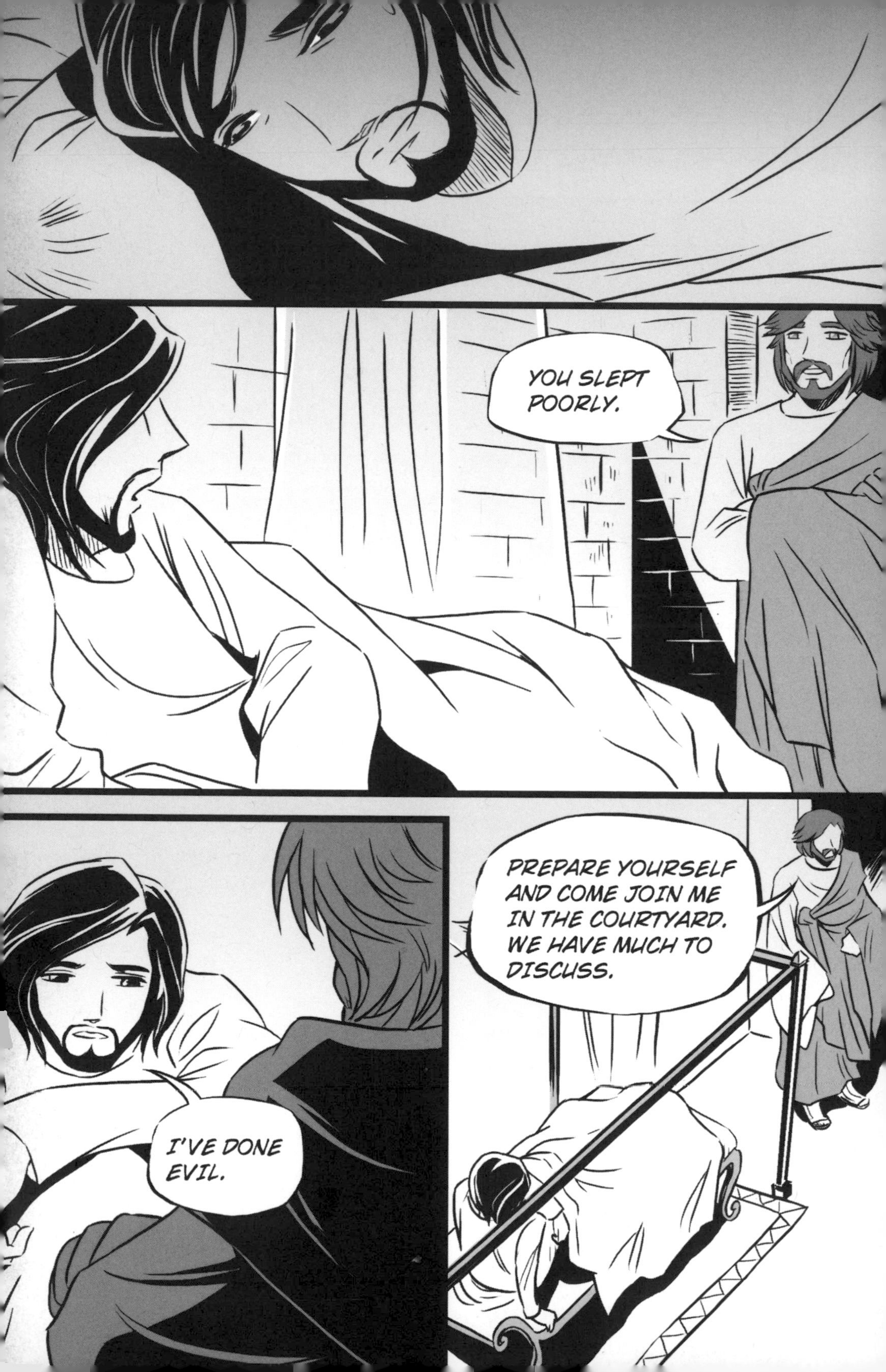
YOU SLEPT POORLY.
I'VE DONE EVIL.
PREPARE YOURSELF AND COME JOIN ME IN THE COURTYARD. WE HAVE MUCH TO DISCUSS.

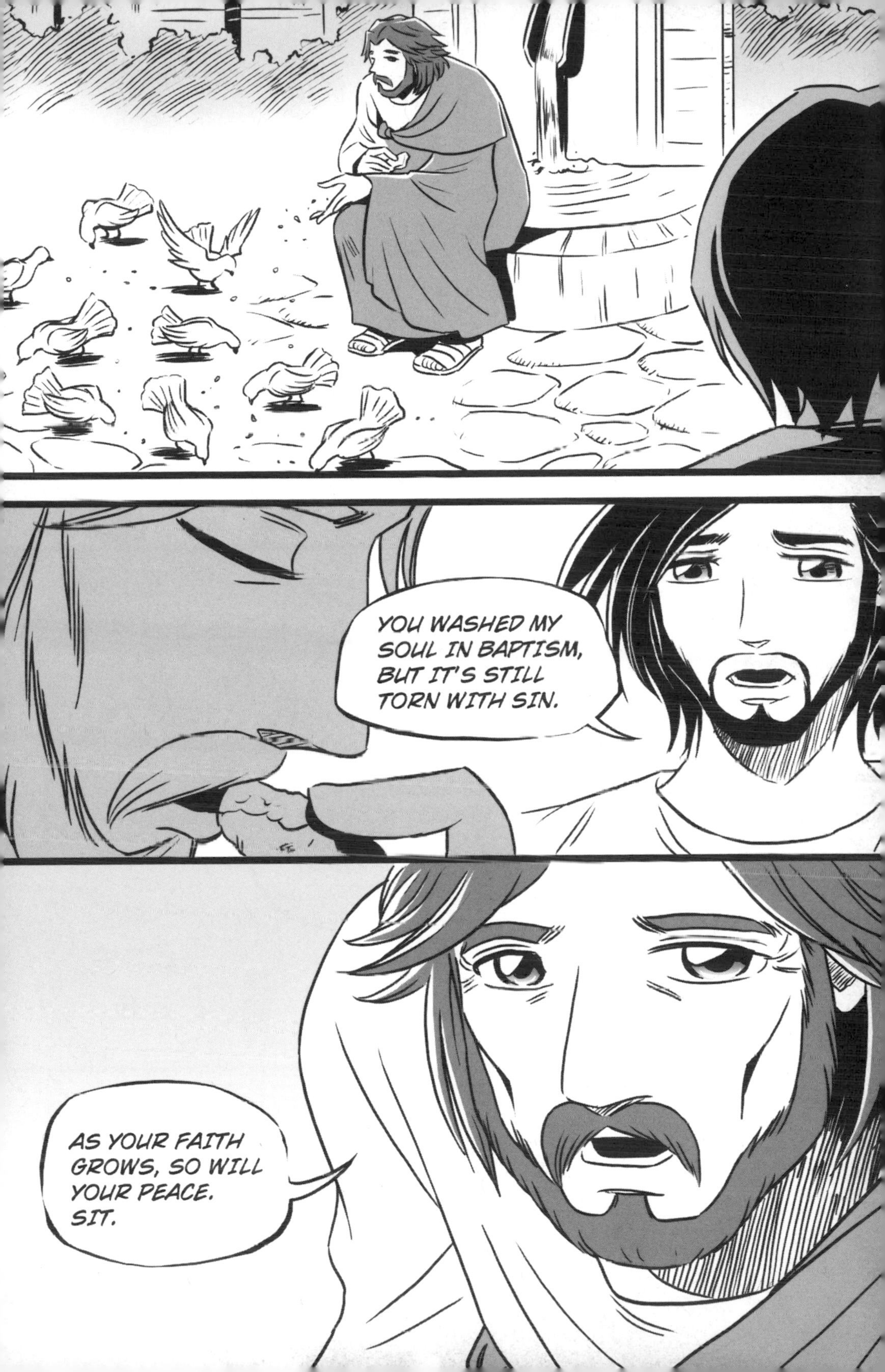
YOU WASHED MY SOUL IN BAPTISM, BUT IT'S STILL TORN WITH SIN.
AS YOUR FAITH GROWS, SO WILL YOUR PEACE. SIT.

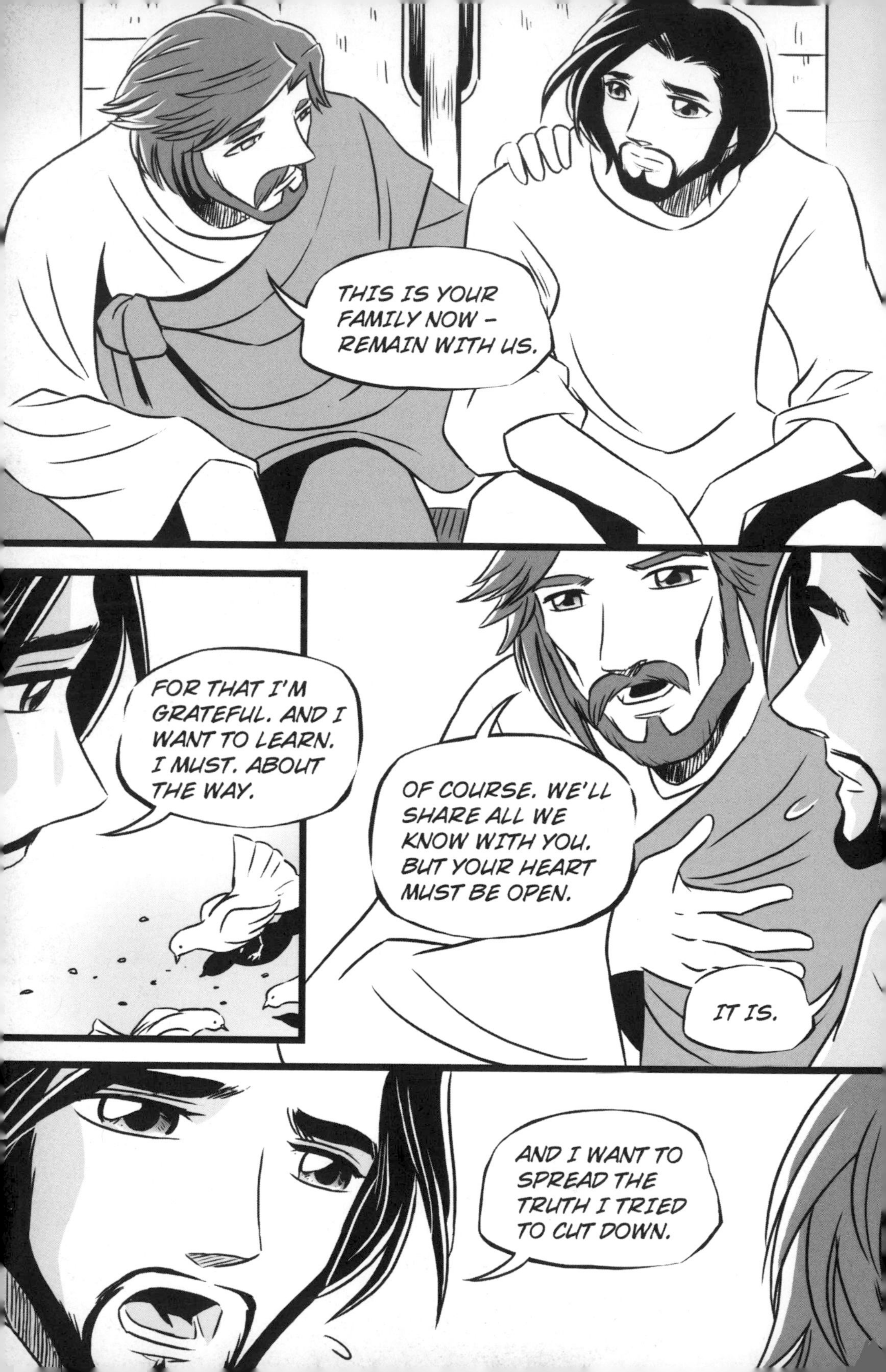

THIS IS YOUR FAMILY NOW - REMAIN WITH US.
FOR THAT I'M GRATEFUL. AND I WANT TO LEARN. I MUST. ABOUT THE WAY.
OF COURSE. WE'LL SHARE ALL WE KNOW WITH YOU. BUT YOUR HEART MUST BE OPEN.
IT IS.
AND I WANT TO SPREAD THE TRUTH I TRIED TO CUT DOWN.

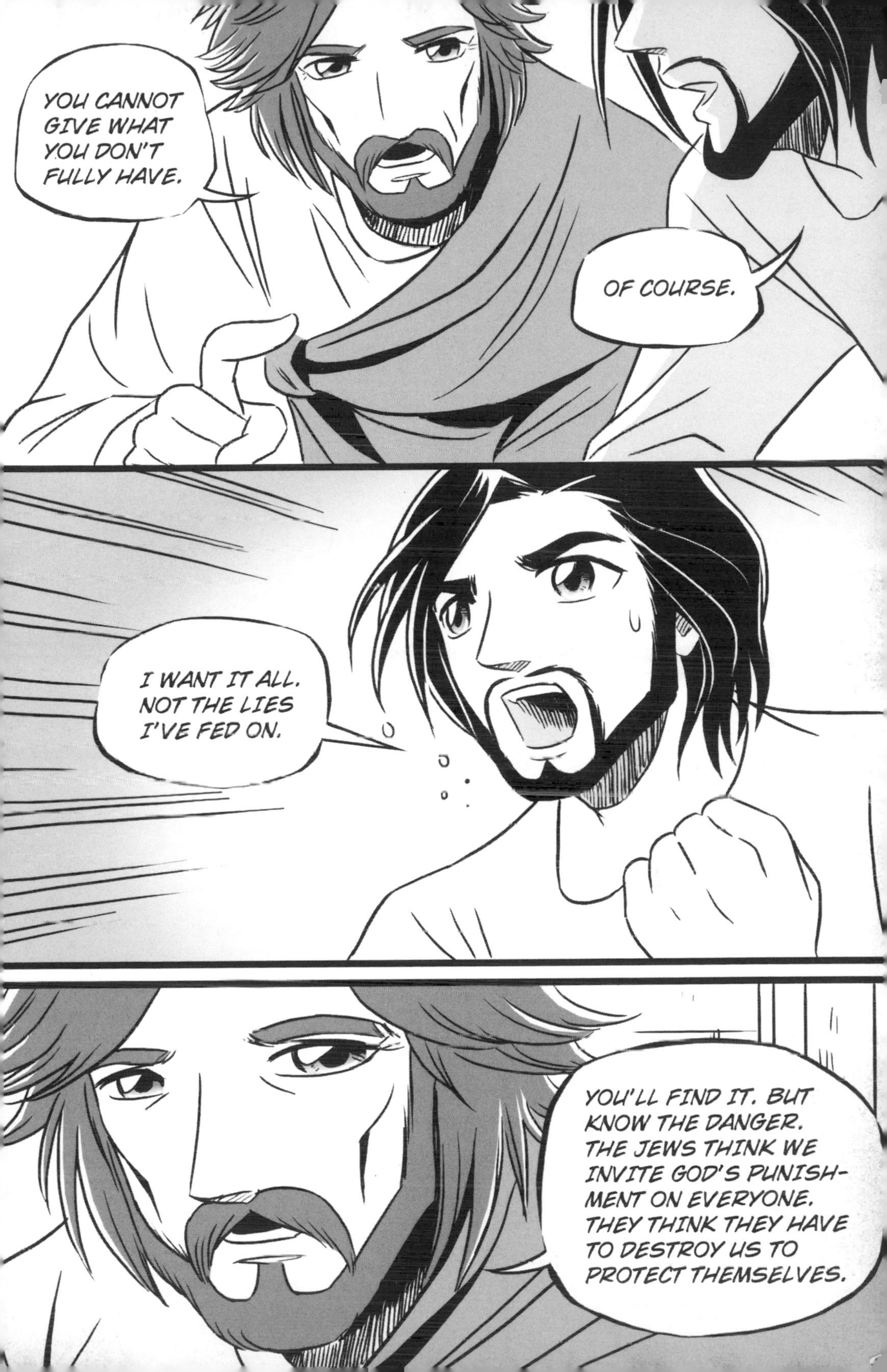
YOU CANNOT GIVE WHAT YOU DON'T FULLY HAVE.
OF COURSE.
I WANT IT ALL. NOT THE LIES I'VE FED ON.
YOU'LL FIND IT. BUT KNOW THE DANGER. THE JEWS THINK WE INVITE GOD'S PUNISHMENT ON EVERYONE. THEY THINK THEY HAVE TO DESTROY US TO PROTECT THEMSELVES.

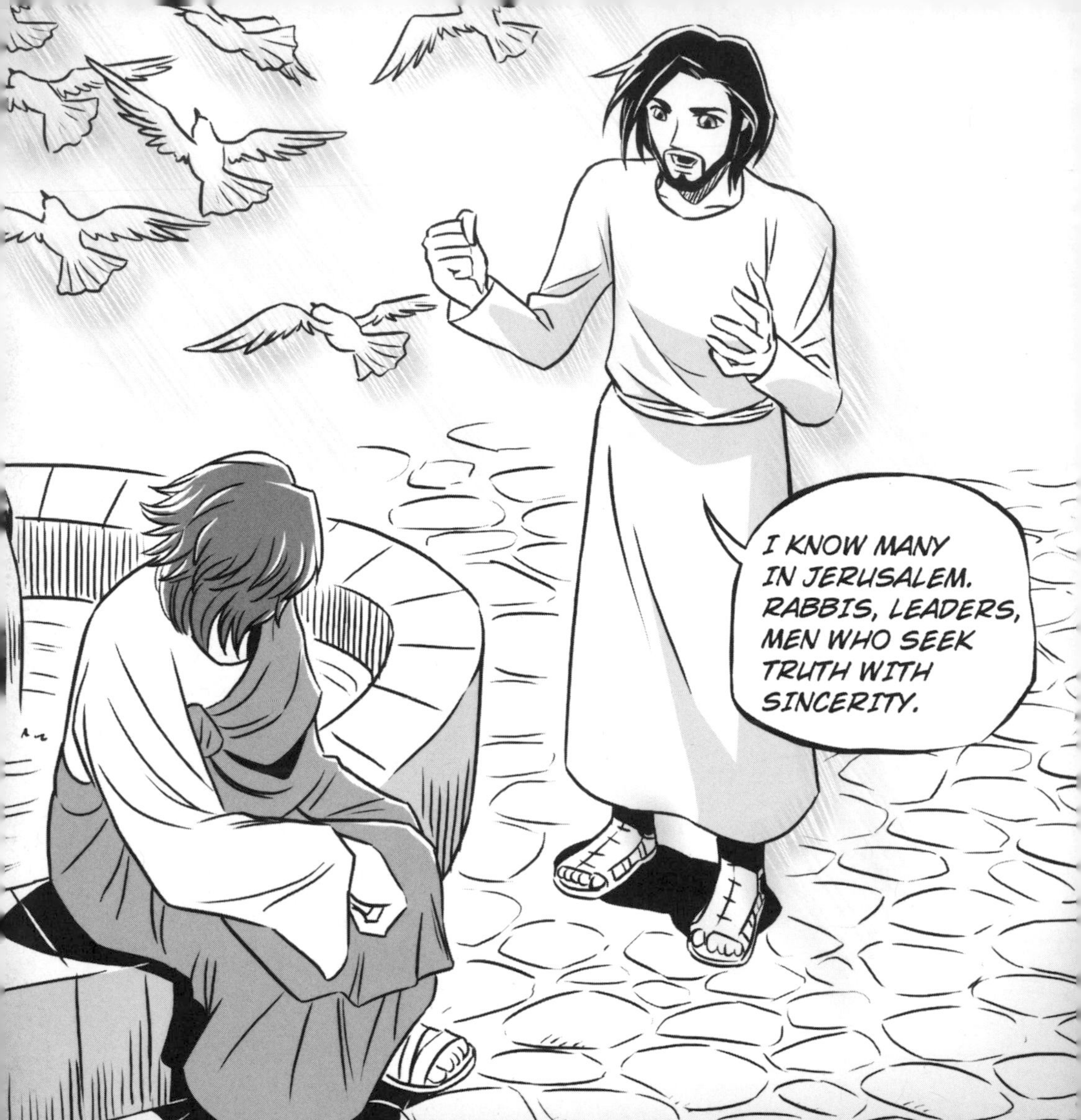
I KNOW MANY IN JERUSALEM. RABBIS, LEADERS, MEN WHO SEEK TRUTH WITH SINCERITY.

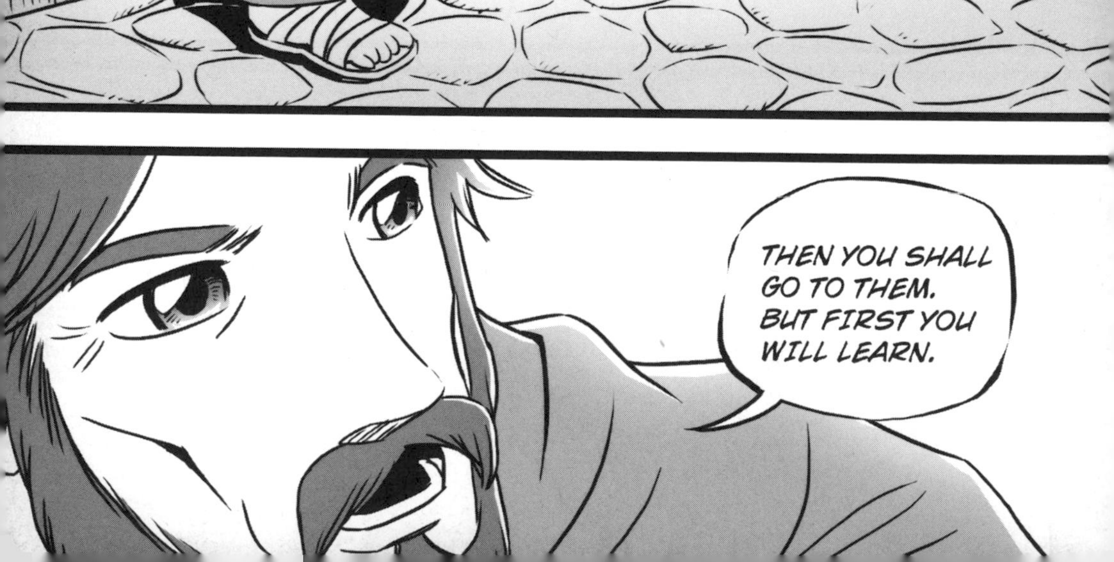
THEN YOU SHALL GO TO THEM. BUT FIRST YOU WILL LEARN.

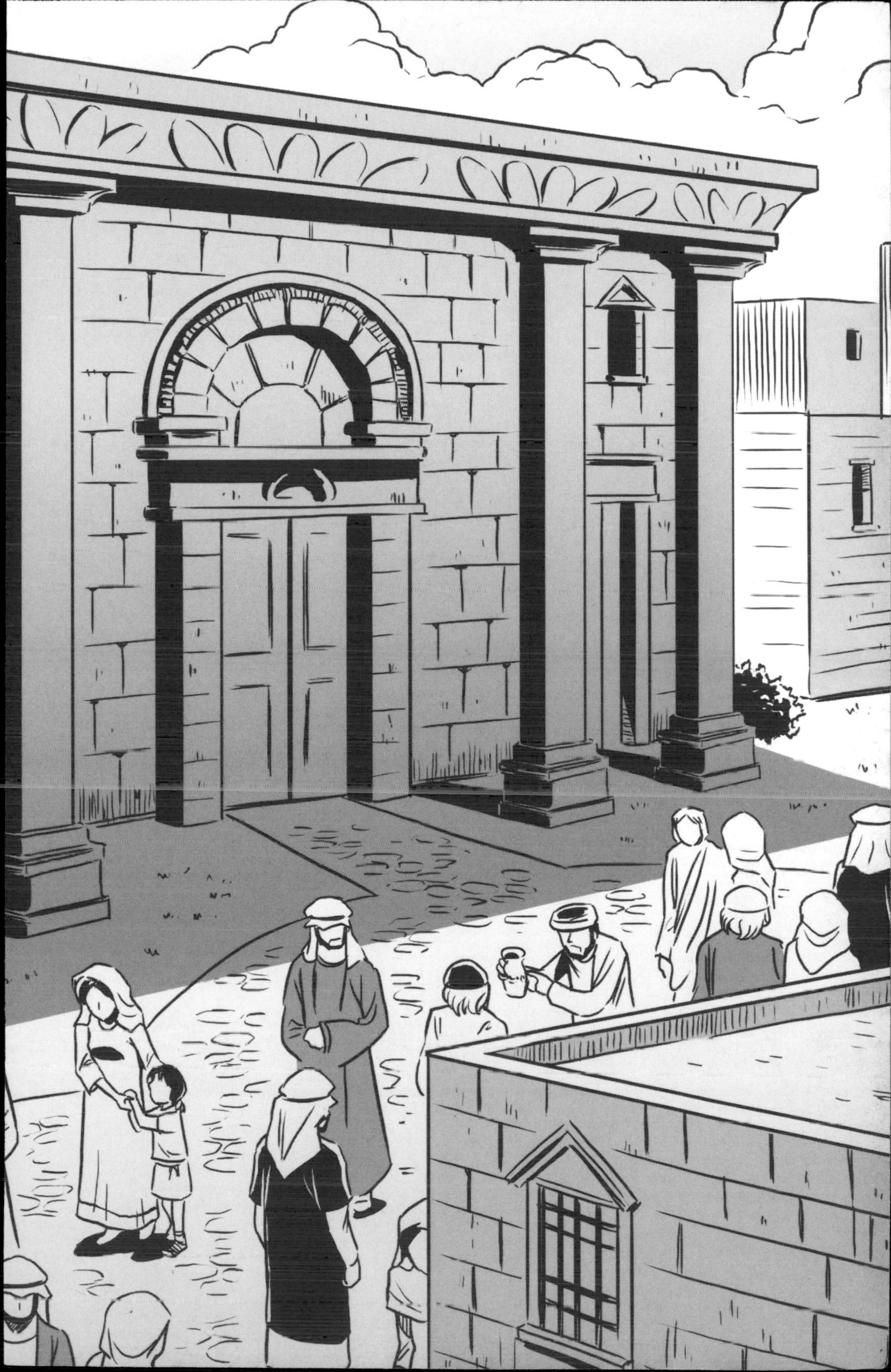

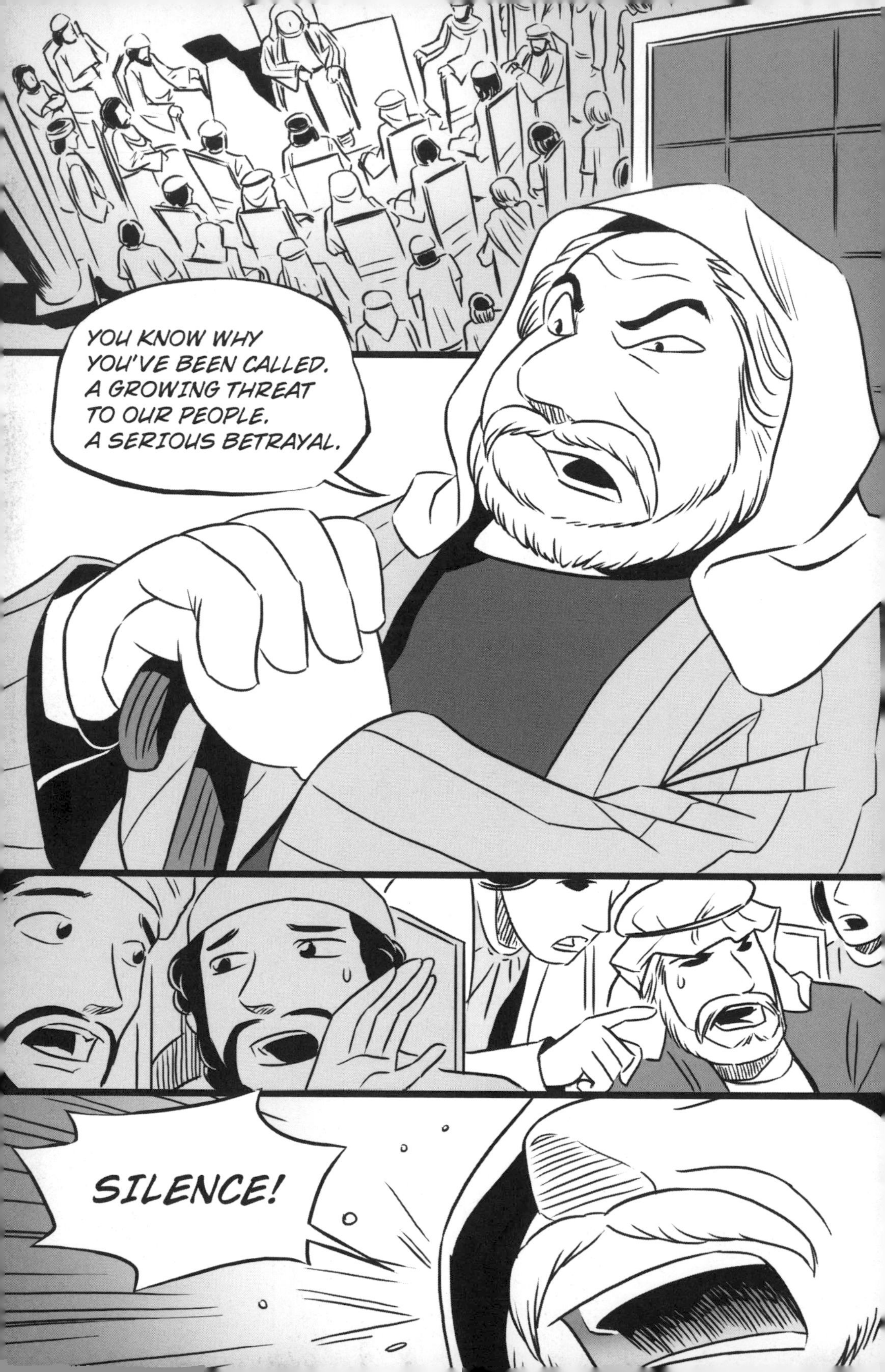
YOU KNOW WHY YOU'VE BEEN CALLED. A GROWING THREAT TO OUR PEOPLE. A SERIOUS BETRAYAL.
SILENCE!

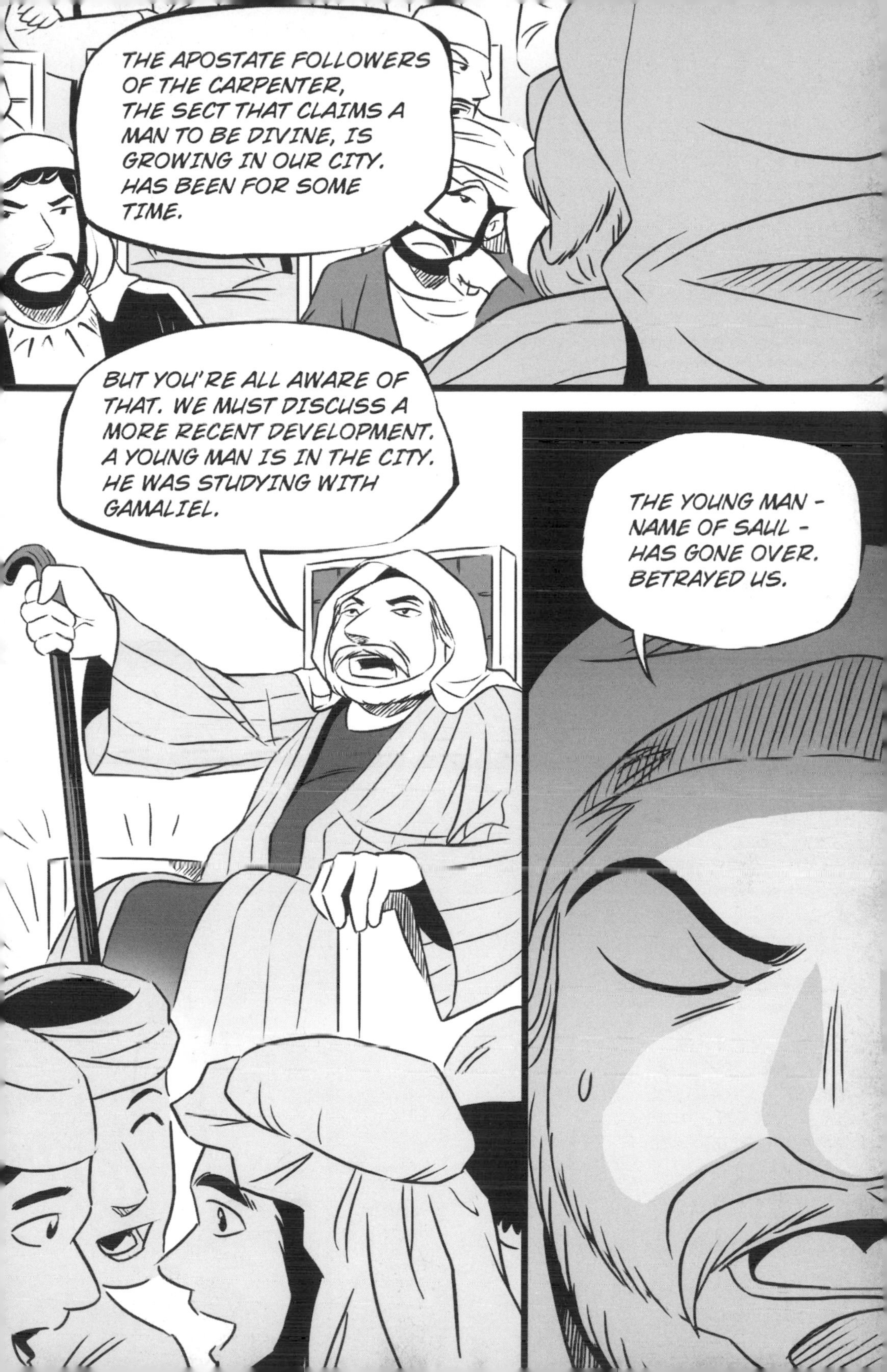
THE APOSTATE FOLLOWERS OF THE CARPENTER, THE SECT THAT CLAIMS A MAN TO BE DIVINE, IS GROWING IN OUR CITY. HAS BEEN FOR SOME TIME.
BUT YOU'RE ALL AWARE OF THAT. WE MUST DISCUSS A MORE RECENT DEVELOPMENT. A YOUNG MAN IS IN THE CITY. HE WAS STUDYING WITH GAMALIEL.
THE YOUNG MAN - NAME OF SAUL - HAS GONE OVER. BETRAYED US.

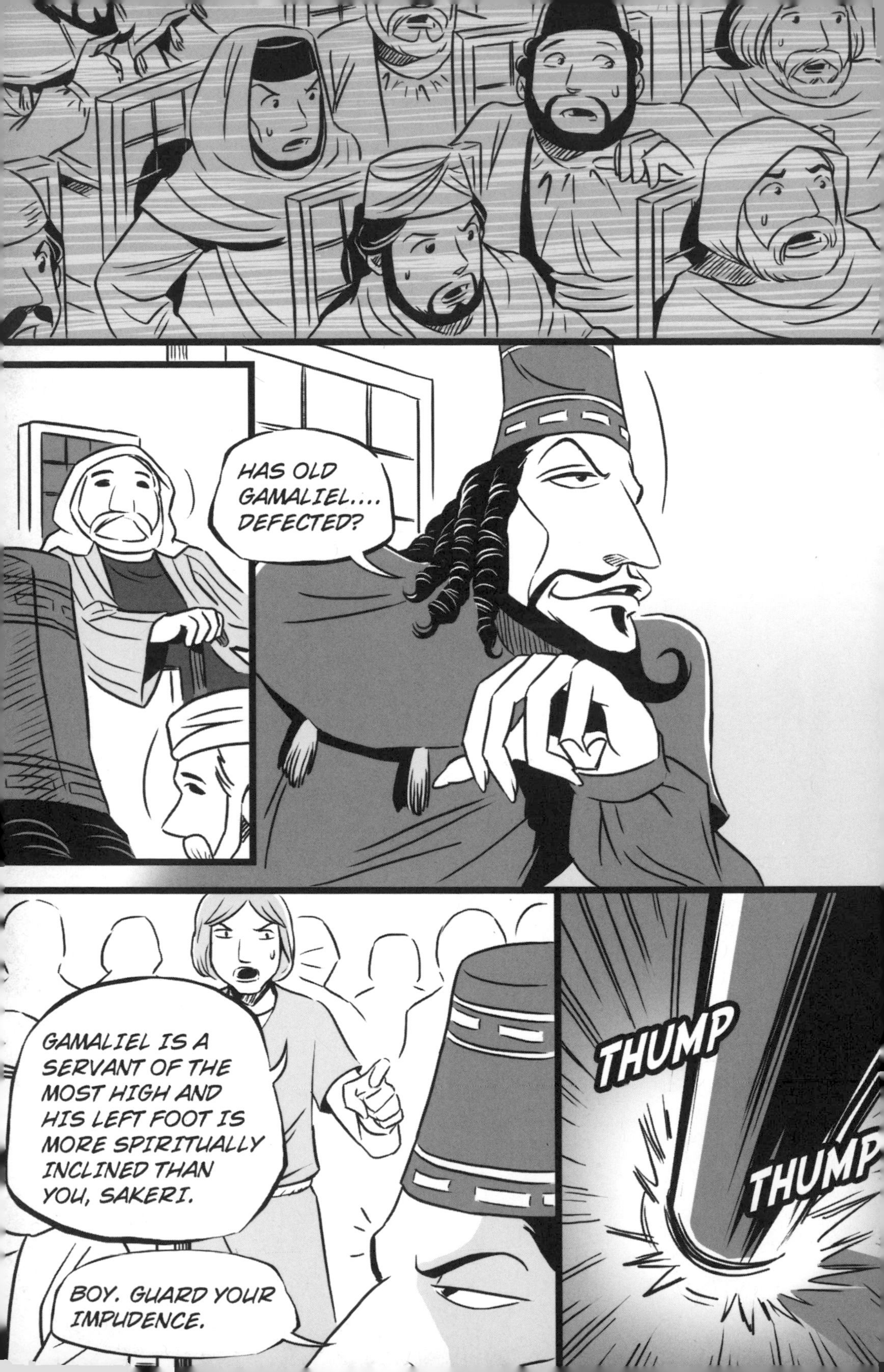

HAS OLD GAMALIEL.... DEFECTED?
GAMALIEL IS A SERVANT OF THE MOST HIGH AND HIS LEFT FOOT IS MORE SPIRITUALLY INCLINED THAN YOU, SAKERI.
BOY. GUARD YOUR IMPUDENCE.
THUMP
THUMP

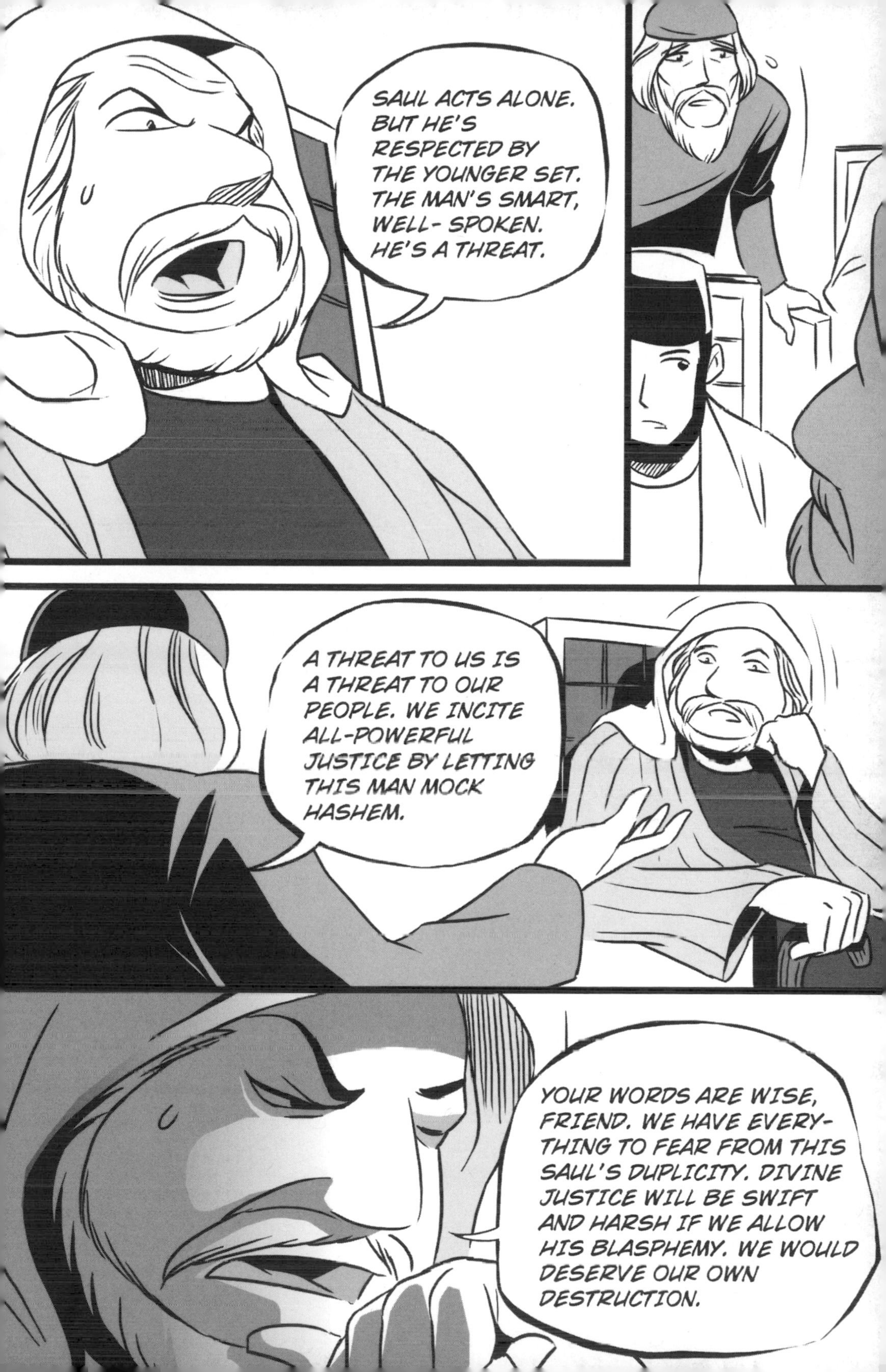
SAUL ACTS ALONE. BUT HE'S RESPECTED BY THE YOUNGER SET. THE MAN'S SMART, WELL- SPOKEN. HE'S A THREAT.
A THREAT TO US IS A THREAT TO OUR PEOPLE. WE INCITE ALL-POWERFUL JUSTICE BY LETTING THIS MAN MOCK HASHEM.
YOUR WORDS ARE WISE, FRIEND. WE HAVE EVERY-THING TO FEAR FROM THIS SAUL'S DUPLICITY. DIVINE JUSTICE WILL BE SWIFT AND HARSH IF WE ALLOW HIS BLASPHEMY. WE WOULD DESERVE OUR OWN DESTRUCTION.

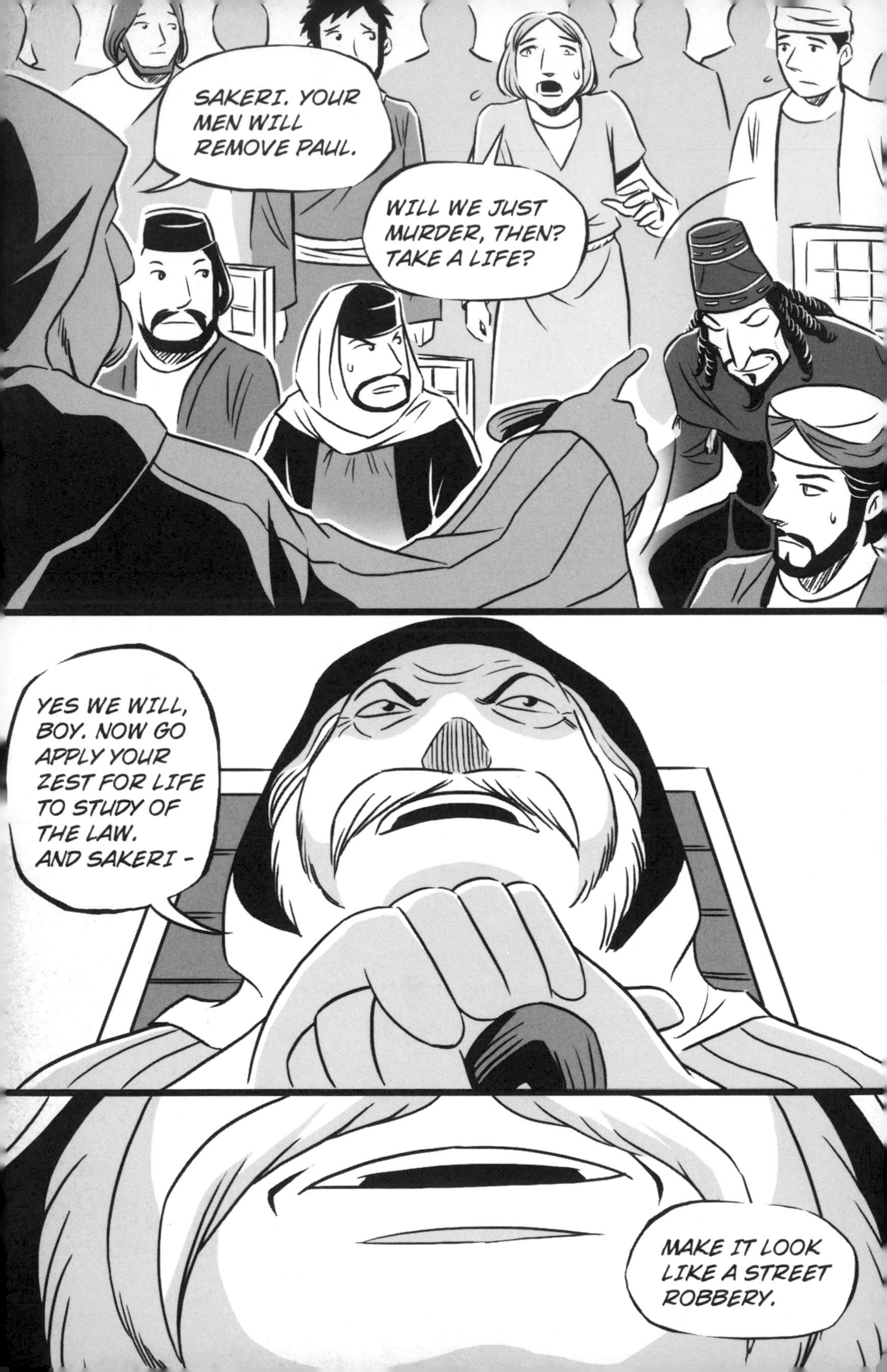
SAKERI. YOUR MEN WILL REMOVE PAUL.
WILL WE JUST MURDER, THEN? TAKE A LIFE?
YES WE WILL, BOY. NOW GO APPLY YOUR ZEST FOR LIFE TO STUDY OF THE LAW. AND SAKERI -
MAKE IT LOOK LIKE A STREET ROBBERY.

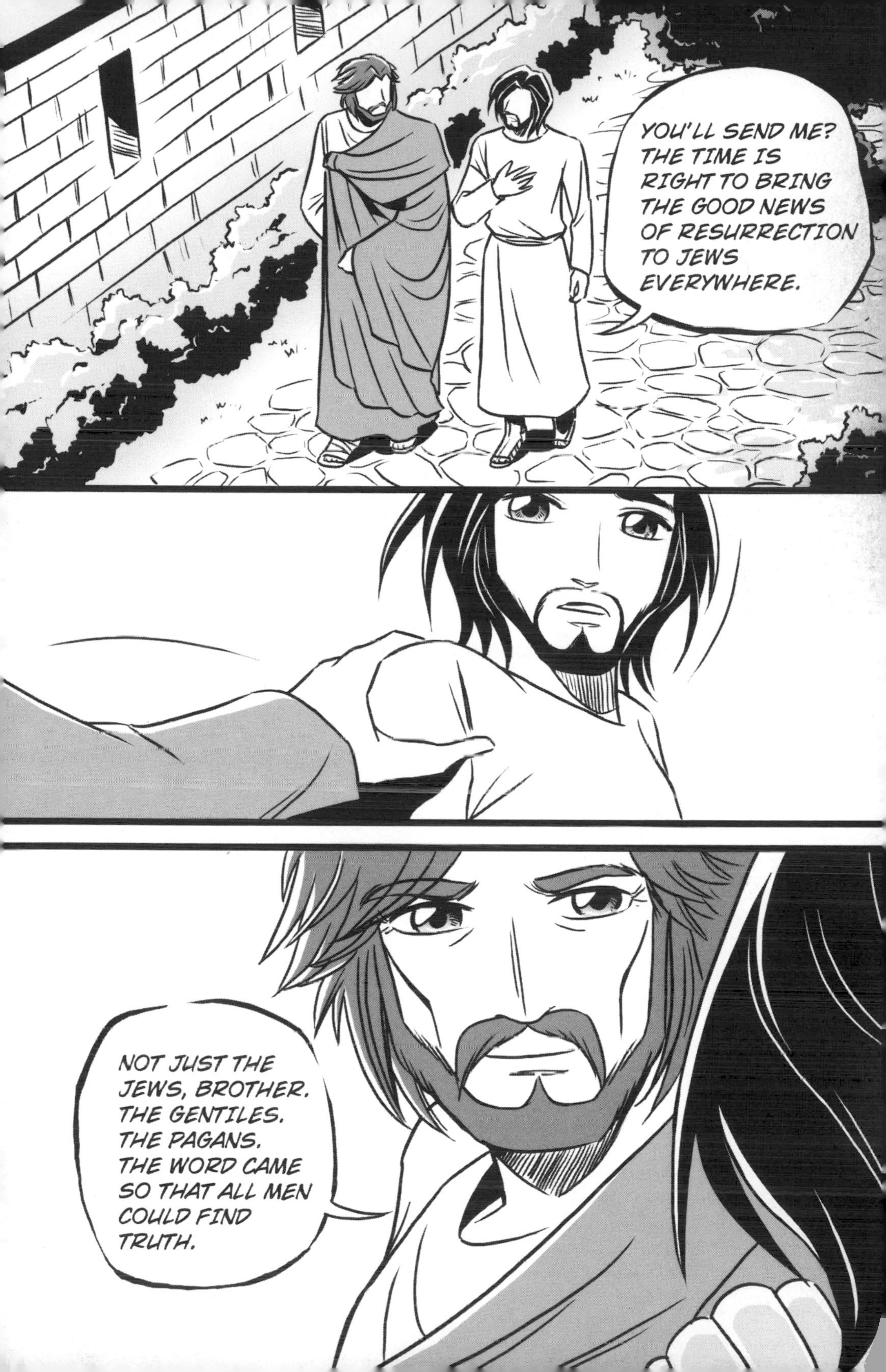
YOU'LL SEND ME? THE TIME IS RIGHT TO BRING THE GOOD NEWS OF RESURRECTION TO JEWS EVERYWHERE.
NOT JUST THE JEWS, BROTHER. THE GENTILES. THE PAGANS. THE WORD CAME SO THAT ALL MEN COULD FIND TRUTH.

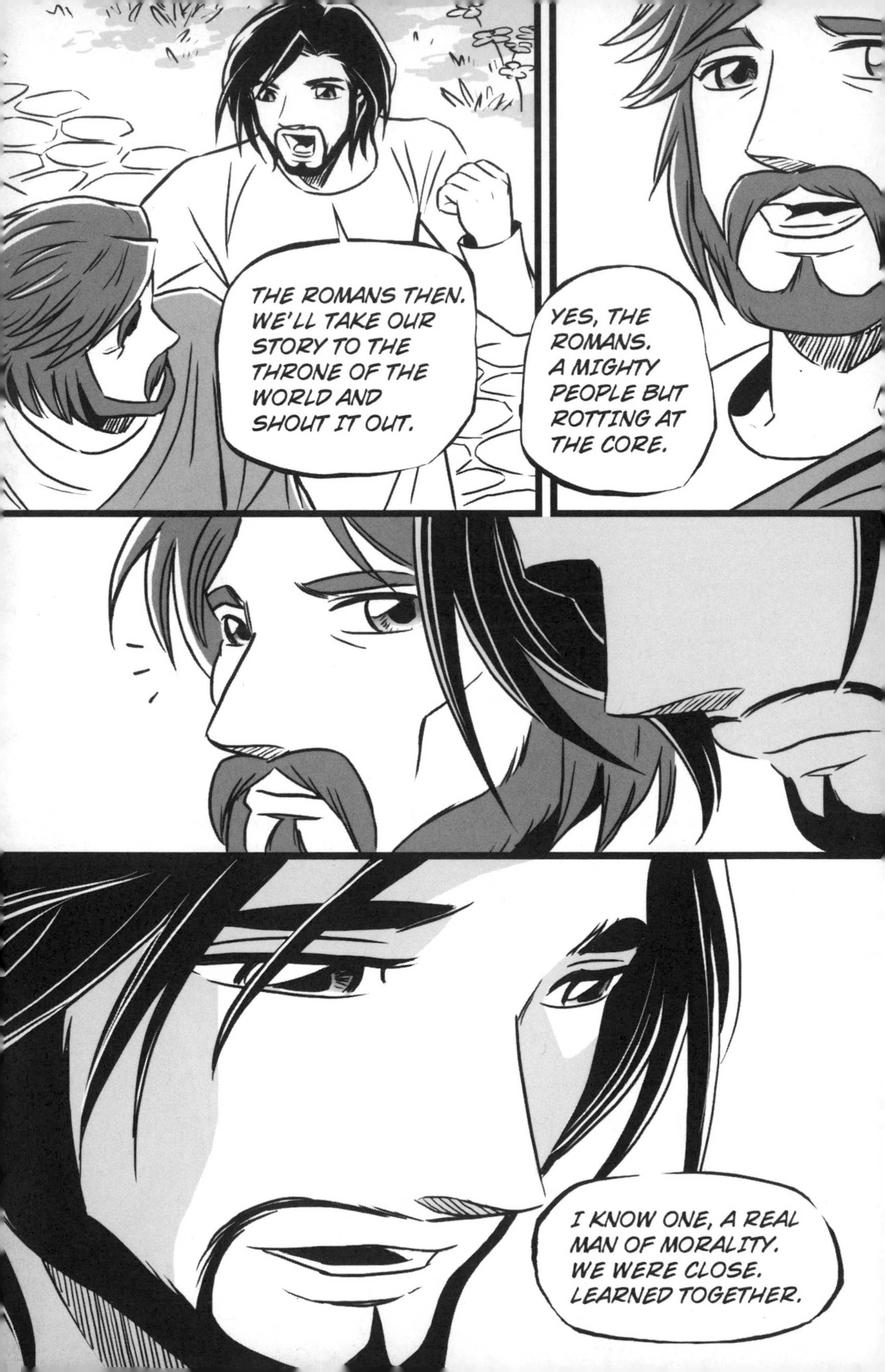
THE ROMANS THEN. WE'LL TAKE OUR STORY TO THE THRONE OF THE WORLD AND SHOUT IT OUT.
YES, THE ROMANS. A MIGHTY PEOPLE BUT ROTTING AT THE CORE.
I KNOW ONE, A REAL MAN OF MORALITY. WE WERE CLOSE. LEARNED TOGETHER.

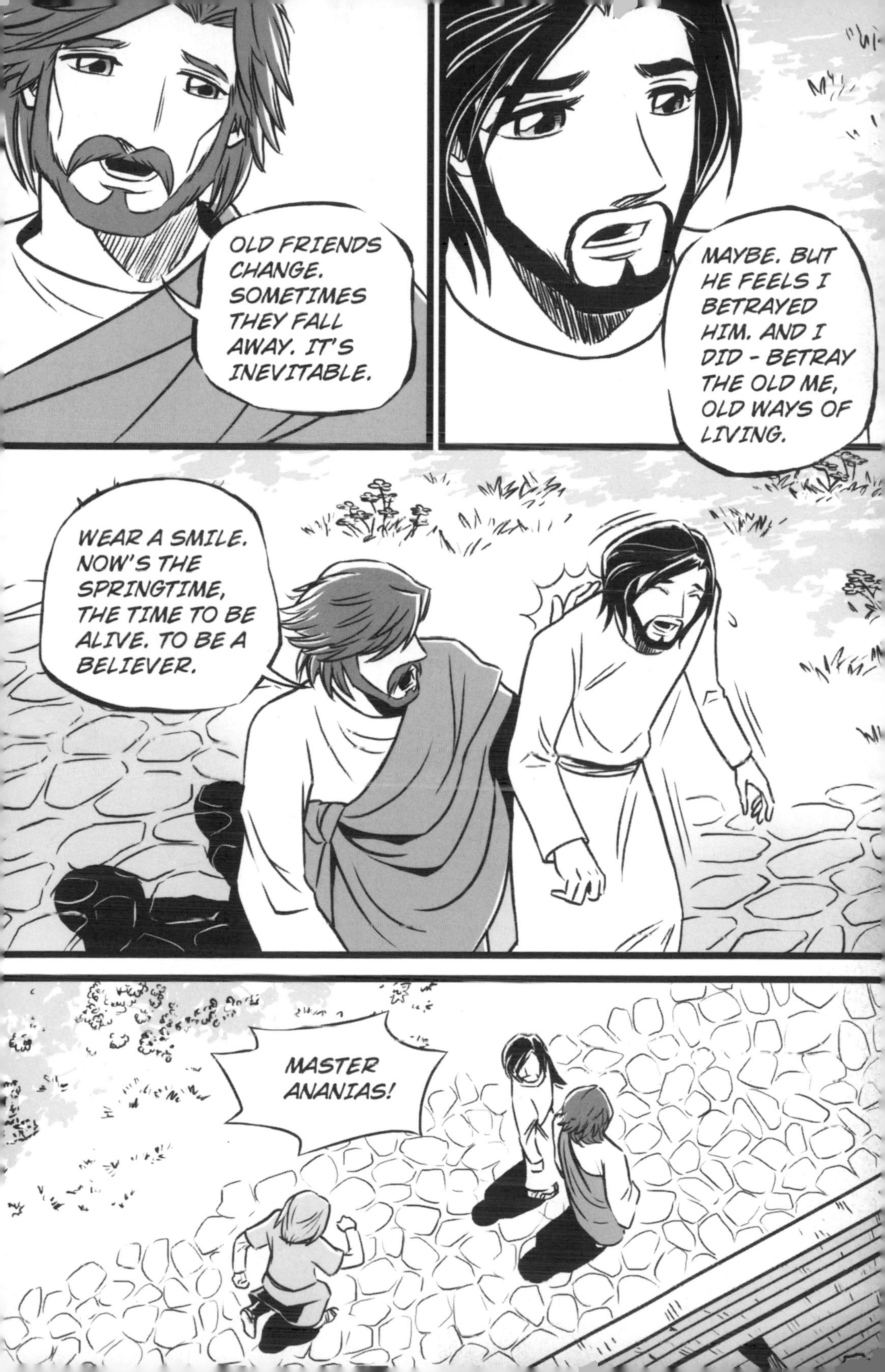
OLD FRIENDS CHANGE. SOMETIMES THEY FALL AWAY. IT'S INEVITABLE.
MAYBE. BUT HE FEELS I BETRAYED HIM. AND I DID - BETRAY THE OLD ME, OLD WAYS OF LIVING.
WEAR A SMILE. NOW'S THE SPRINGTIME, THE TIME TO BE ALIVE. TO BE A BELIEVER.
MASTER ANANIAS!

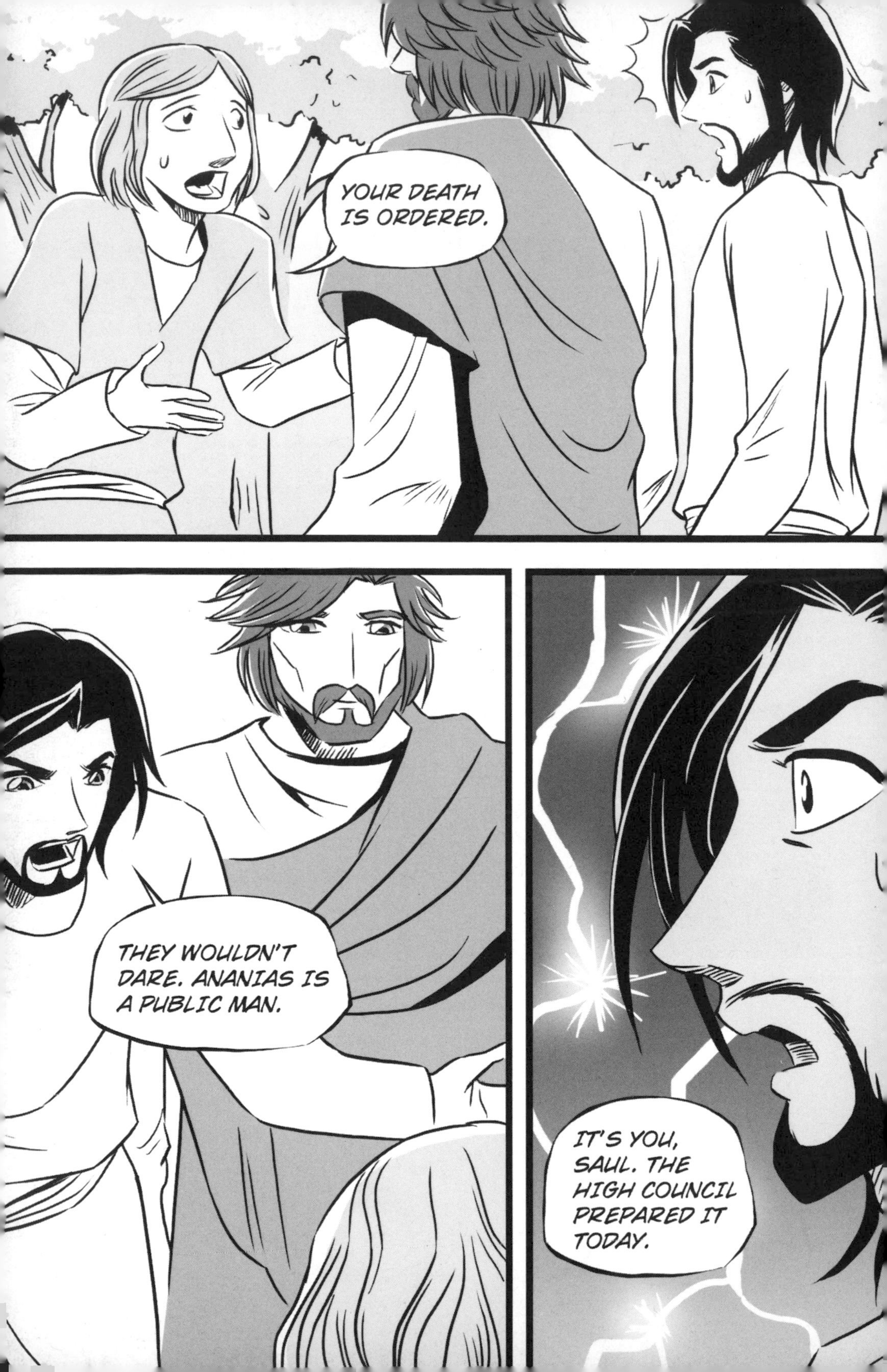
YOUR DEATH IS ORDERED.
THEY WOULDN'T DARE. ANANIAS IS A PUBLIC MAN.
IT'S YOU, SAUL. THE HIGH COUNCIL PREPARED IT TODAY.

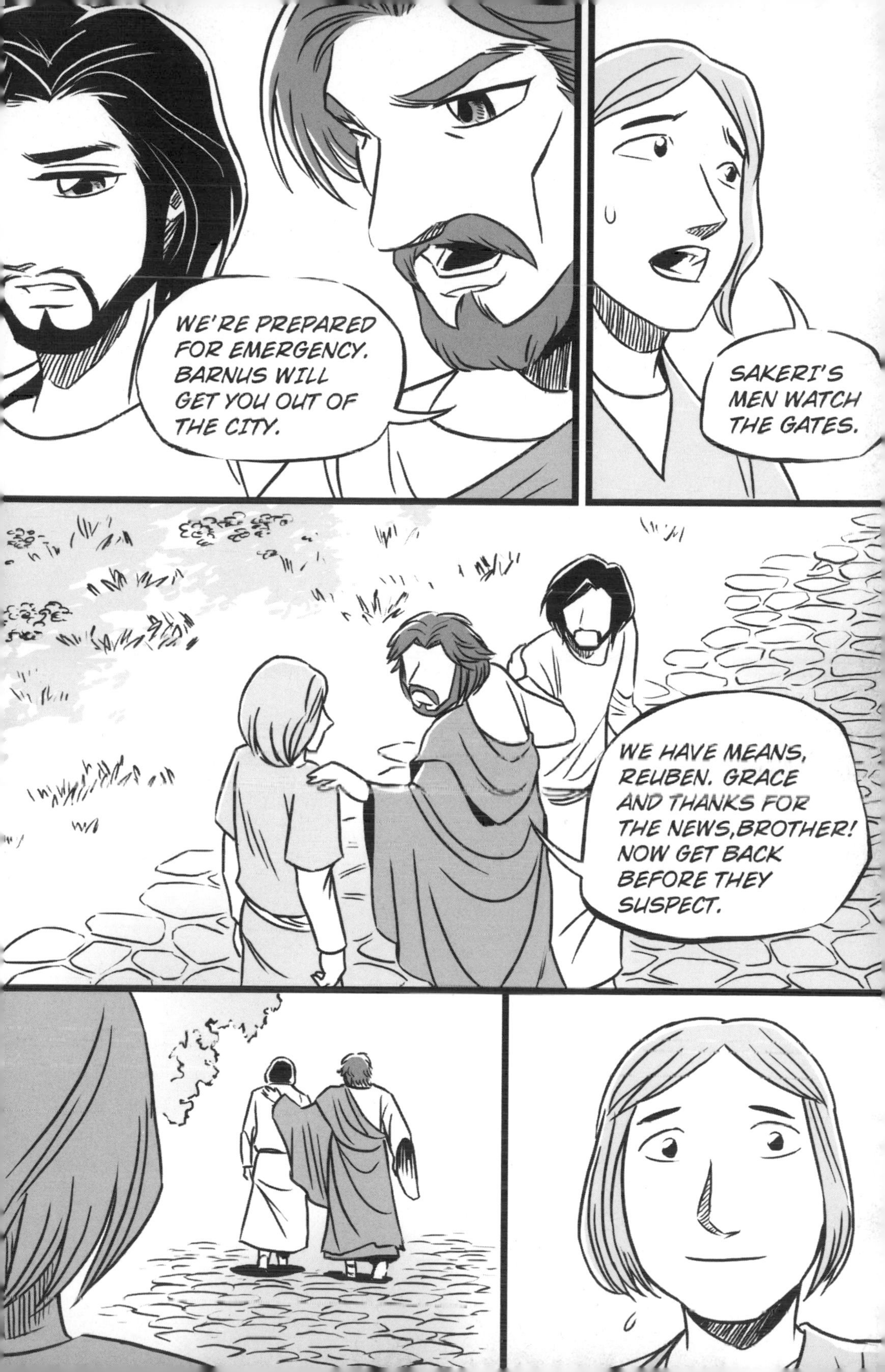
WE'RE PREPARED FOR EMERGENCY. BARNUS WILL GET YOU OUT OF THE CITY.
SAKERI'S MEN WATCH THE GATES.
WE HAVE MEANS, REUBEN. GRACE AND THANKS FOR THE NEWS,BROTHER! NOW GET BACK BEFORE THEY SUSPECT.

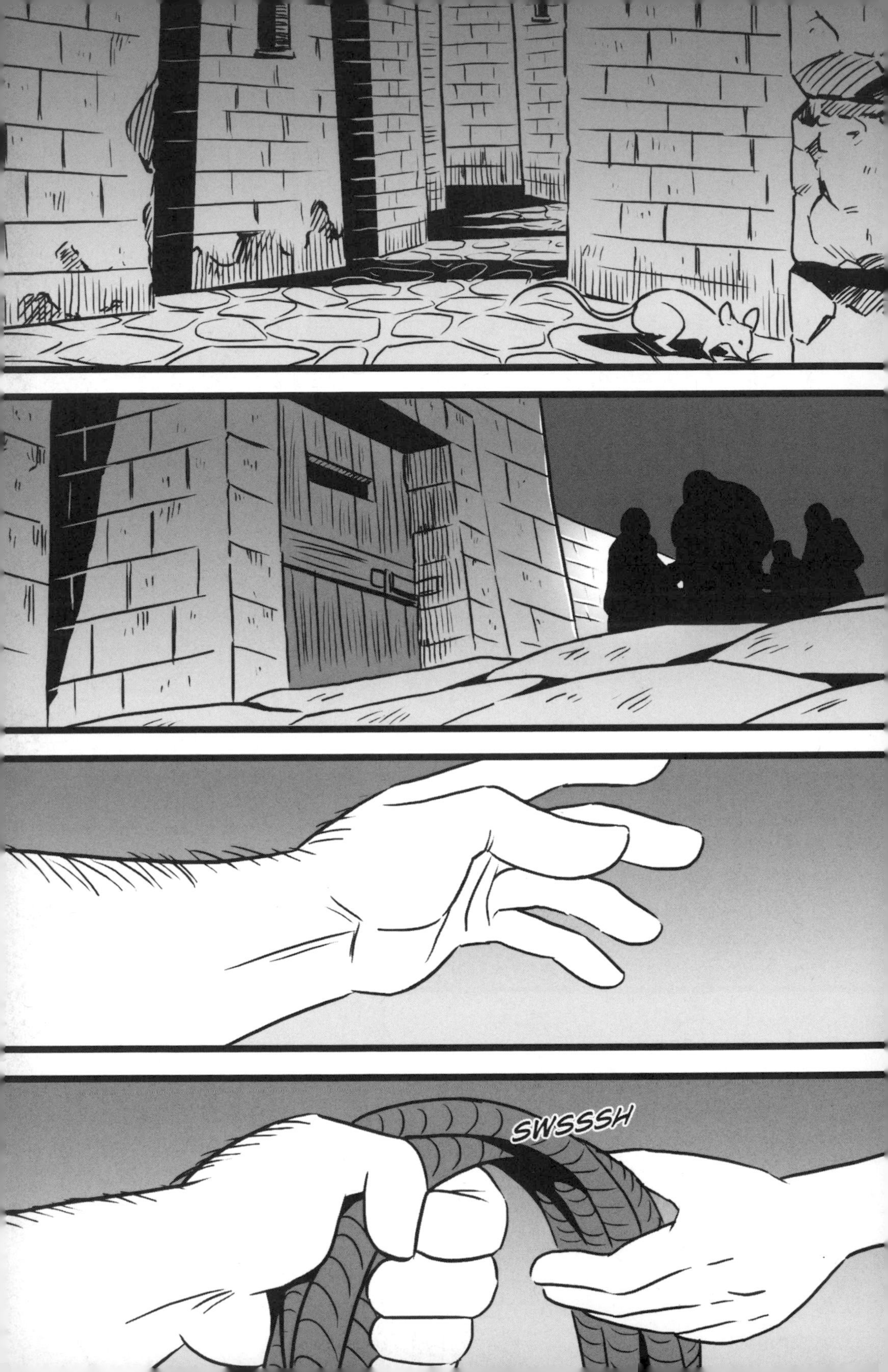
SWSSSH

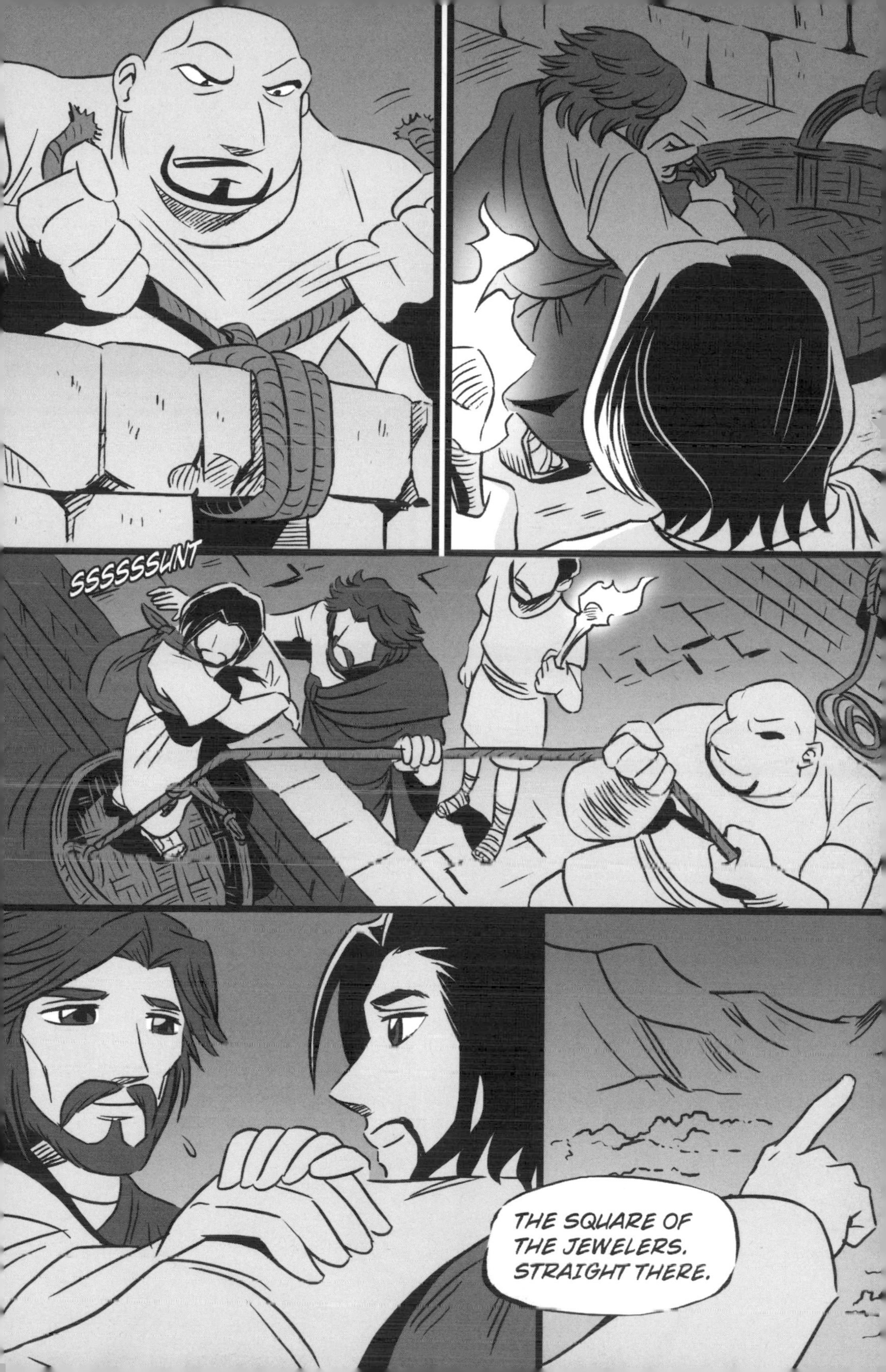
SSSSSSLINT
THE SQUARE OF THE JEWELERS. STRAIGHT THERE.

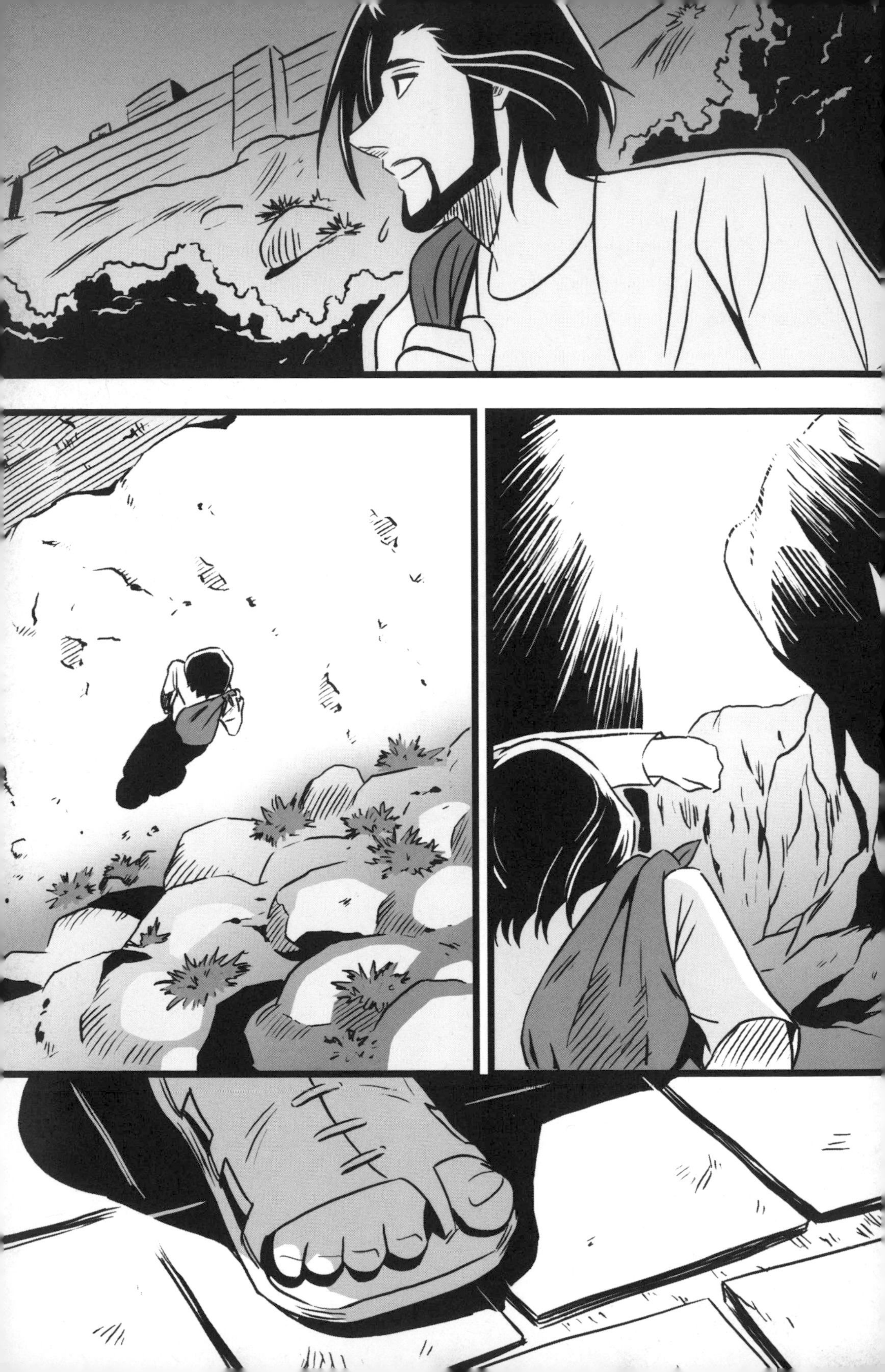

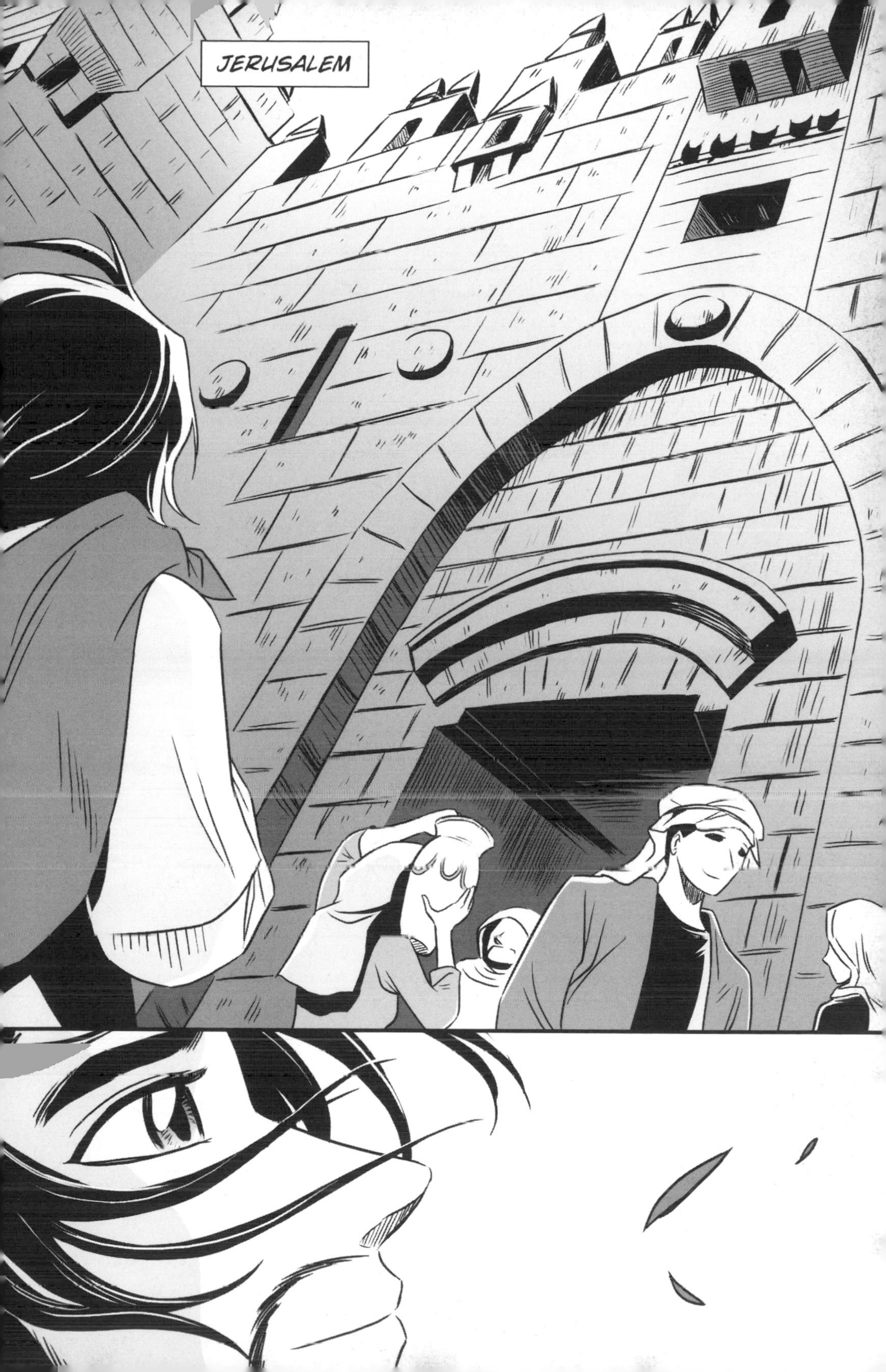
JERUSALEM

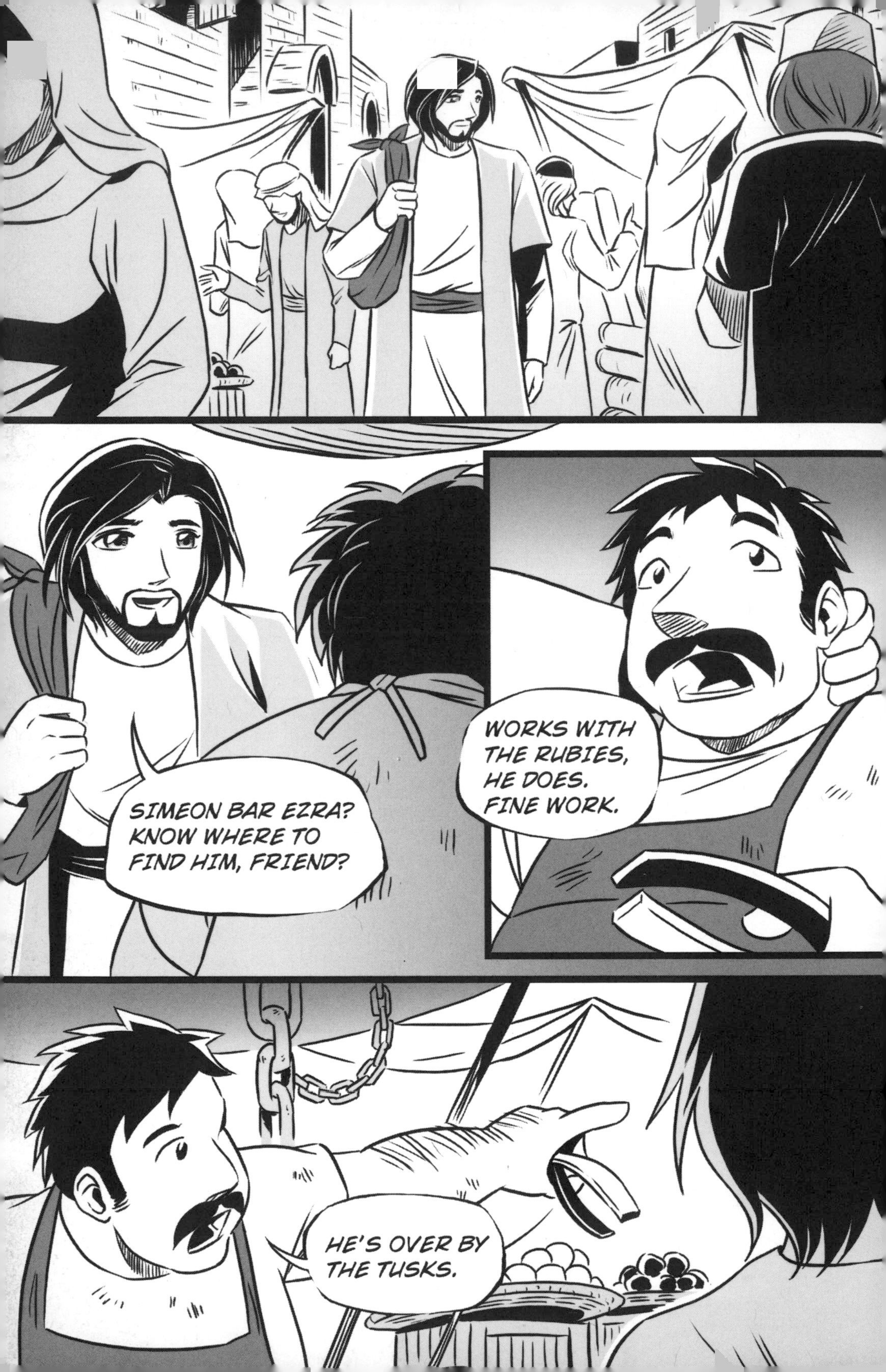
SIMEON BAR EZRA? KNOW WHERE TO FIND HIM, FRIEND?
WORKS WITH THE RUBIES, HE DOES. FINE WORK.
HE'S OVER BY THE TUSKS.

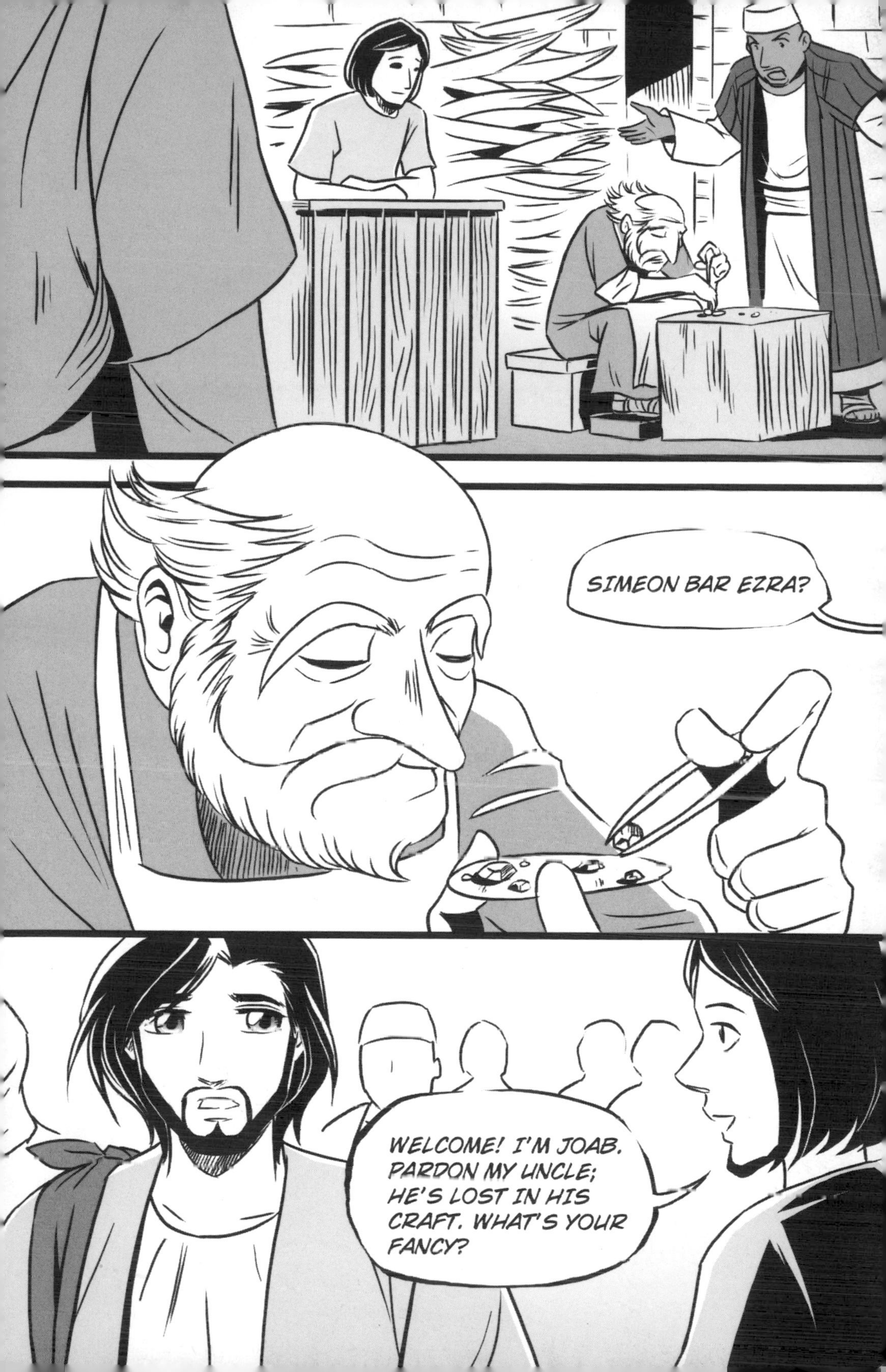
SIMEON BAR EZRA?
WELCOME! I'M JOAB. PARDON MY UNCLE; HE'S LOST IN HIS CRAFT. WHAT'S YOUR FANCY?

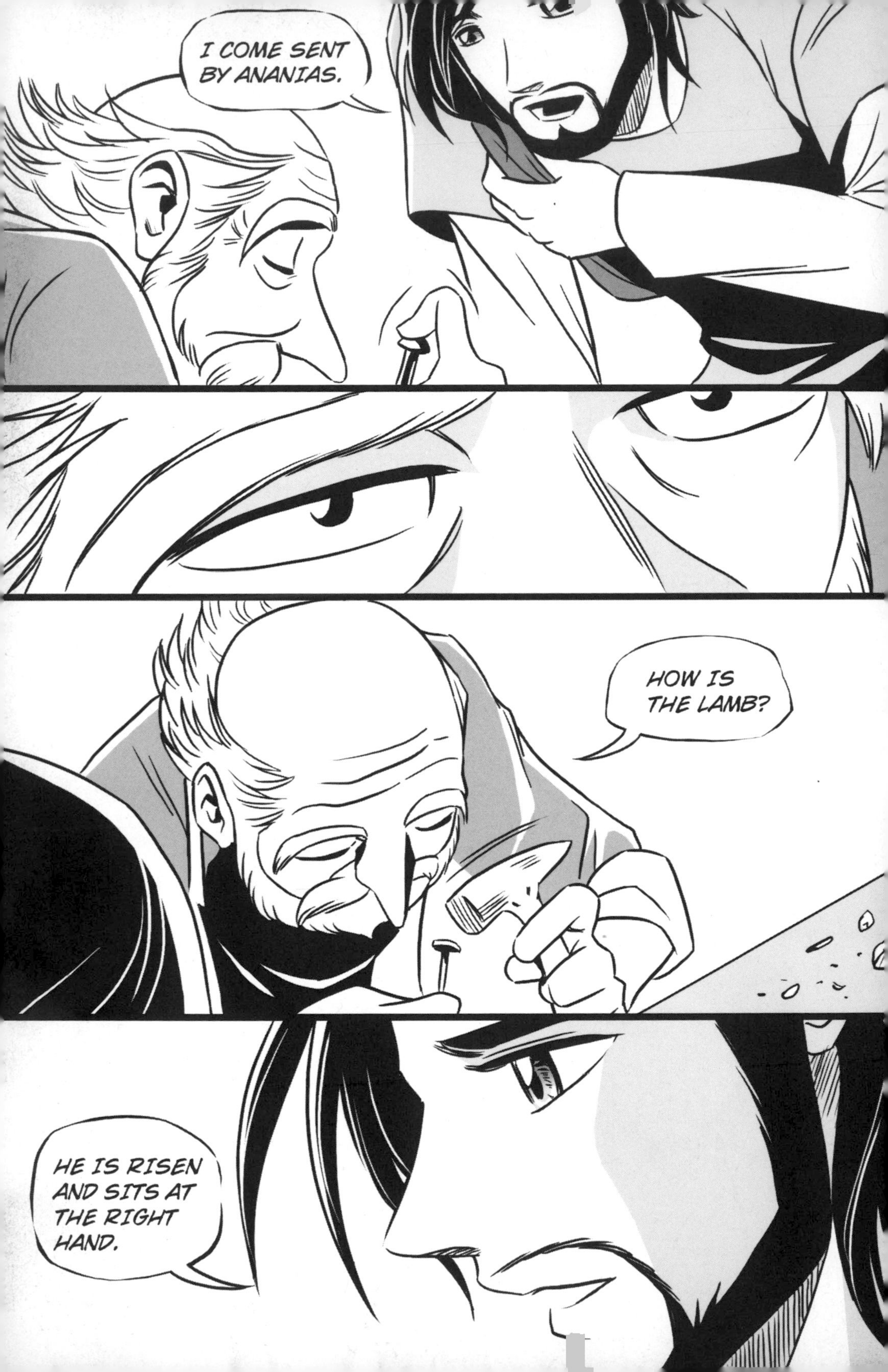
I COME SENT BY ANANIAS.
HOW IS THE LAMB?
HE IS RISEN AND SITS AT THE RIGHT HAND.

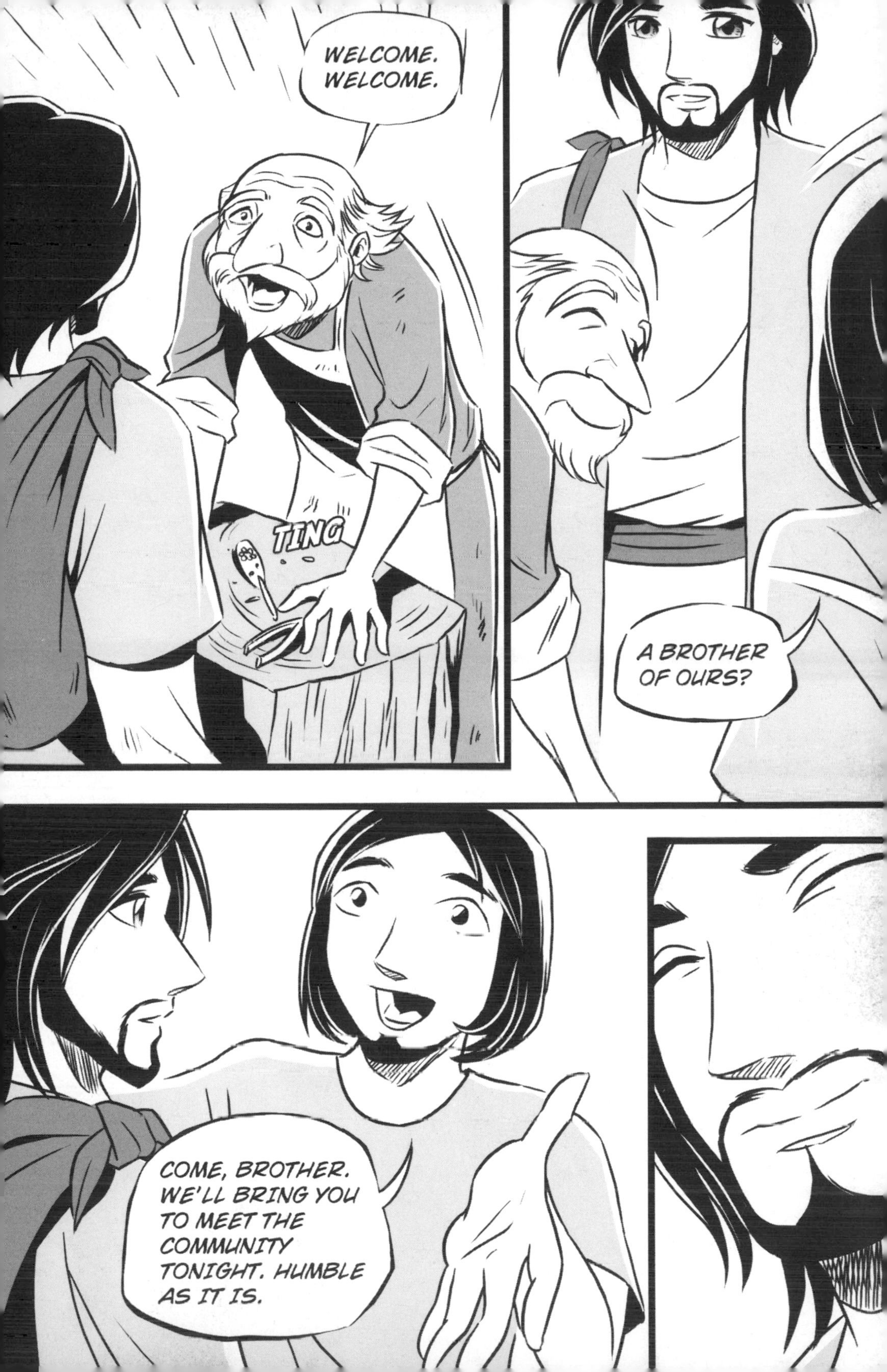
WELCOME. WELCOME.
TING
A BROTHER OF OURS?
COME, BROTHER. WE'LL BRING YOU TO MEET THE COMMUNITY TONIGHT. HUMBLE AS IT IS.

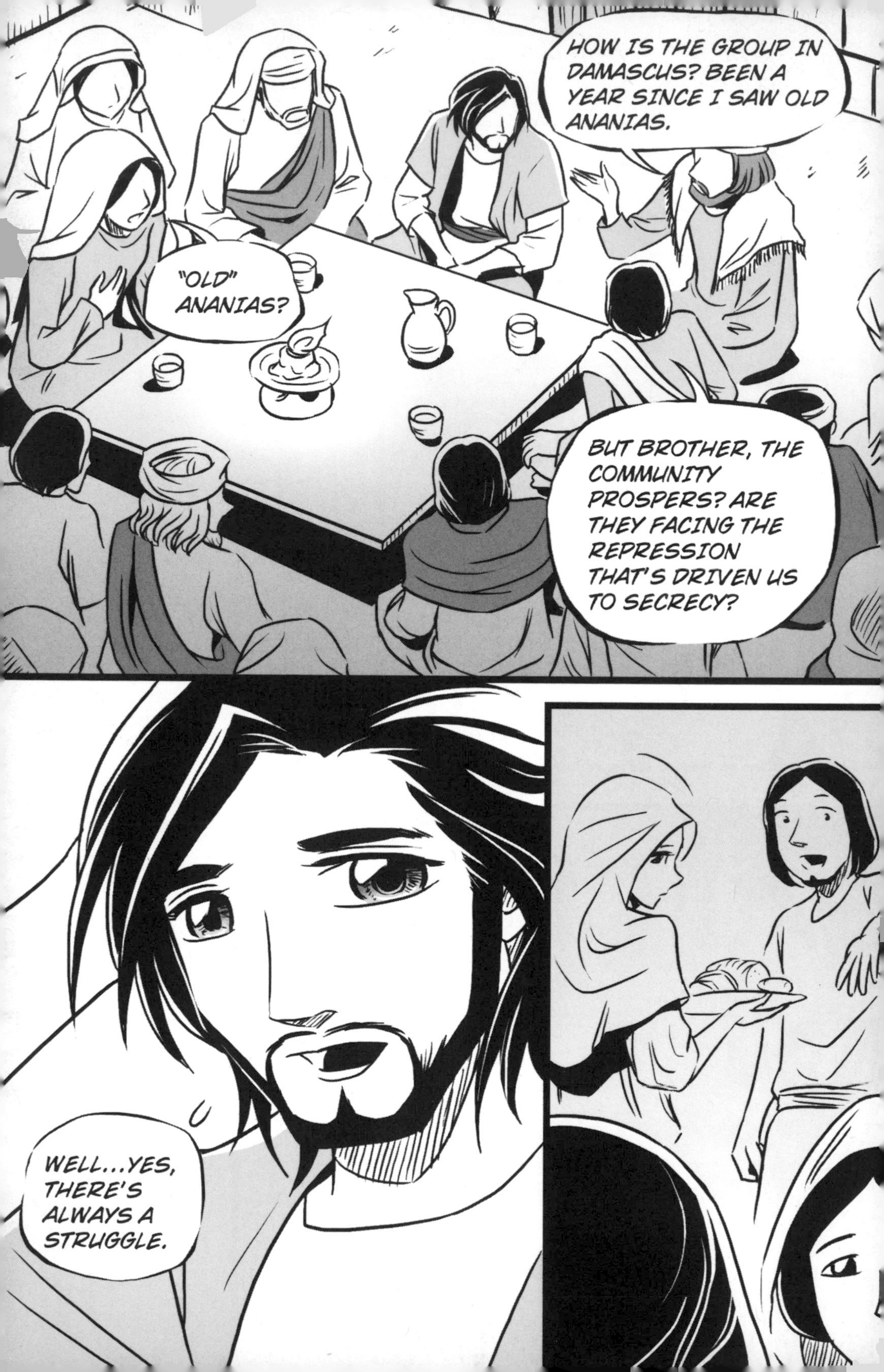
HOW IS THE GROUP IN DAMASCUS? BEEN A YEAR SINCE I SAW OLD ANANIAS.
"OLD" ANANIAS?
BUT BROTHER, THE COMMUNITY PROSPERS? ARE THEY FACING THE REPRESSION THAT'S DRIVEN US TO SECRECY?
WELL...YES, THERE'S ALWAYS A STRUGGLE.

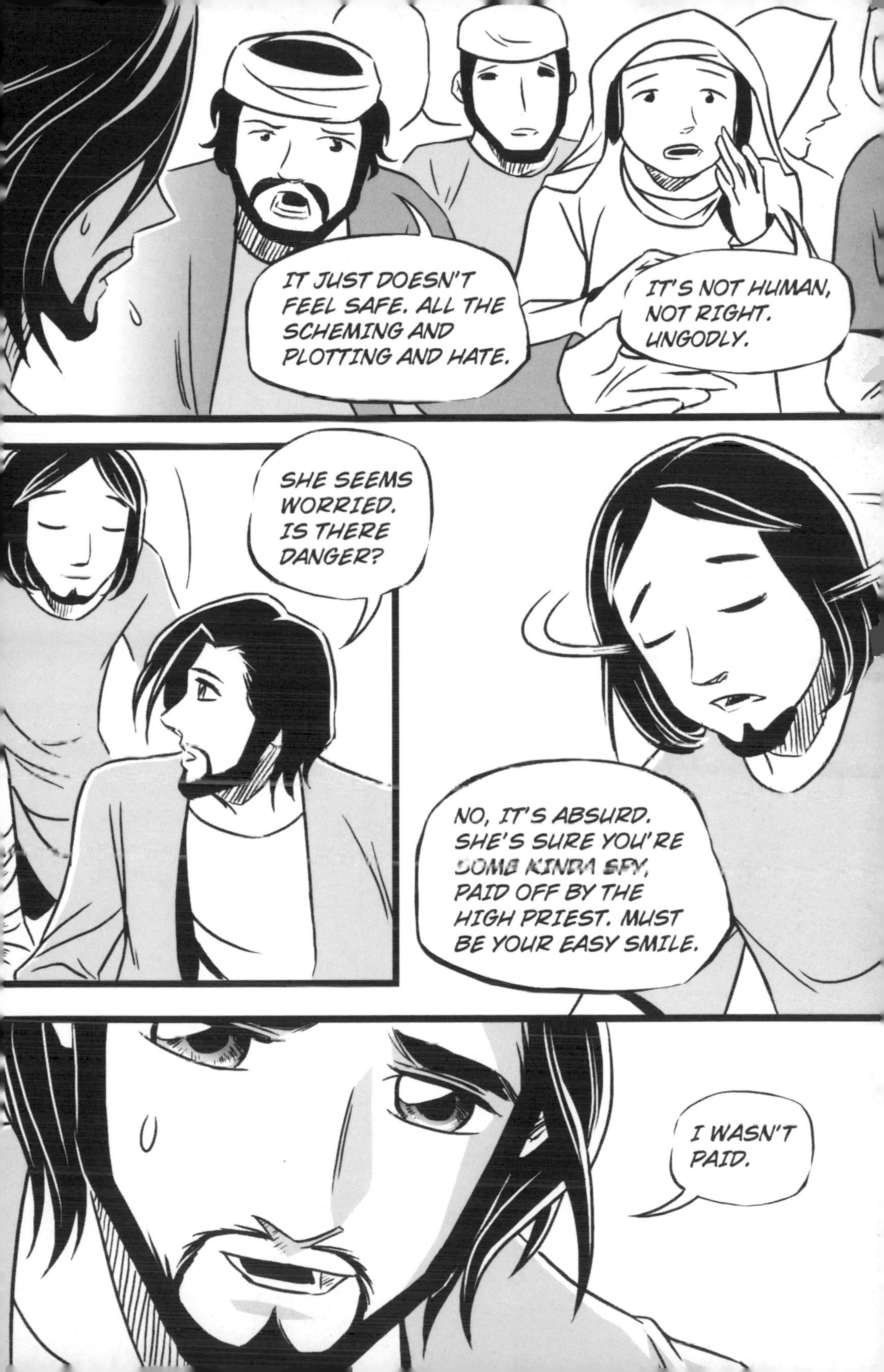
IT JUST DOESN'T FEEL SAFE. ALL THE SCHEMING AND PLOTTING AND HATE.
IT'S NOT HUMAN, NOT RIGHT. UNGODLY.
SHE SEEMS WORRIED. IS THERE DANGER?
NO, IT'S ABSURD. SHE'S SURE YOU'RE SOME KINDA SPY, PAID OFF BY THE HIGH PRIEST. MUST BE YOUR EASY SMILE.
I WASN'T PAID.

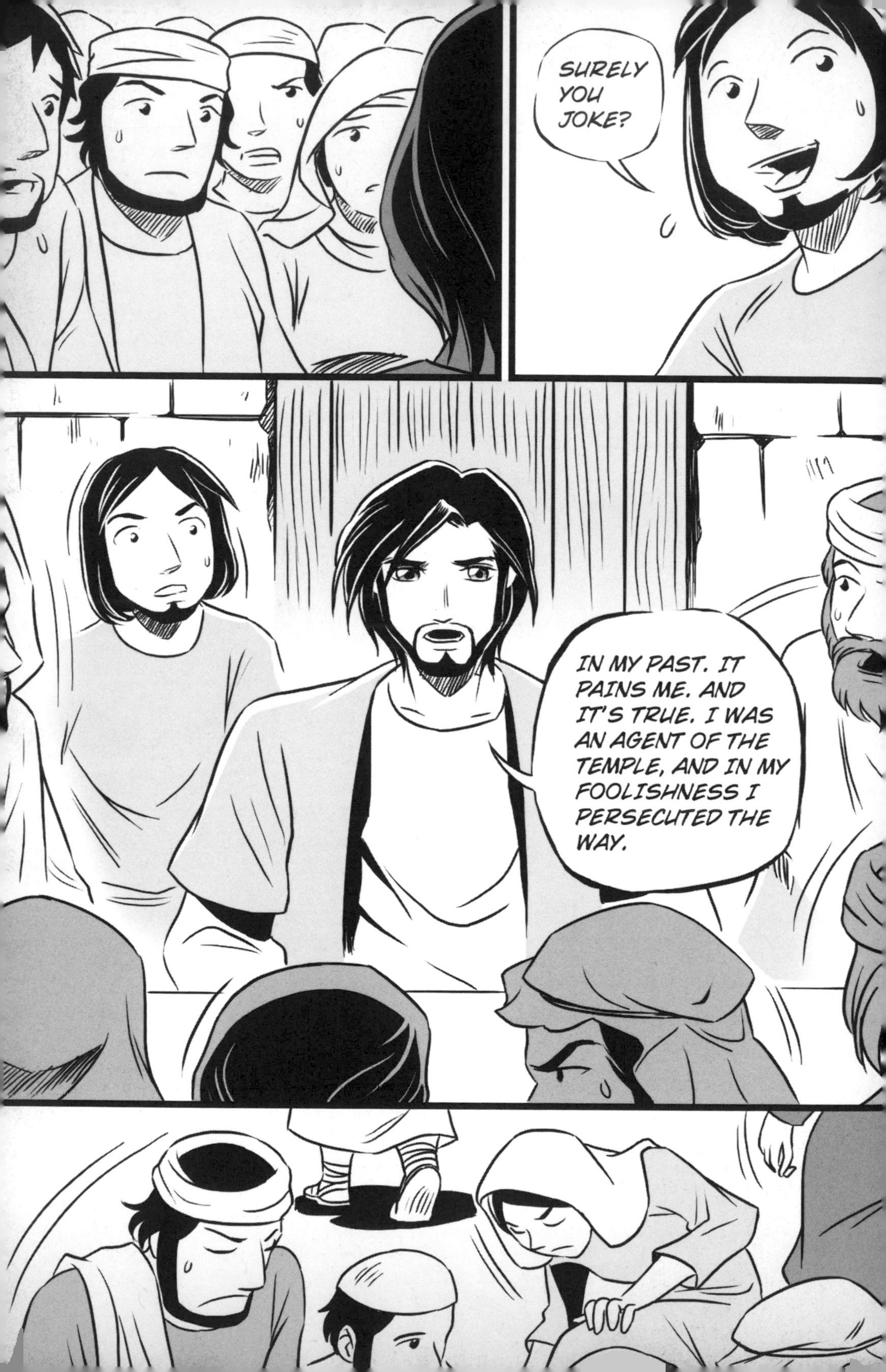
SURELY YOU JOKE?
IN MY PAST. IT PAINS ME. AND IT'S TRUE. I WAS AN AGENT OF THE TEMPLE, AND IN MY FOOLISHNESS I PERSECUTED THE WAY.

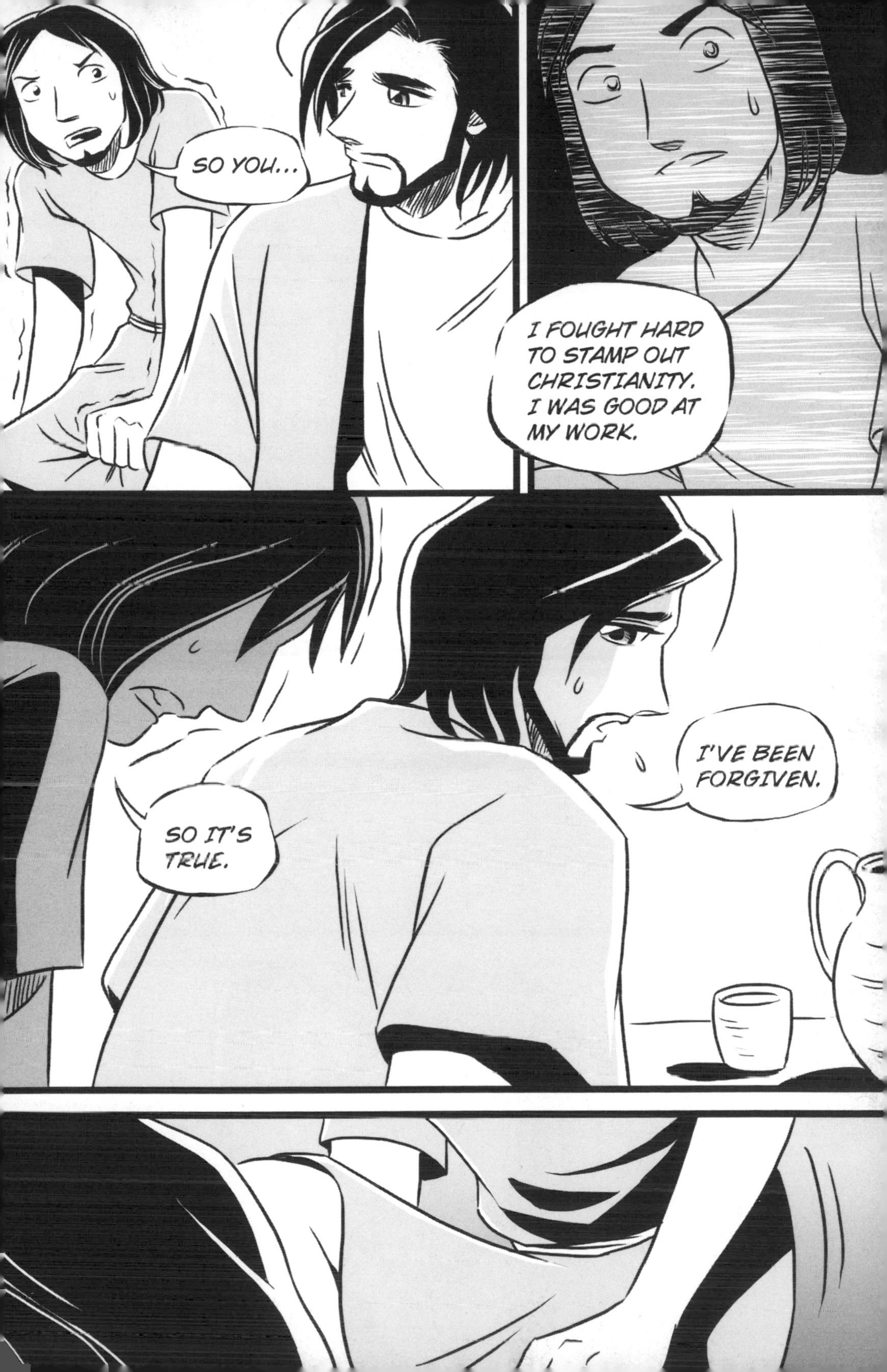
SO YOU...
I FOUGHT HARD TO STAMP OUT CHRISTIANITY. I WAS GOOD AT MY WORK.
I'VE BEEN FORGIVEN.
SO IT'S TRUE.

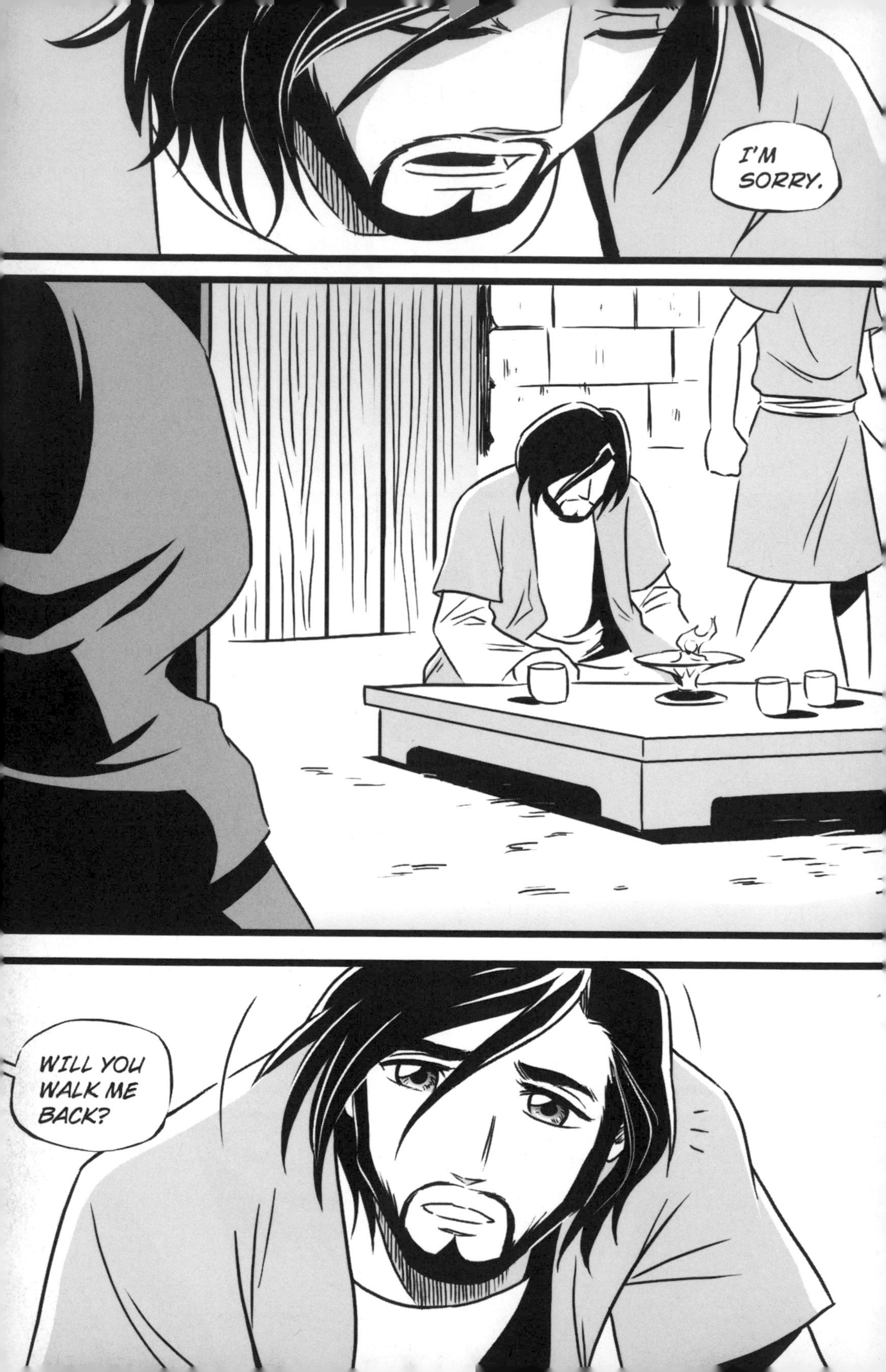
I'M SORRY.
WILL YOU WALK ME BACK?

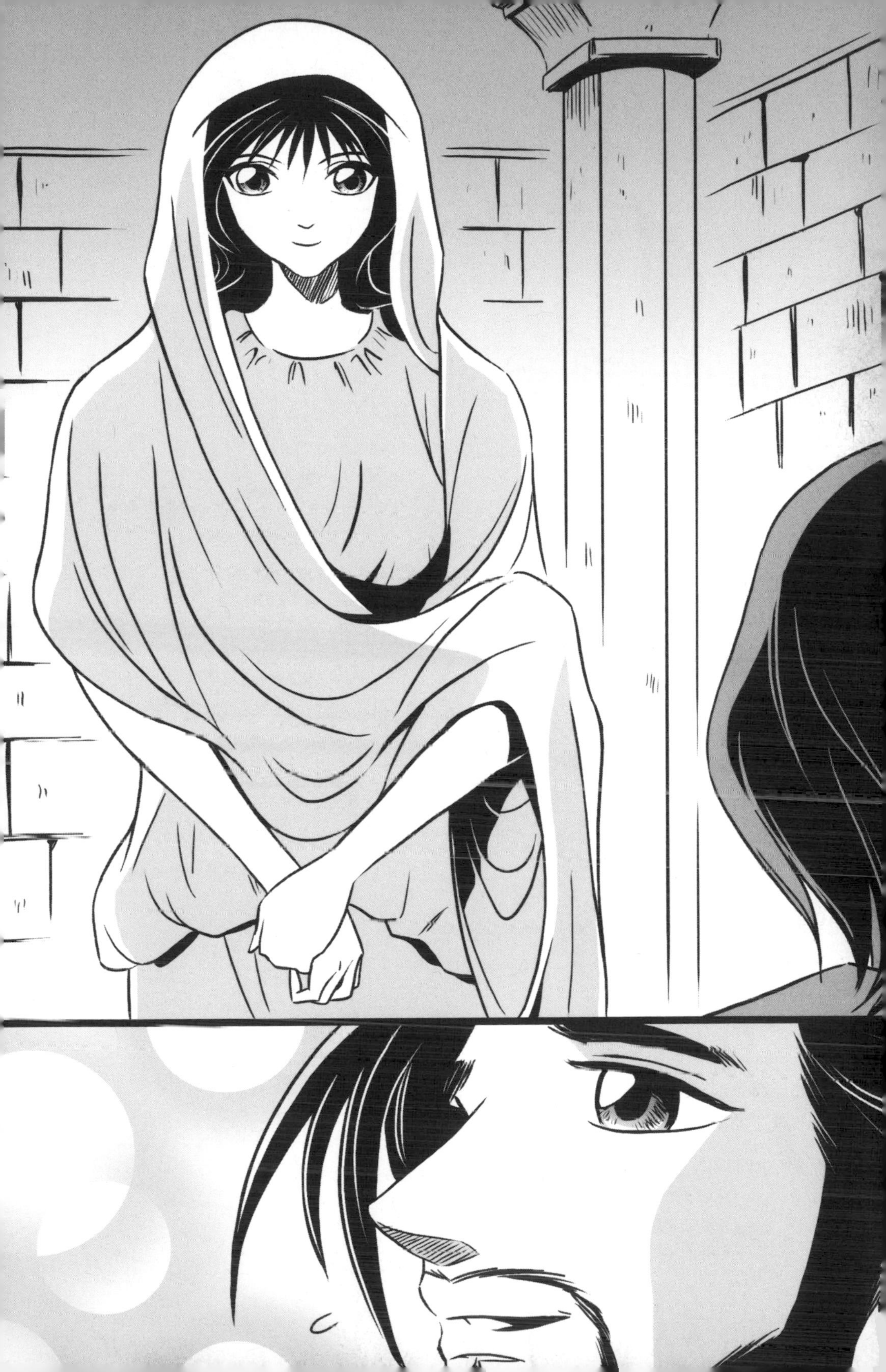

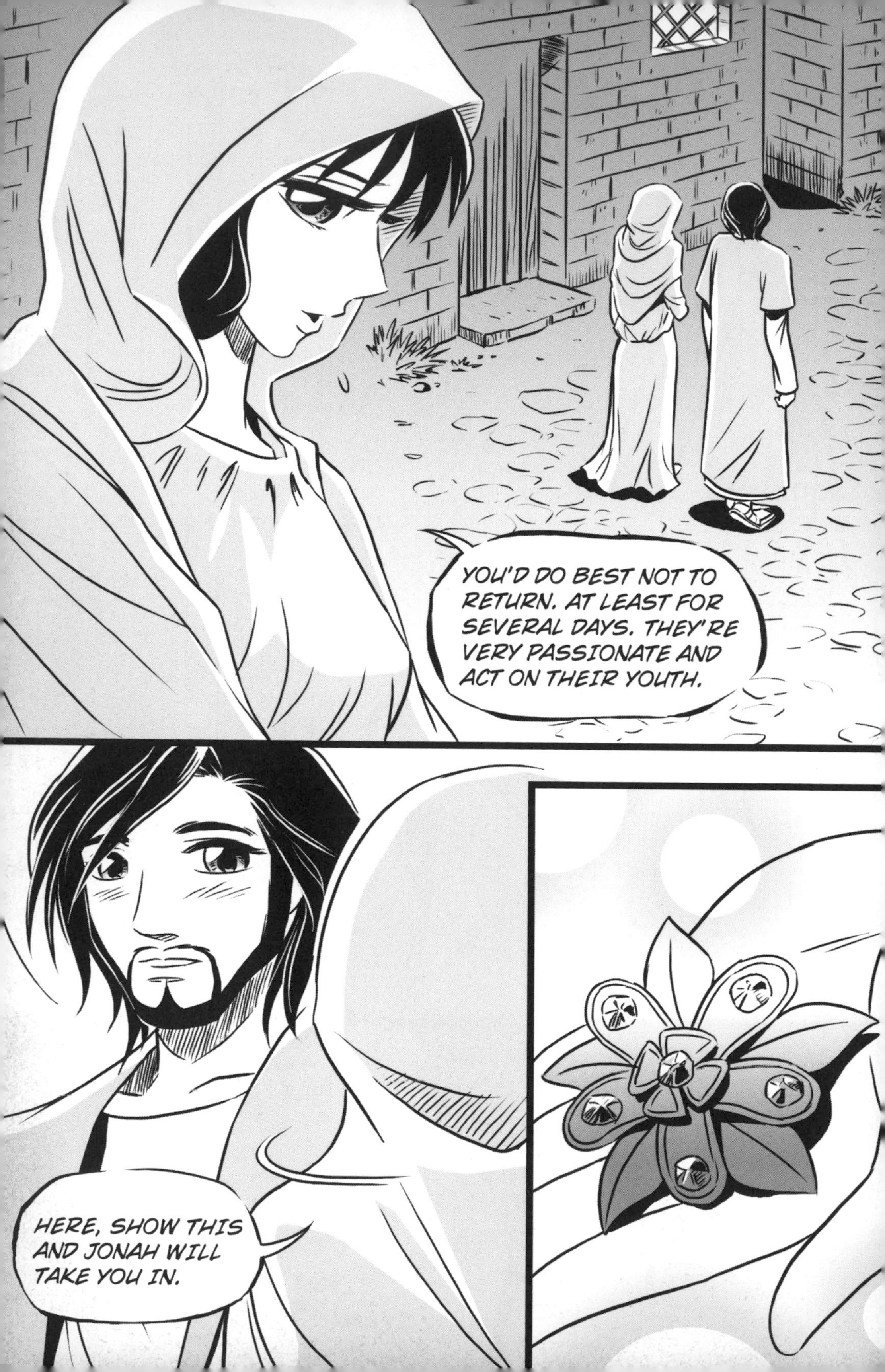
YOU'D DO BEST NOT TO RETURN. AT LEAST FOR SEVERAL DAYS. THEY'RE VERY PASSIONATE AND ACT ON THEIR YOUTH.
HERE, SHOW THIS AND JONAH WILL TAKE YOU IN.

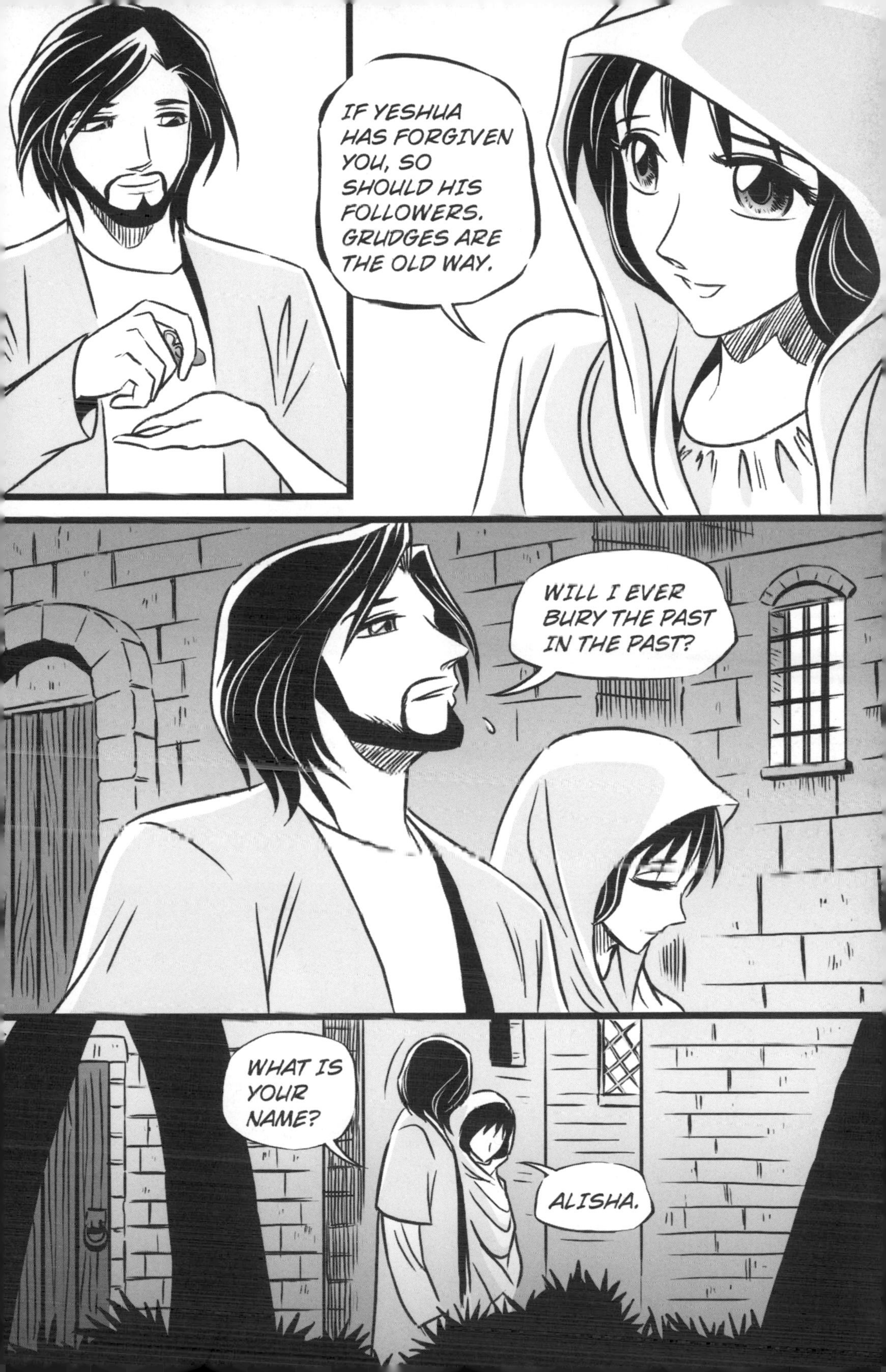
IF YESHUA HAS FORGIVEN YOU, SO SHOULD HIS FOLLOWERS. GRUDGES ARE THE OLD WAY.
WILL I EVER BURY THE PAST IN THE PAST?
WHAT IS YOUR NAME?
ALISHA.

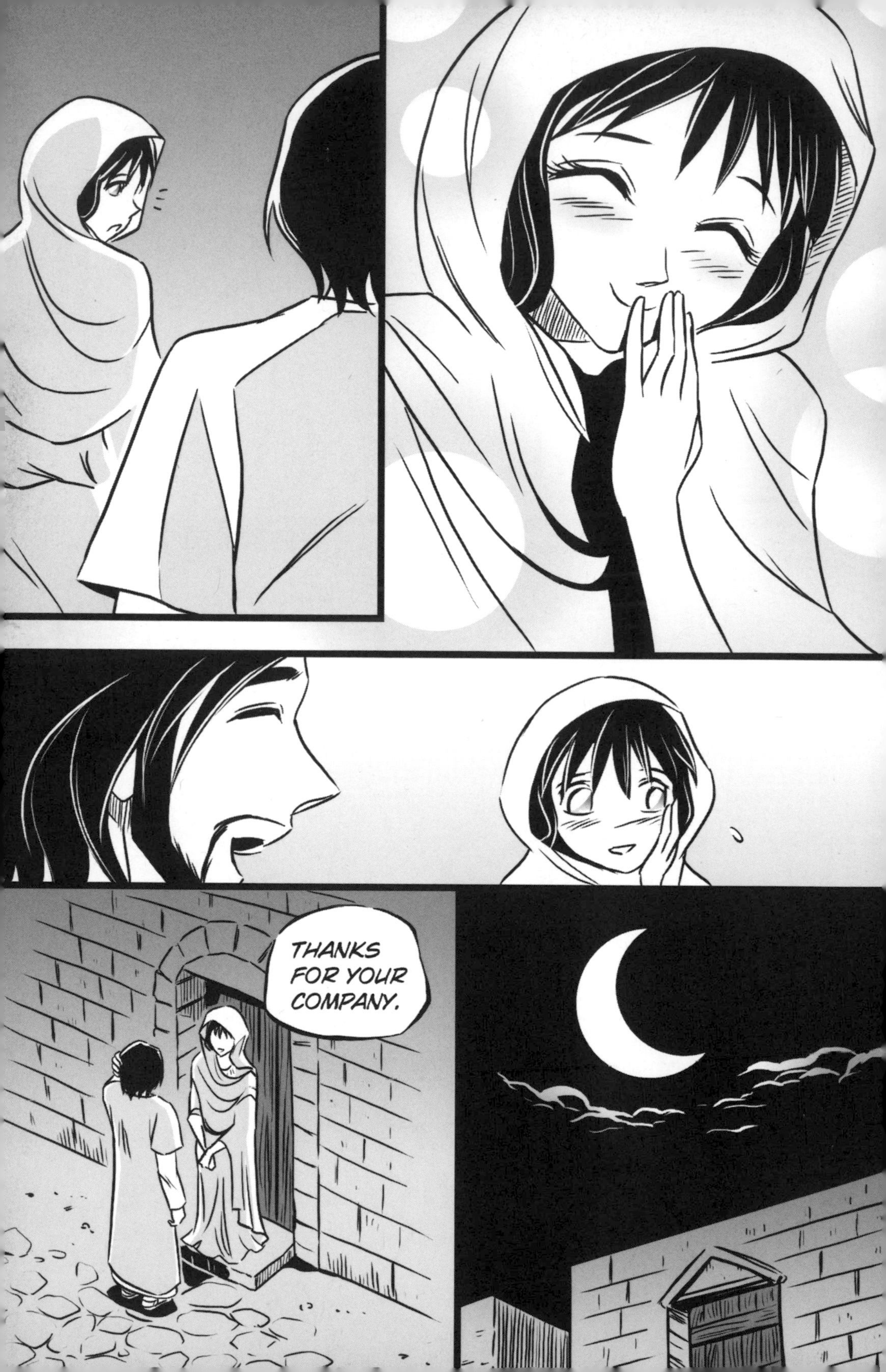
THANKS FOR YOUR COMPANY.

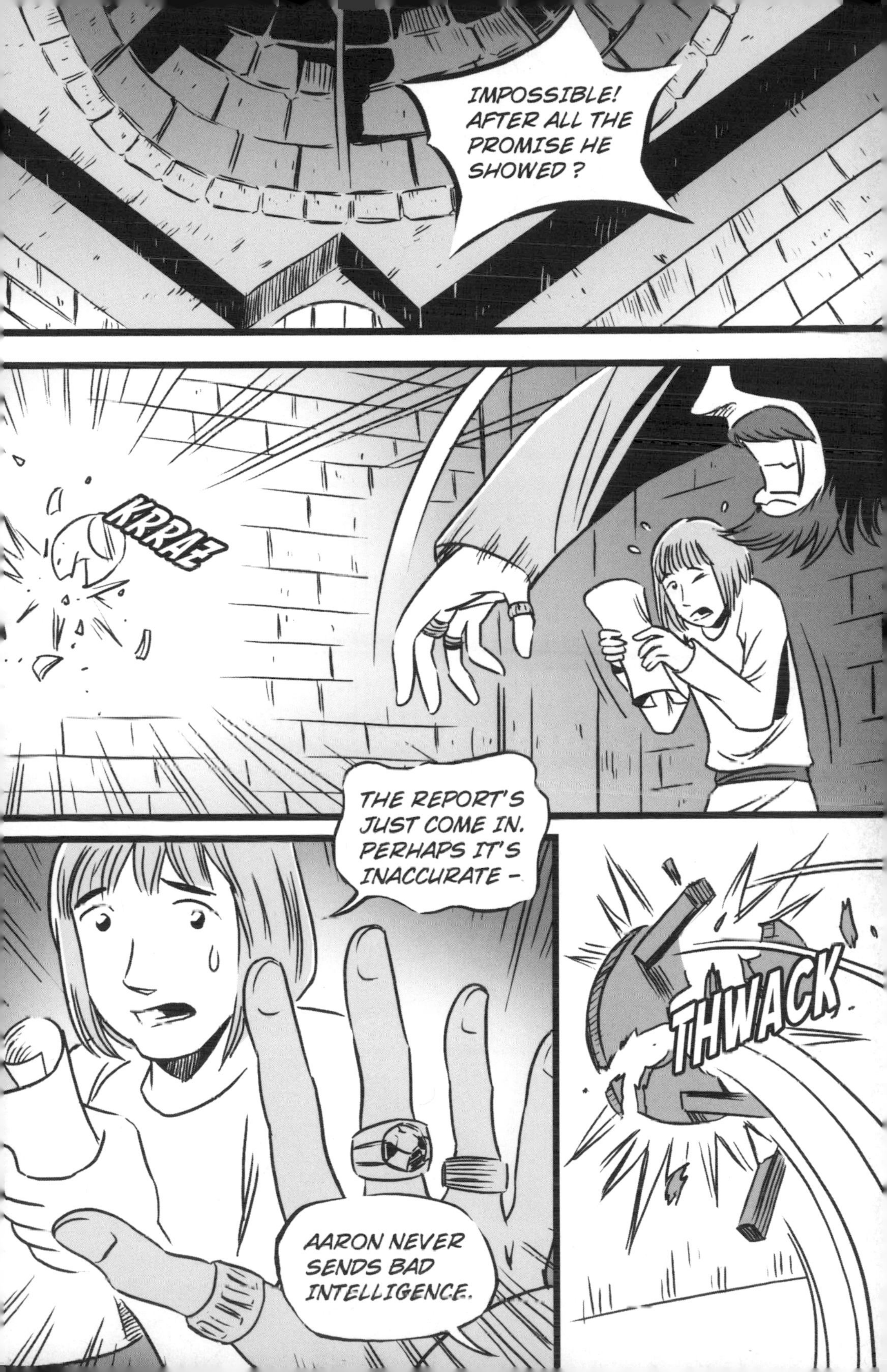
IMPOSSIBLE! AFTER ALL THE PROMISE HE SHOWED?
KRRAZ
THE REPORT'S JUST COME IN. PERHAPS IT'S INACCURATE -
THWACK
AARON NEVER SENDS BAD INTELLIGENCE.

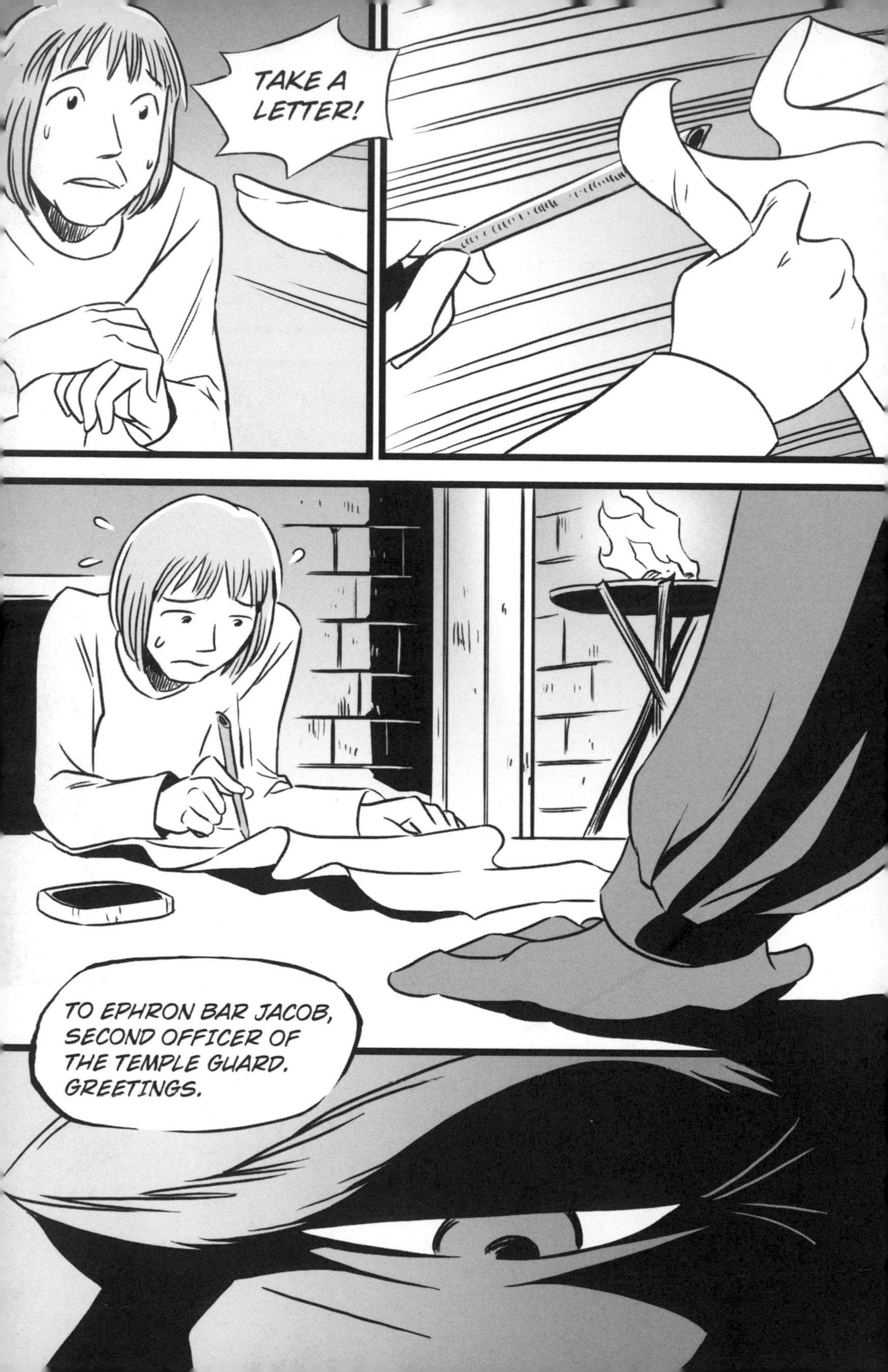
TAKE A LETTER!
TO EPHRON BAR JACOB, SECOND OFFICER OF THE TEMPLE GUARD. GREETINGS.

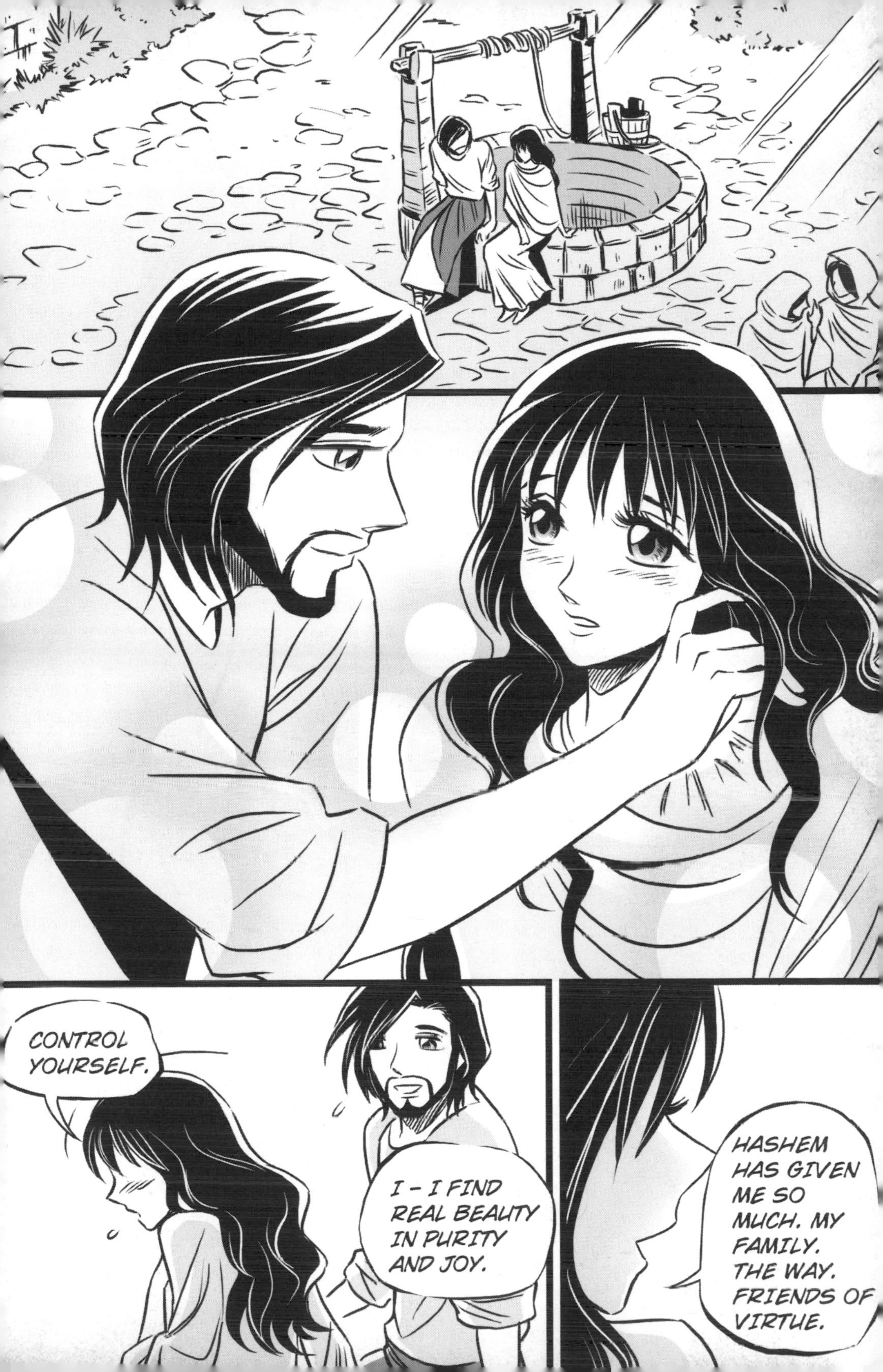
CONTROL YOURSELF.
I - I FIND REAL BEAUTY IN PURITY AND JOY.
HASHEM HAS GIVEN ME SO MUCH. MY FAMILY. THE WAY. FRIENDS OF VIRTUE.

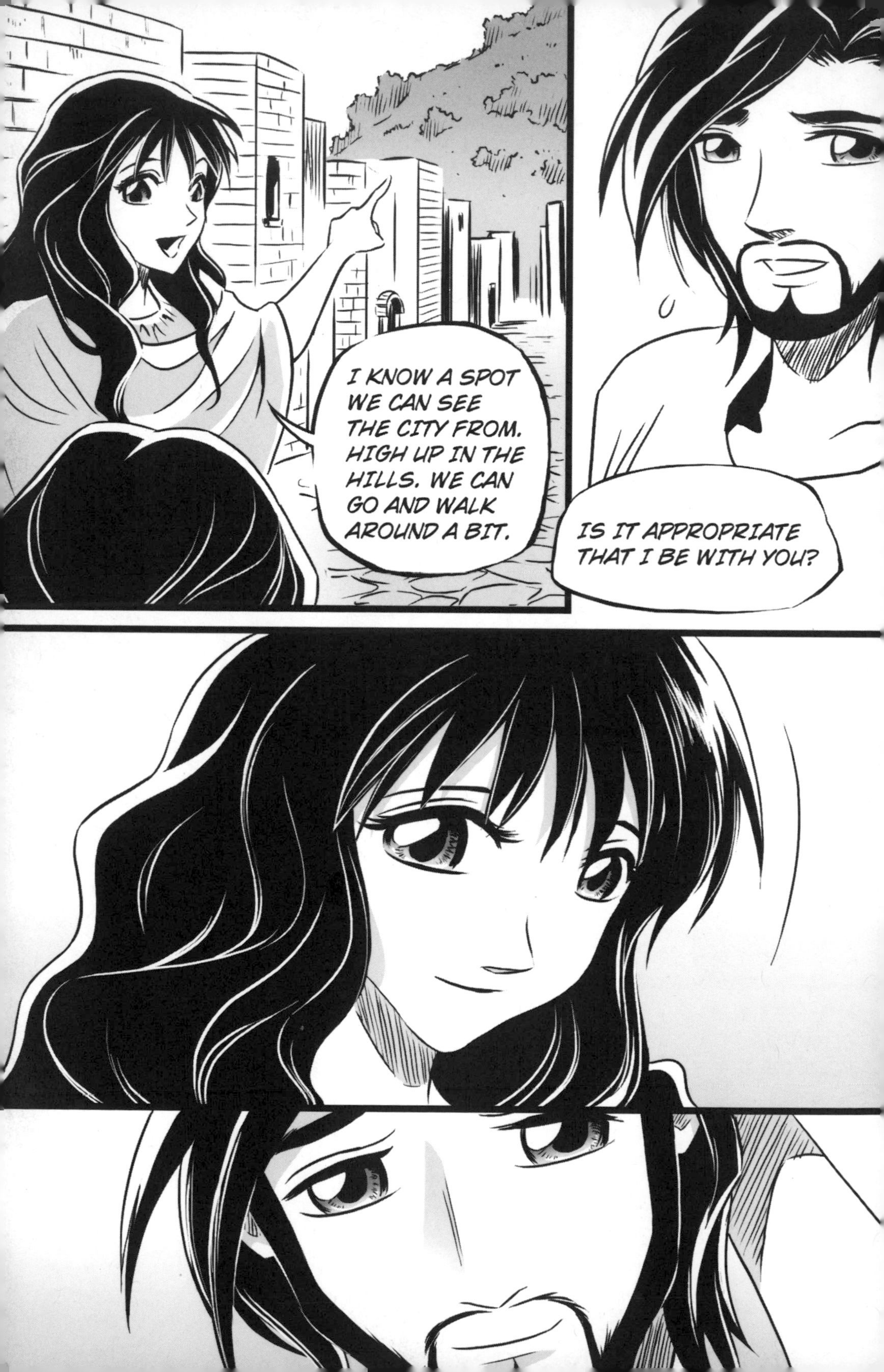
I KNOW A SPOT WE CAN SEE THE CITY FROM. HIGH UP IN THE HILLS. WE CAN GO AND WALK AROUND A BIT.
IS IT APPROPRIATE THAT I BE WITH YOU?

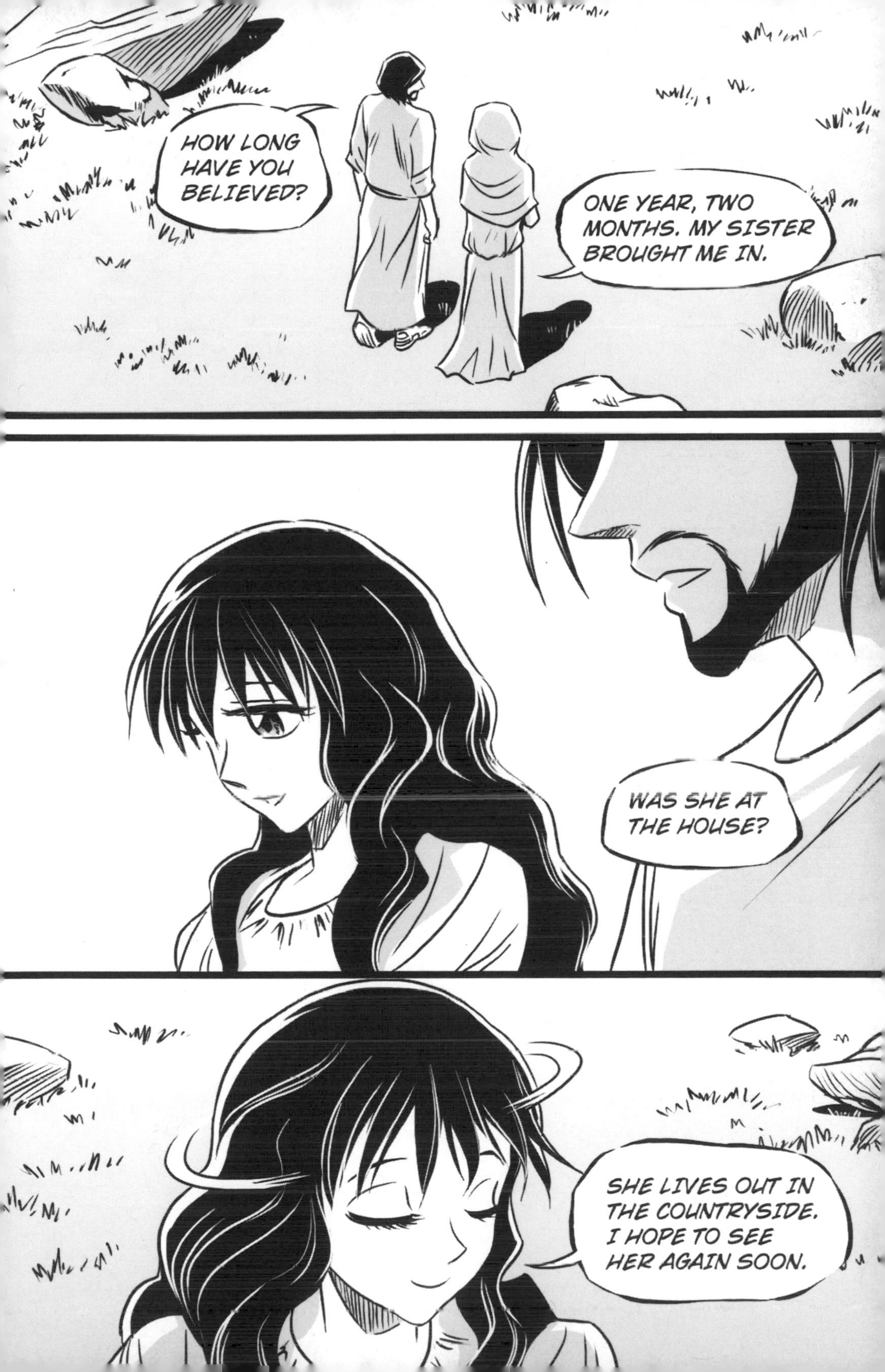

HOW LONG HAVE YOU BELIEVED?
ONE YEAR, TWO MONTHS. MY SISTER BROUGHT ME IN.
WAS SHE AT THE HOUSE?
SHE LIVES OUT IN THE COUNTRYSIDE. I HOPE TO SEE HER AGAIN SOON.

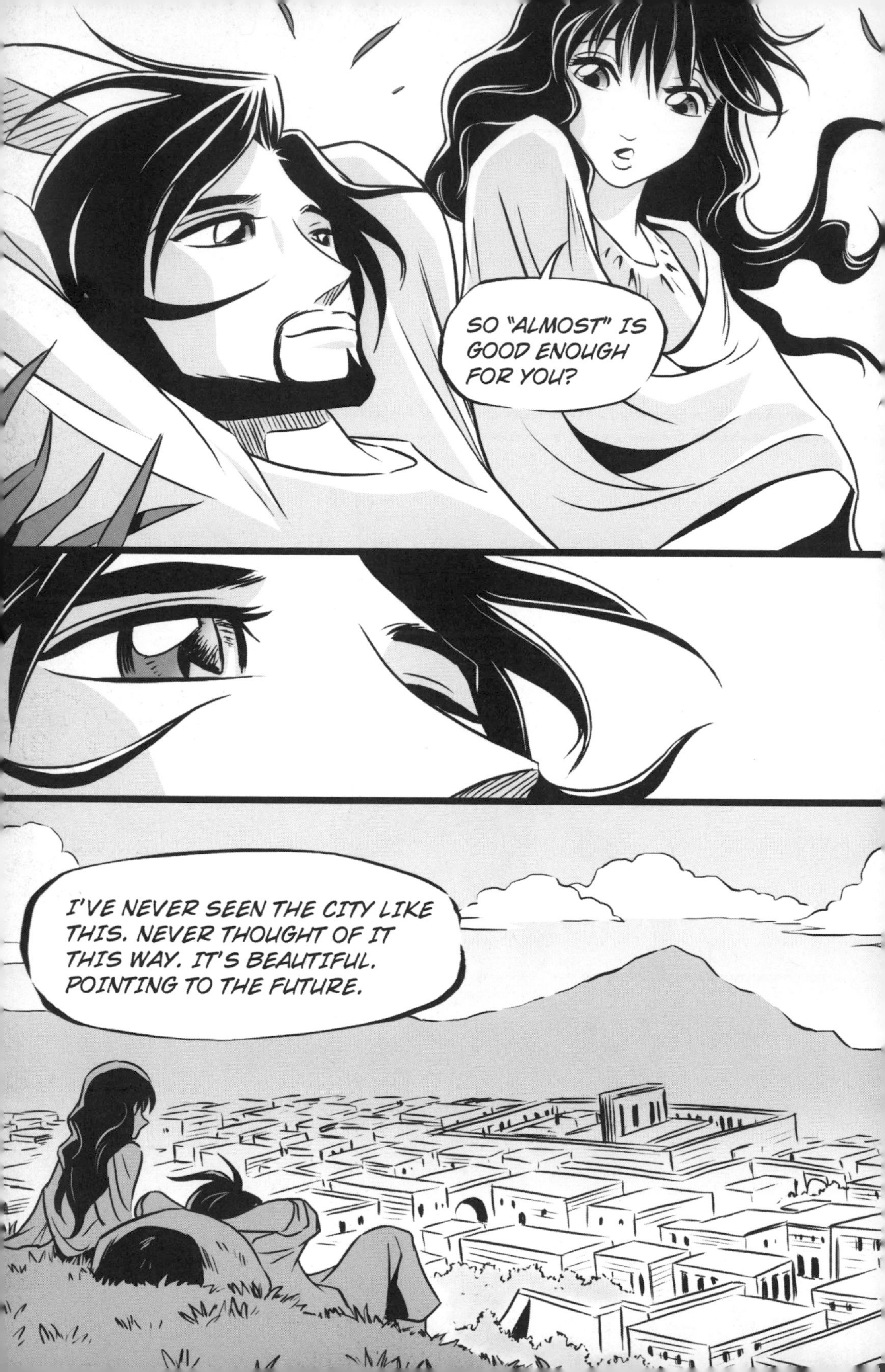
SO "ALMOST" IS GOOD ENOUGH FOR YOU?
I'VE NEVER SEEN THE CITY LIKE THIS. NEVER THOUGHT OF IT THIS WAY. IT'S BEAUTIFUL. POINTING TO THE FUTURE.

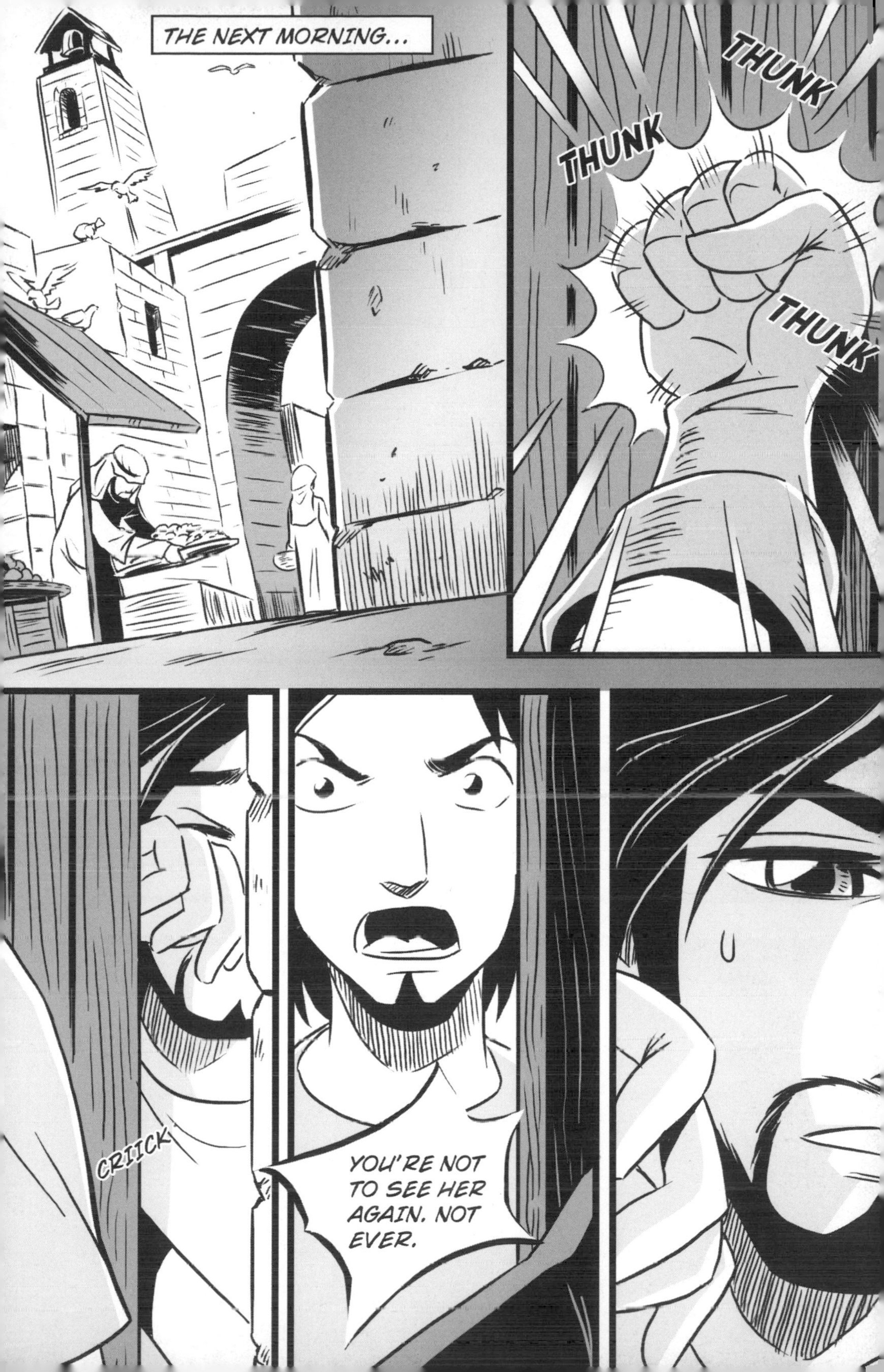

THE NEXT MORNING...
THUNK
THUNK
THUNK
CRIICK
YOU'RE NOT TO SEE HER AGAIN. NOT EVER.

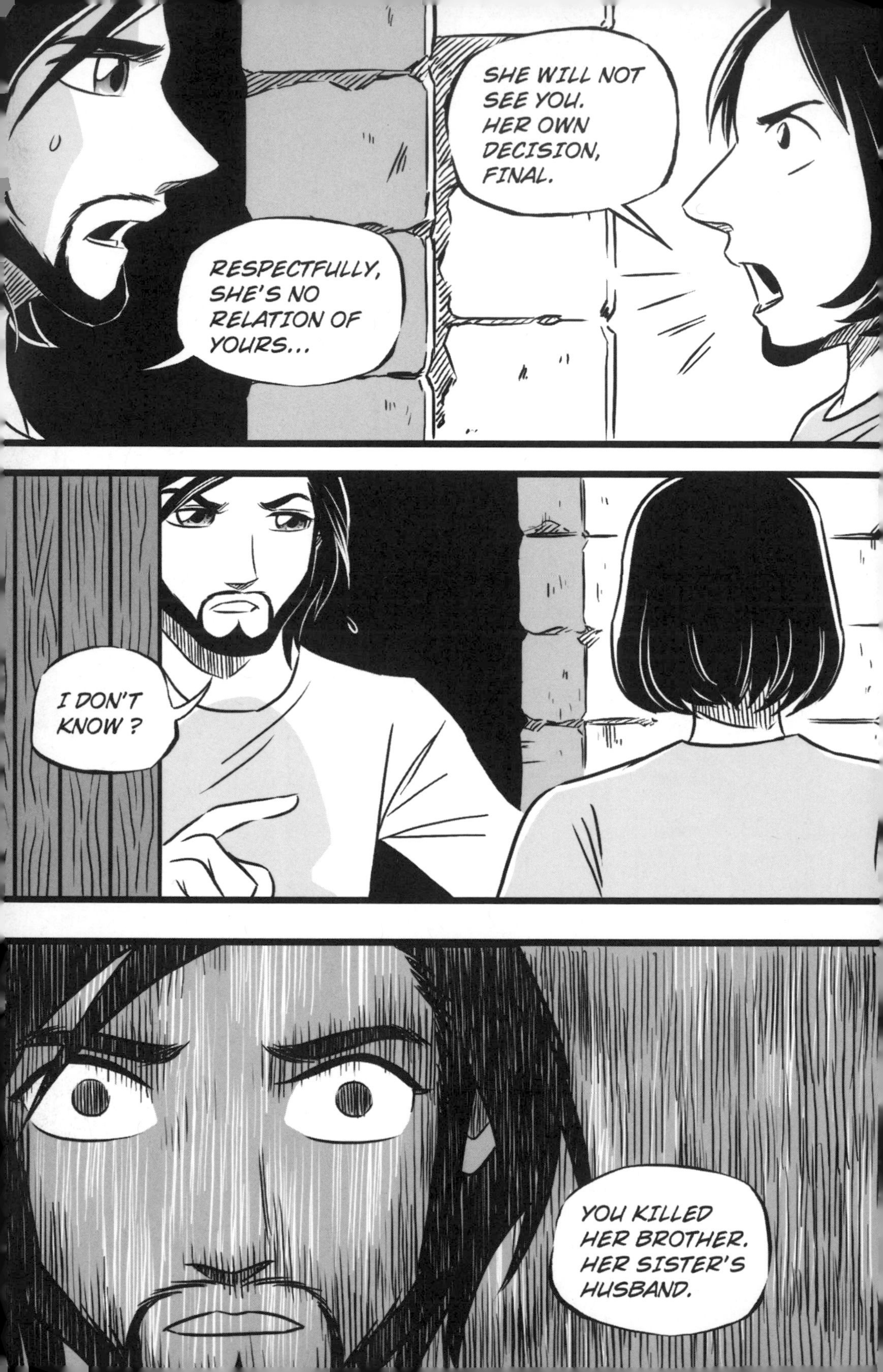
SHE WILL NOT SEE YOU. HER OWN DECISION, FINAL.
RESPECTFULLY, SHE'S NO RELATION OF YOURS...
I DON'T KNOW ?
YOU KILLED HER BROTHER. HER SISTER'S HUSBAND.

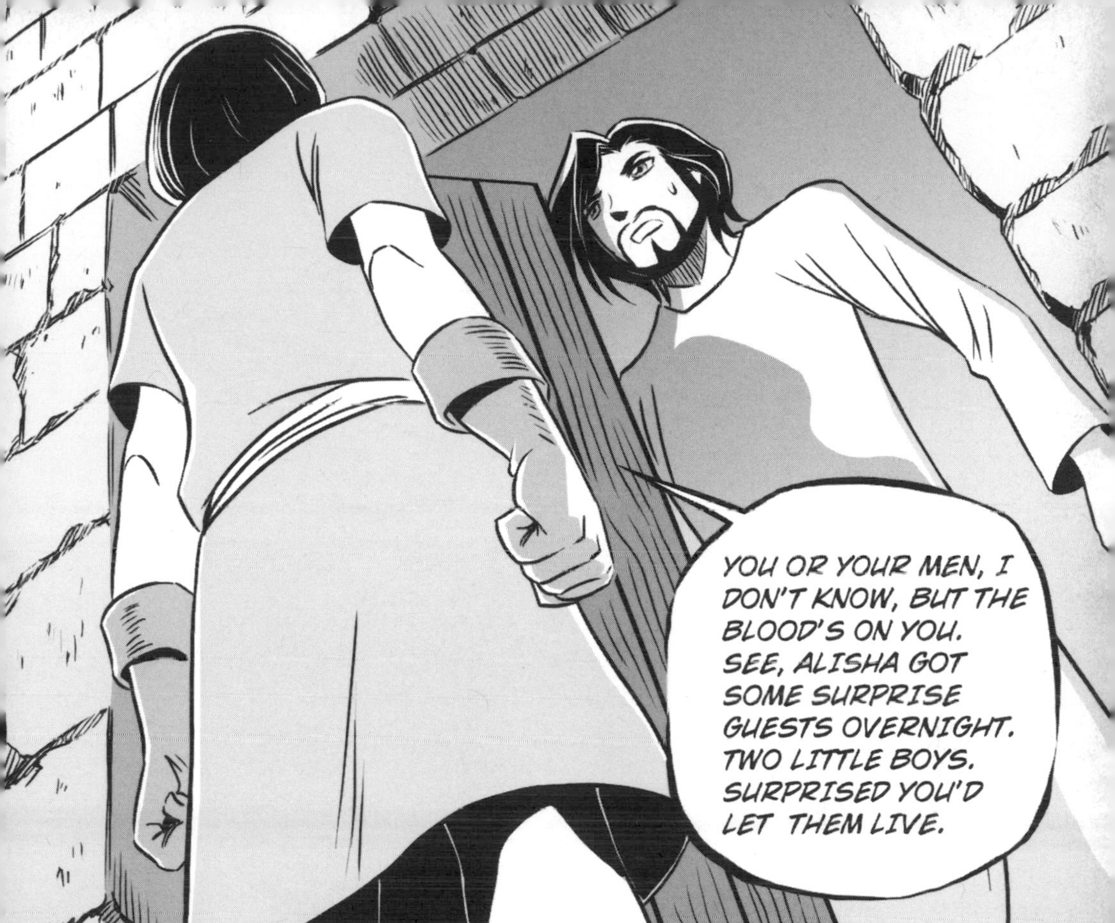
YOU OR YOUR MEN, I DON'T KNOW, BUT THE BLOOD'S ON YOU. SEE, ALISHA GOT SOME SURPRISE GUESTS OVERNIGHT. TWO LITTLE BOYS. SURPRISED YOU'D LET THEM LIVE.

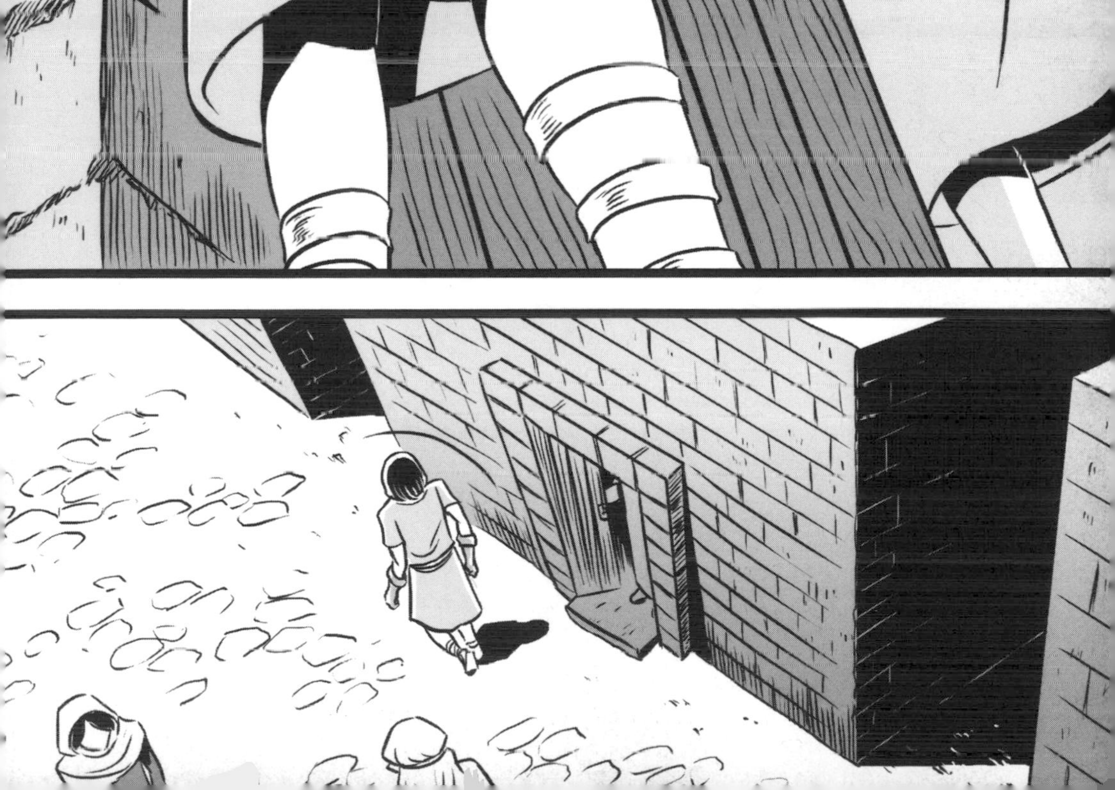

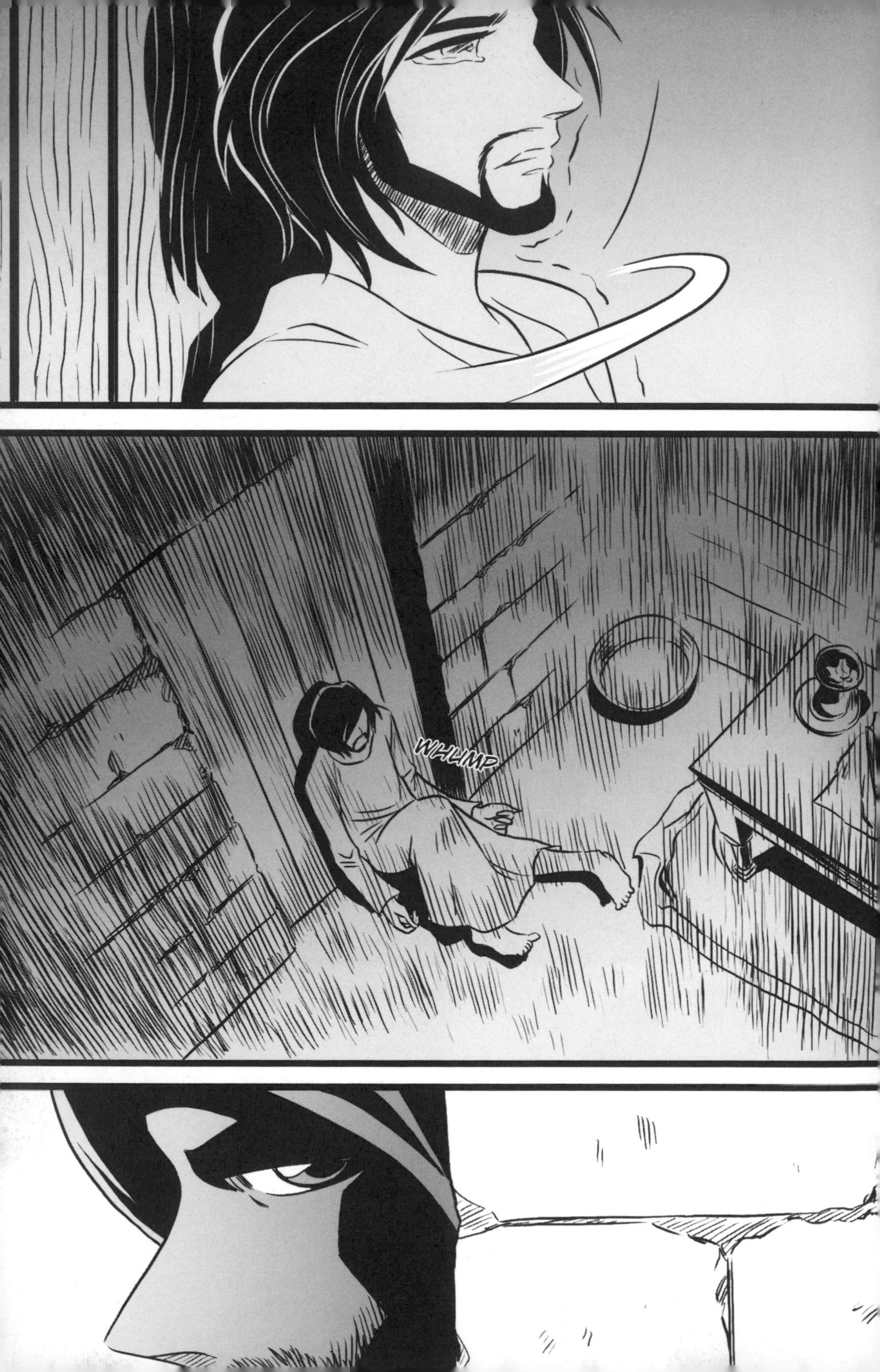
WHUMP

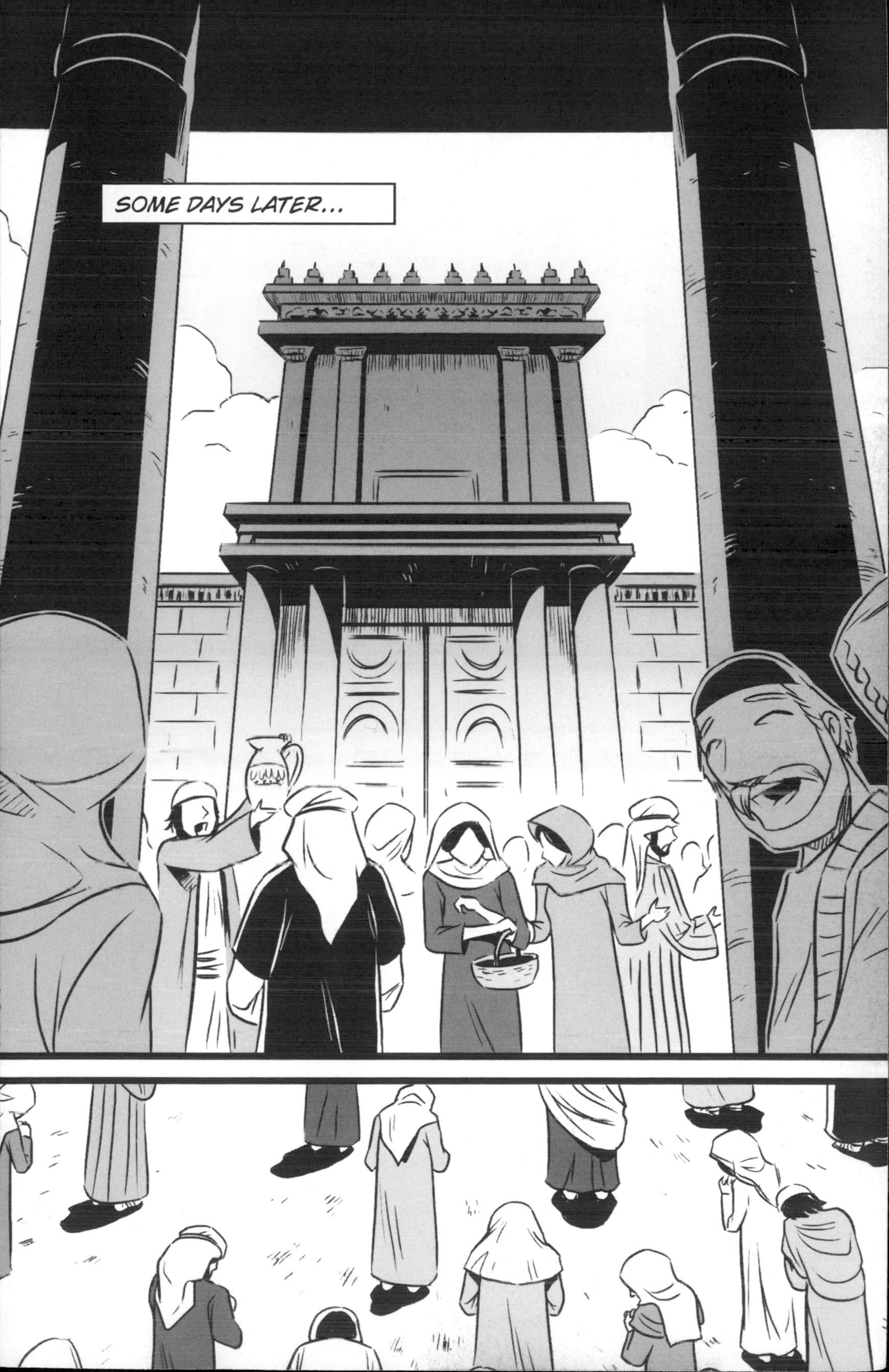
SOME DAYS LATER...

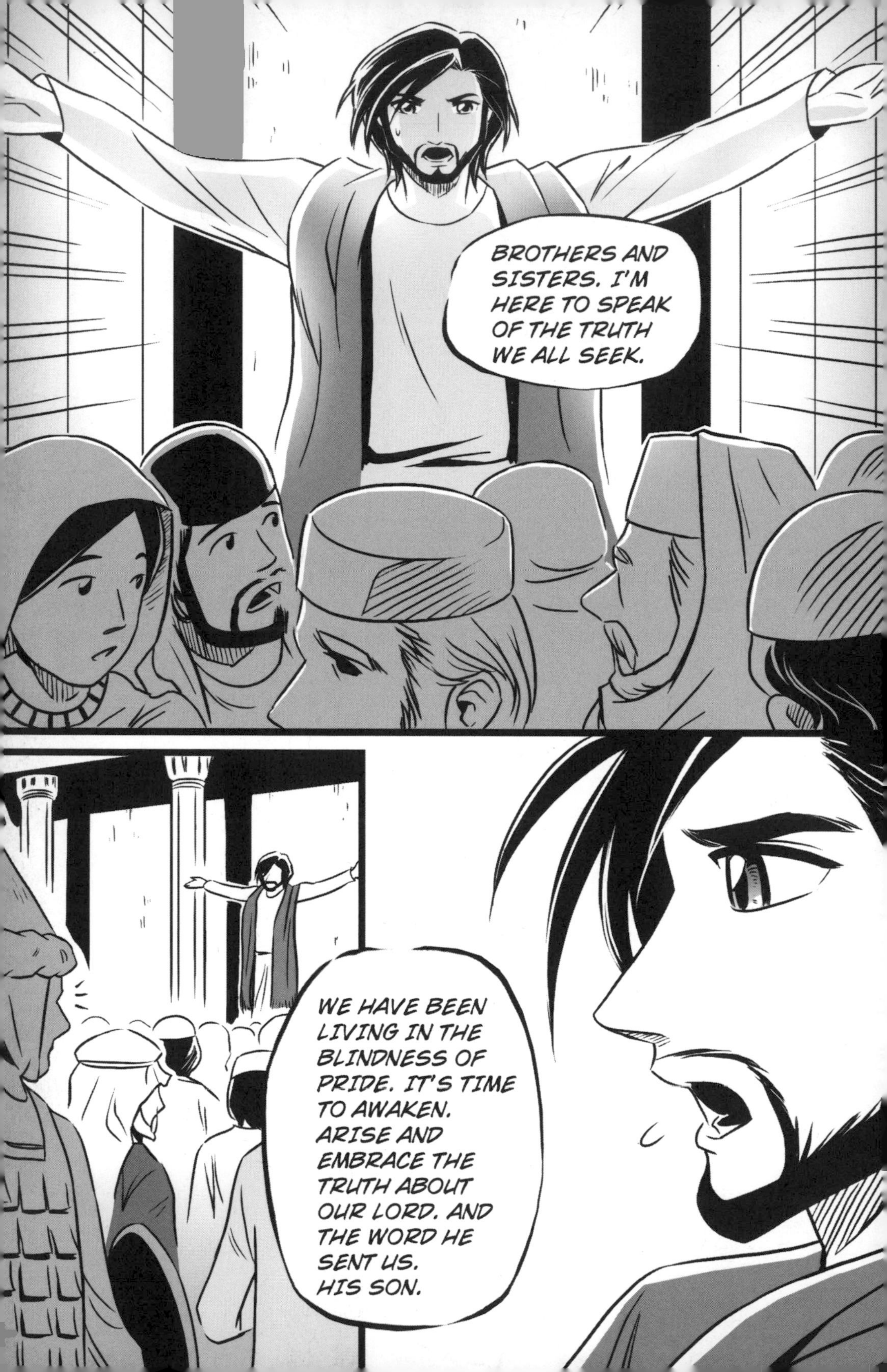
BROTHERS AND SISTERS. I'M HERE TO SPEAK OF THE TRUTH WE ALL SEEK.
WE HAVE BEEN LIVING IN THE BLINDNESS OF PRIDE. IT'S TIME TO AWAKEN. ARISE AND EMBRACE THE TRUTH ABOUT OUR LORD. AND THE WORD HE SENT US. HIS SON.

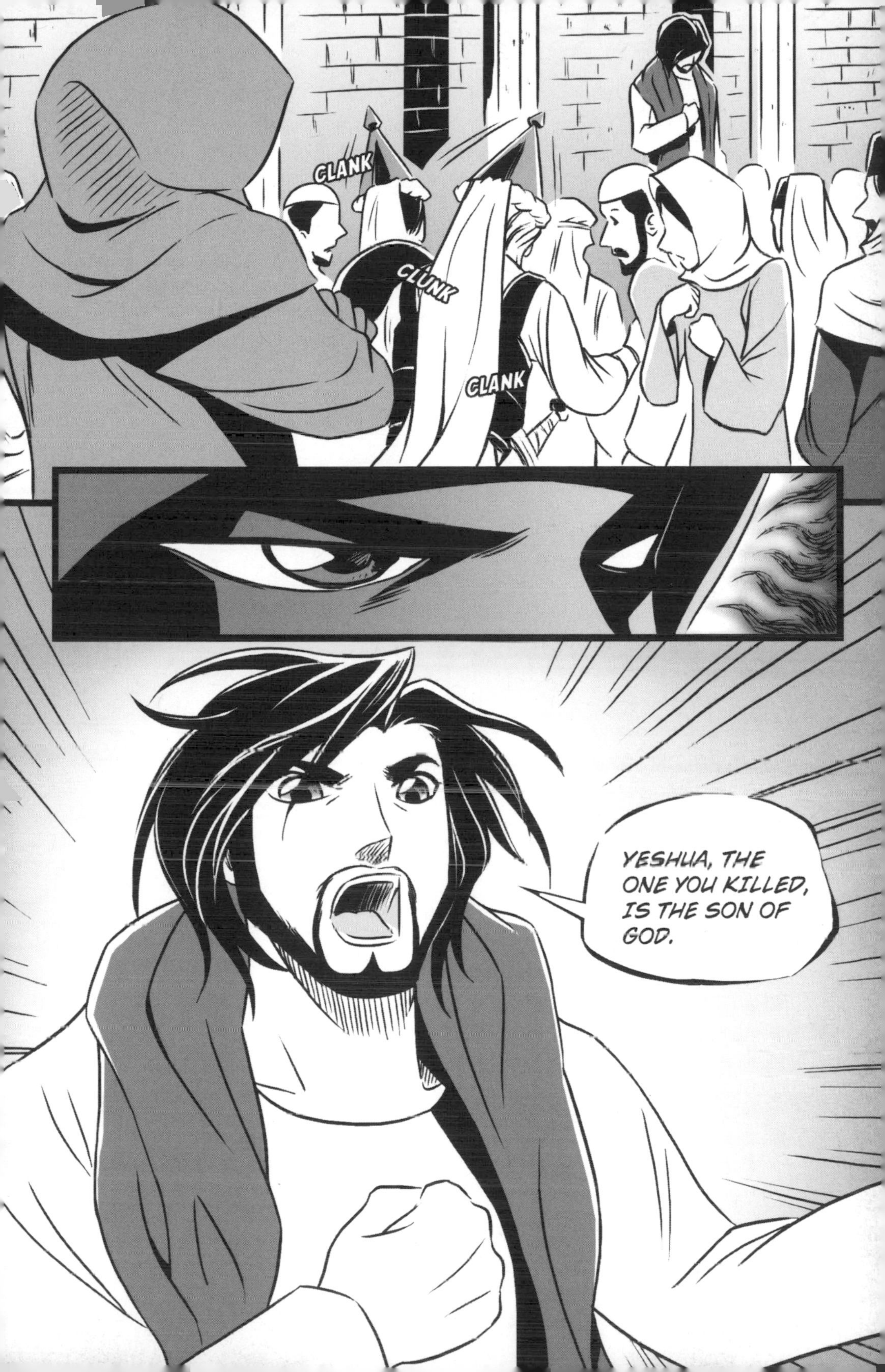
CLANK
CLUNK
CLANK
YESHUA, THE ONE YOU KILLED, IS THE SON OF GOD.

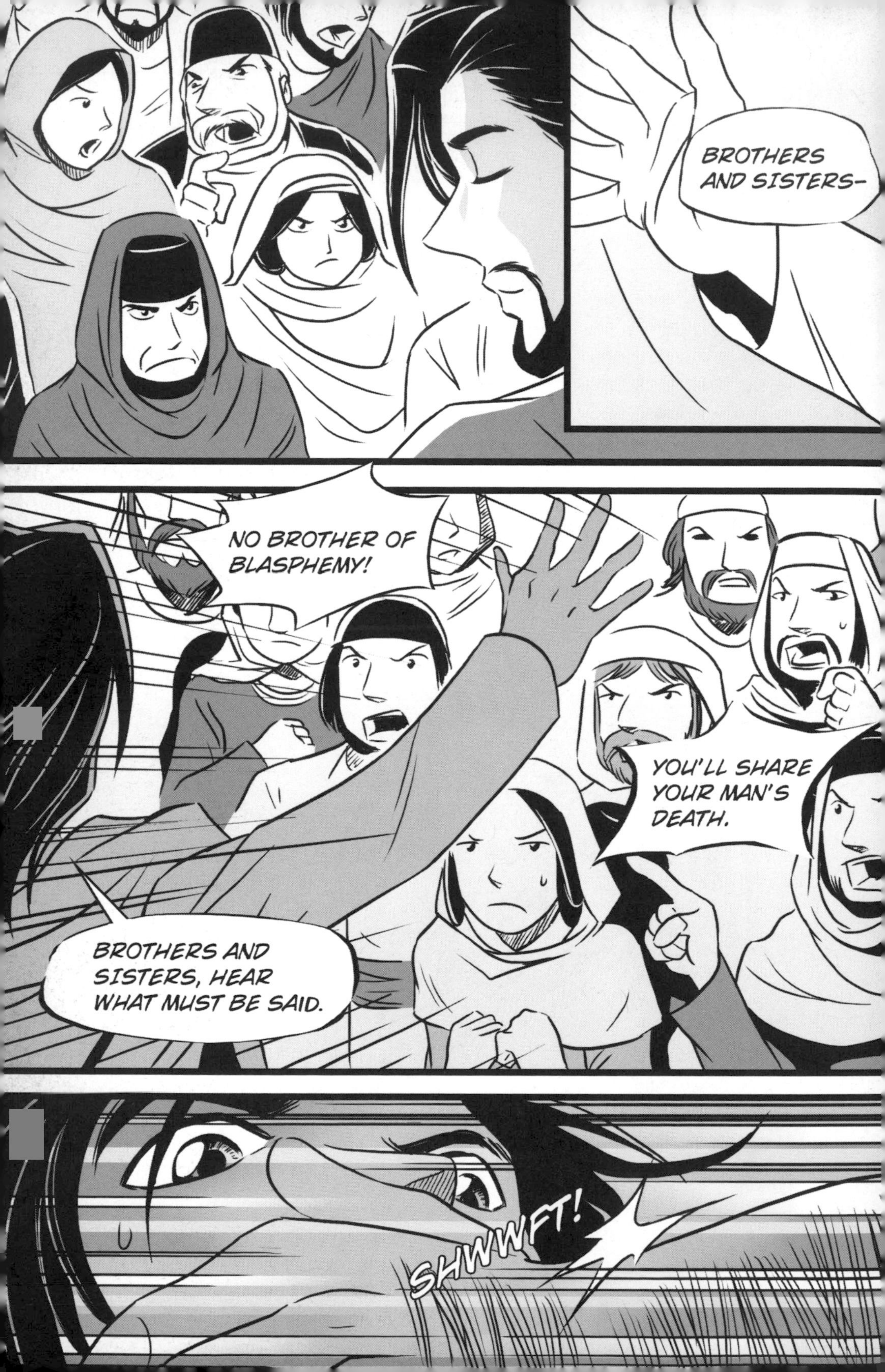
BROTHERS AND SISTERS-
NO BROTHER OF BLASPHEMY!
YOU'LL SHARE YOUR MAN'S DEATH.
BROTHERS AND SISTERS, HEAR WHAT MUST BE SAID.
SHWWFT!

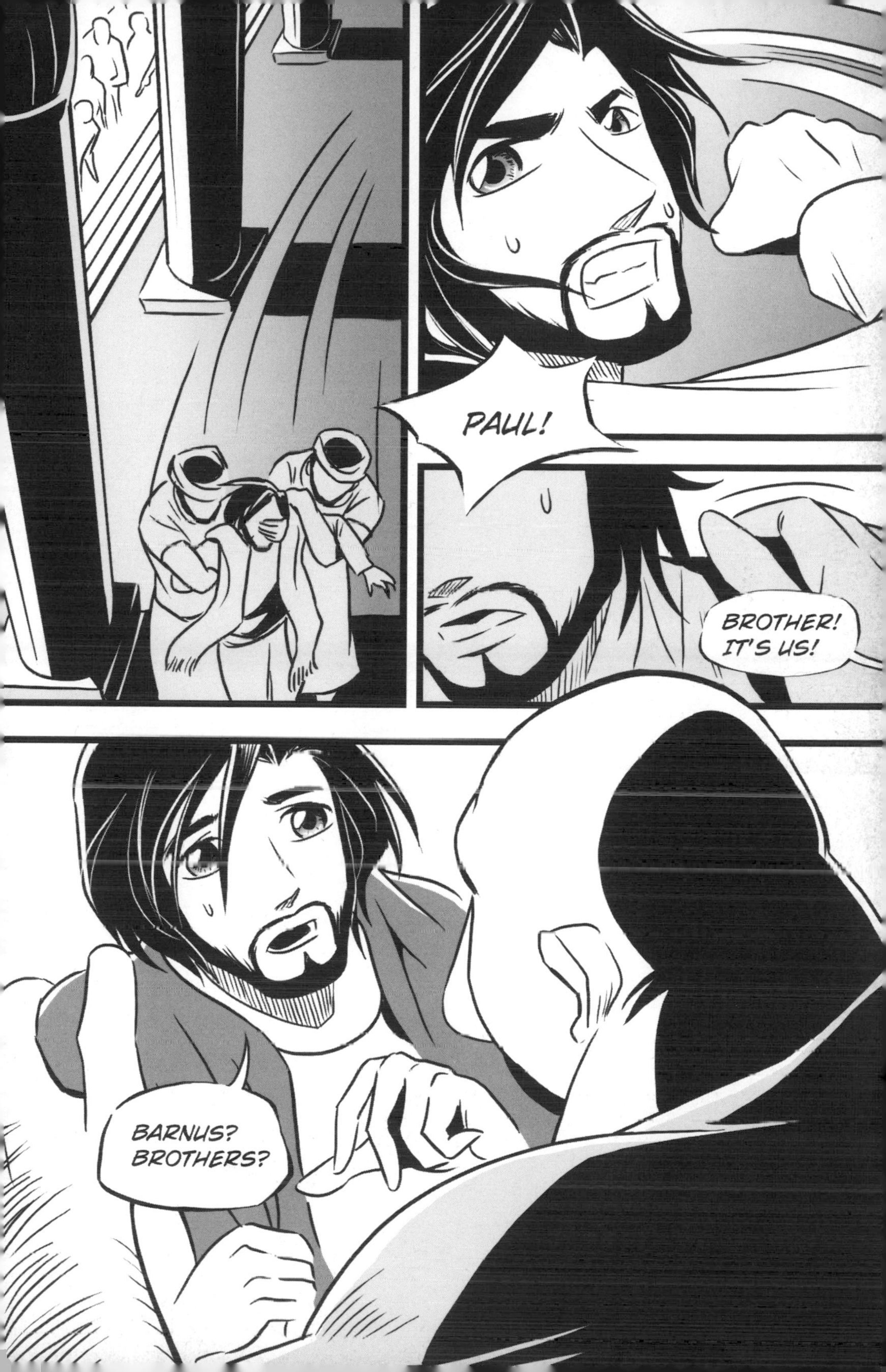
PAUL!
BROTHER! IT'S US!
BARNUS? BROTHERS?

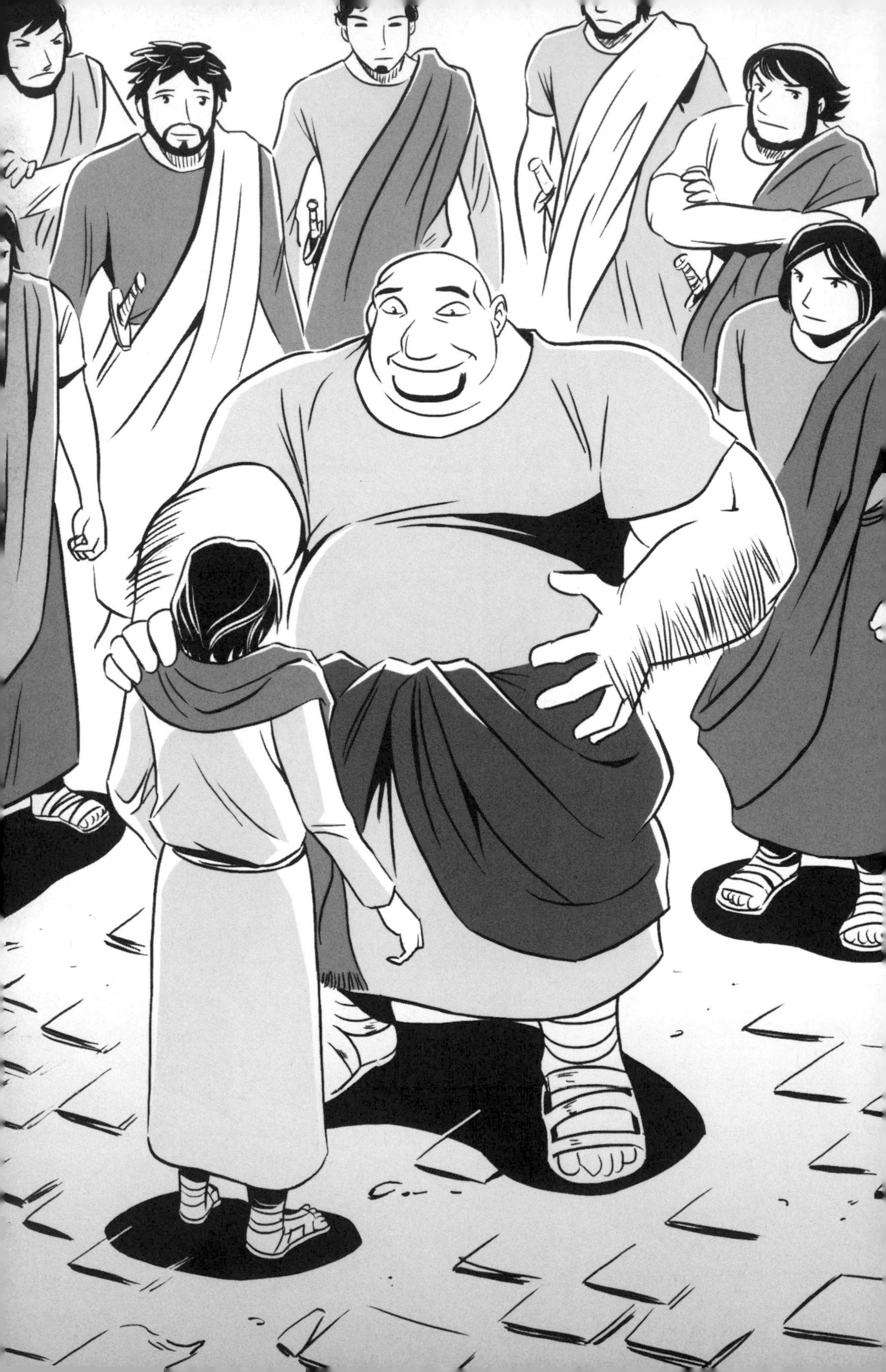

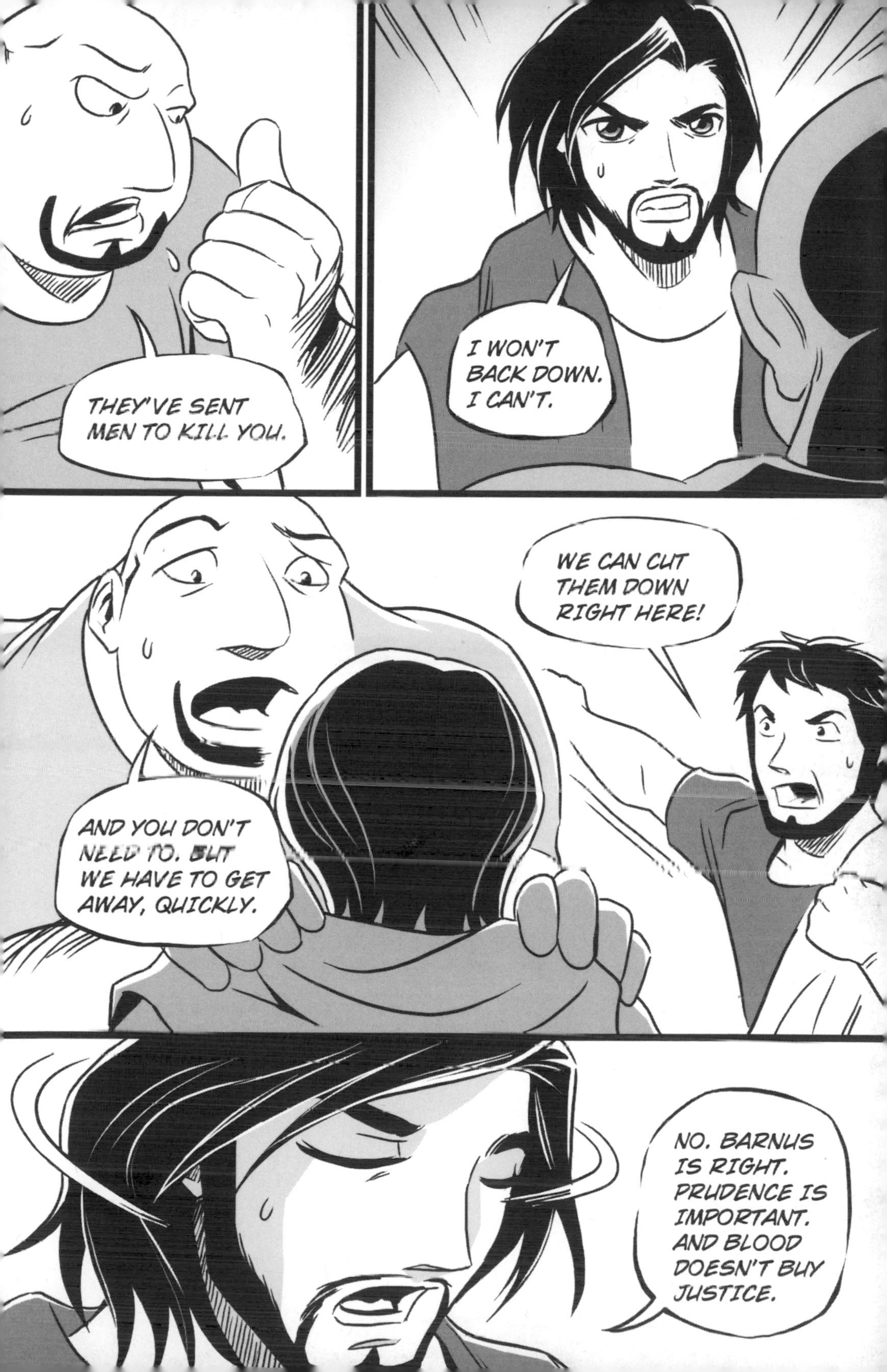
THEY'VE SENT MEN TO KILL YOU.
I WON'T BACK DOWN. I CAN'T.
WE CAN CUT THEM DOWN RIGHT HERE!
AND YOU DON'T NEED TO. BUT WE HAVE TO GET AWAY, QUICKLY.
NO. BARNUS IS RIGHT. PRUDENCE IS IMPORTANT. AND BLOOD DOESN'T BUY JUSTICE.

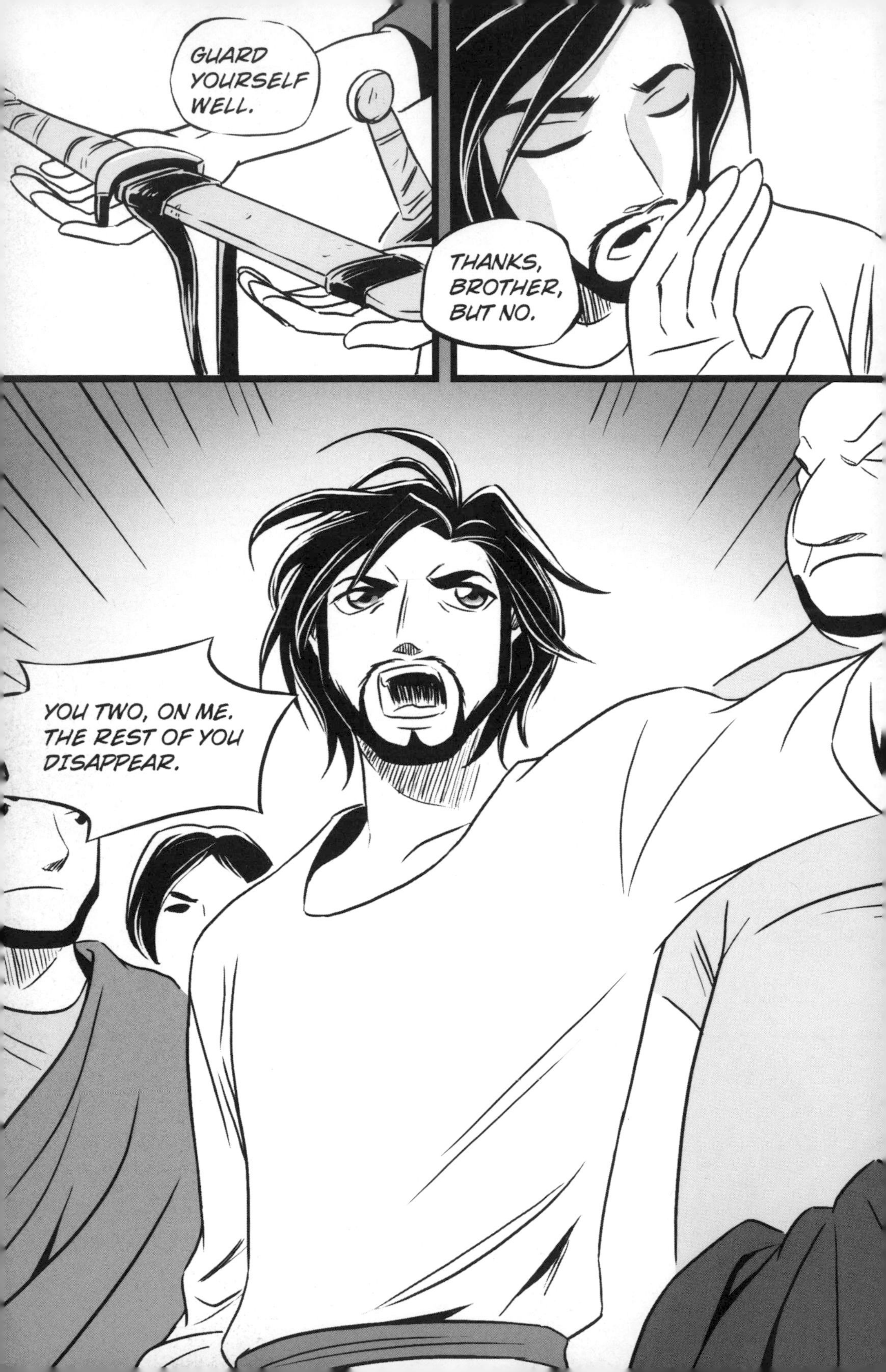
GUARD YOURSELF WELL.
THANKS, BROTHER, BUT NO.
YOU TWO, ON ME. THE REST OF YOU DISAPPEAR.

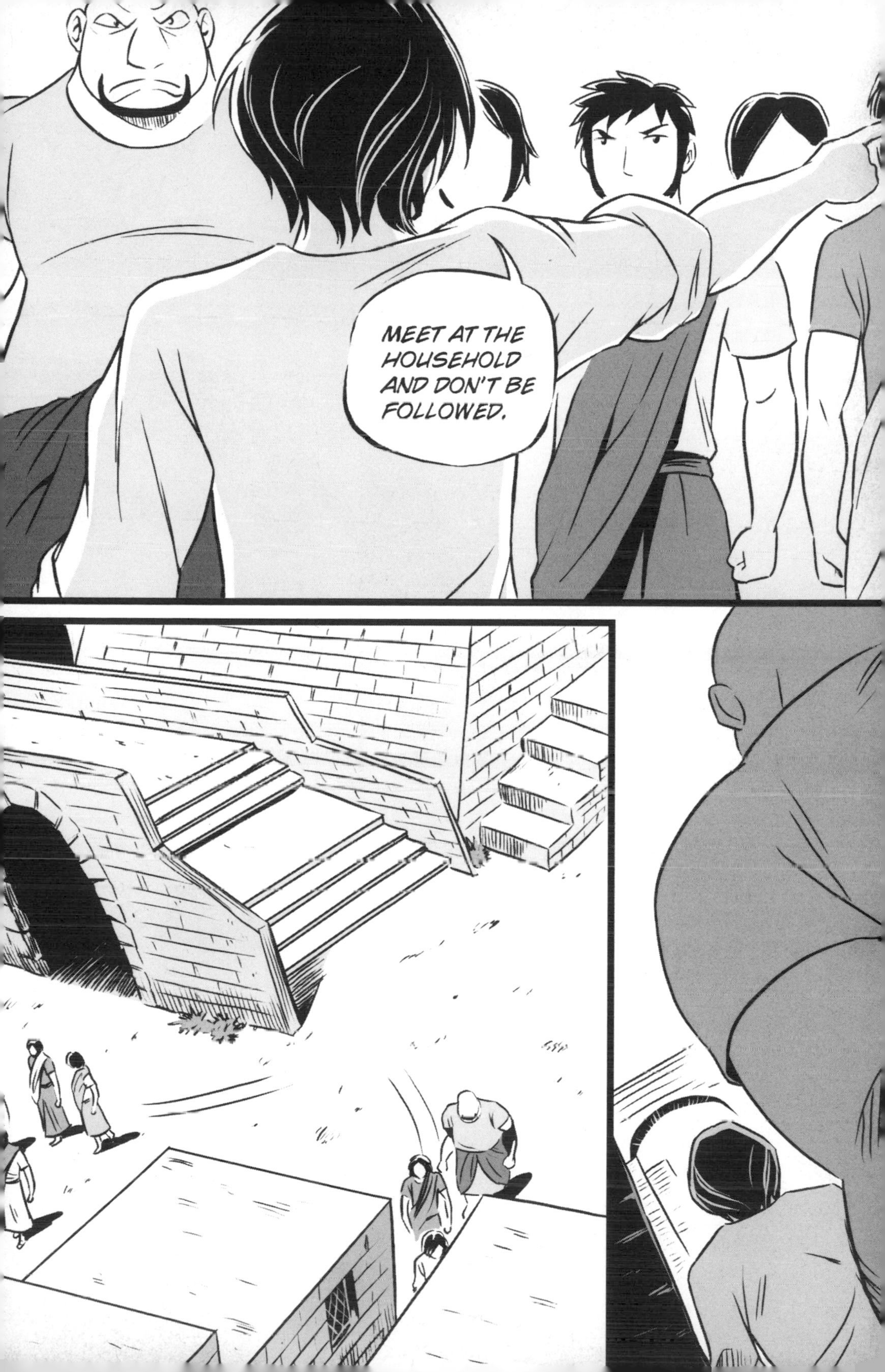
MEET AT THE HOUSEHOLD AND DON'T BE FOLLOWED.

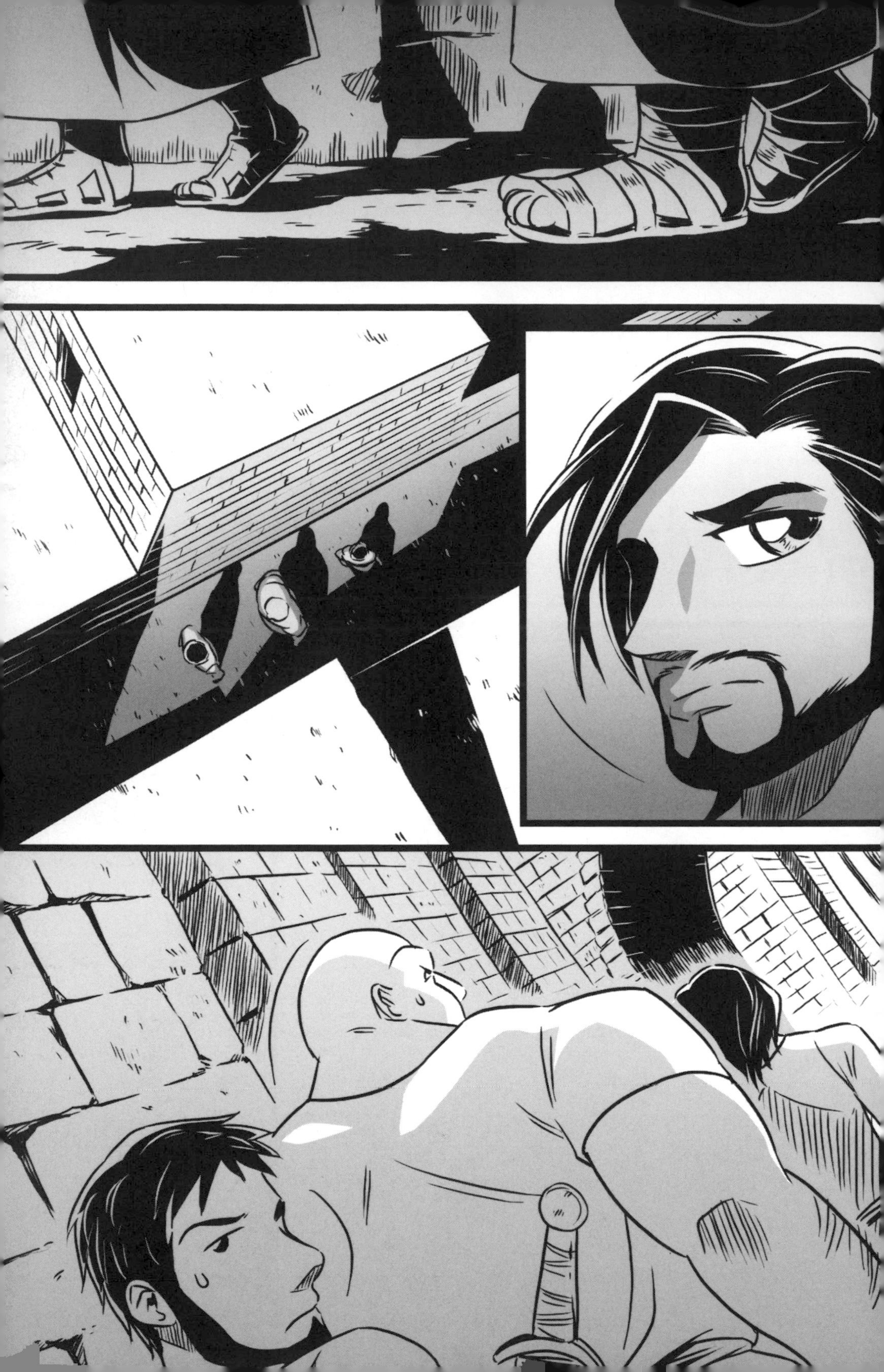

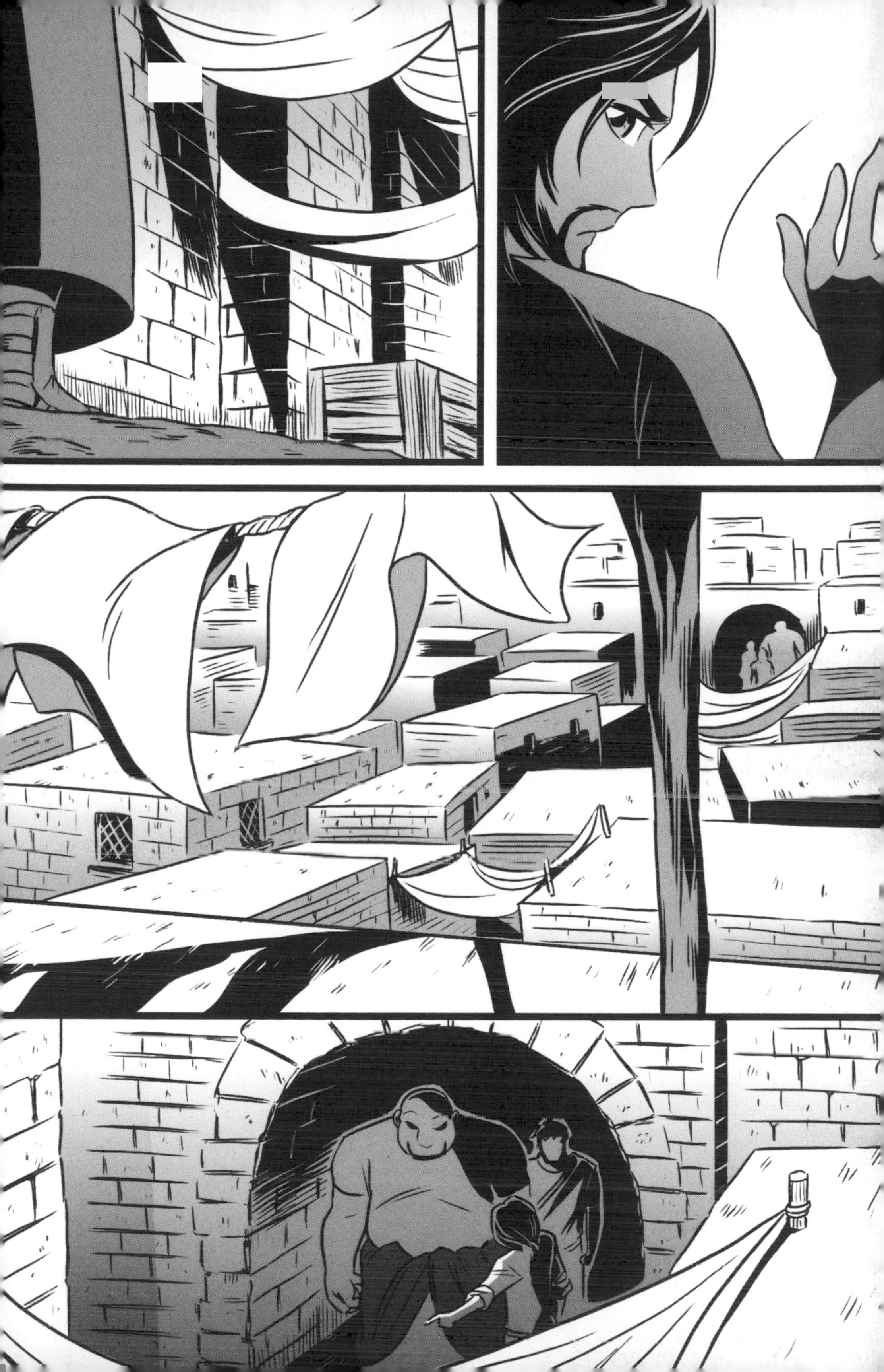

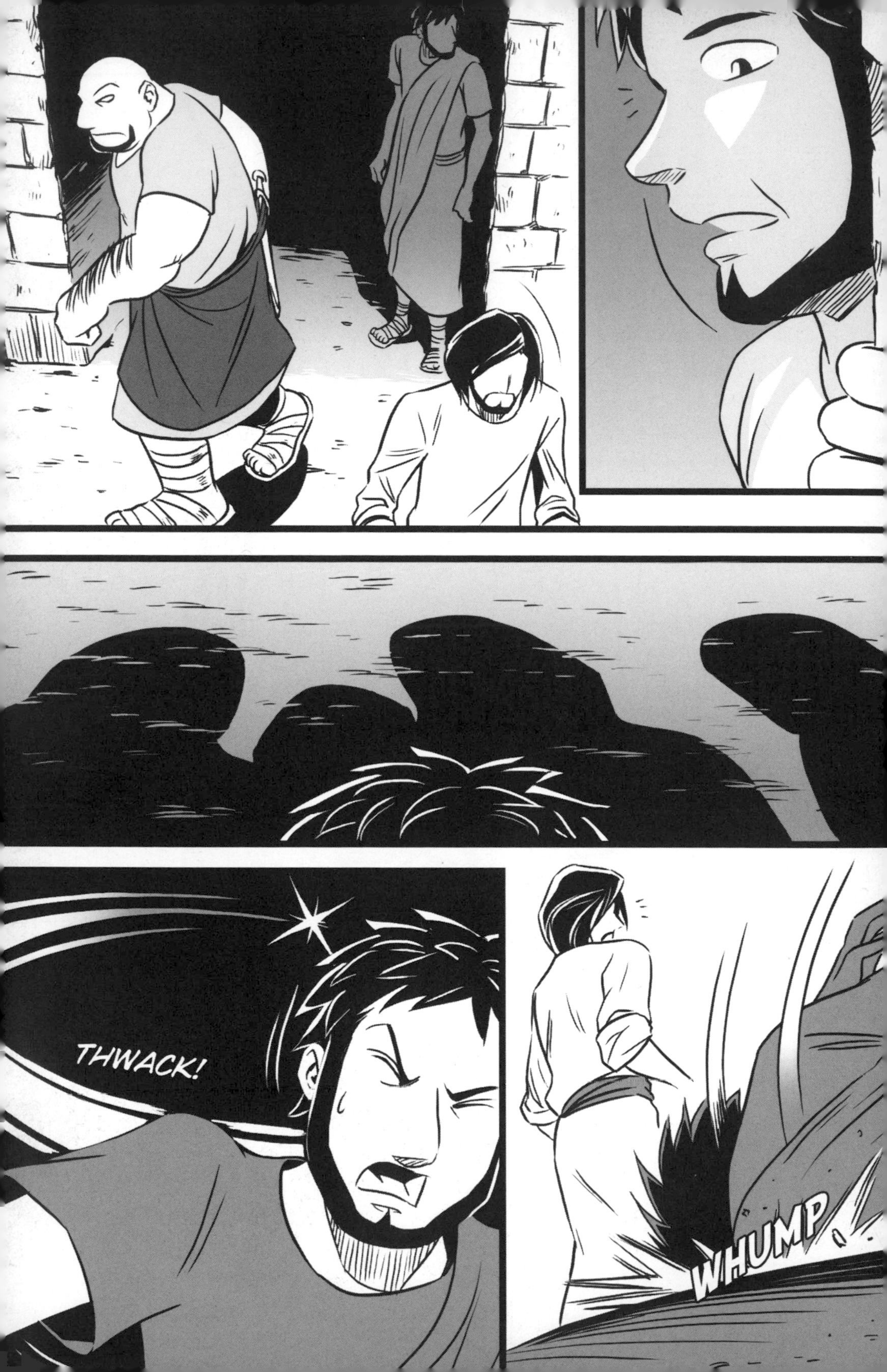
THWACK!
WHUMP

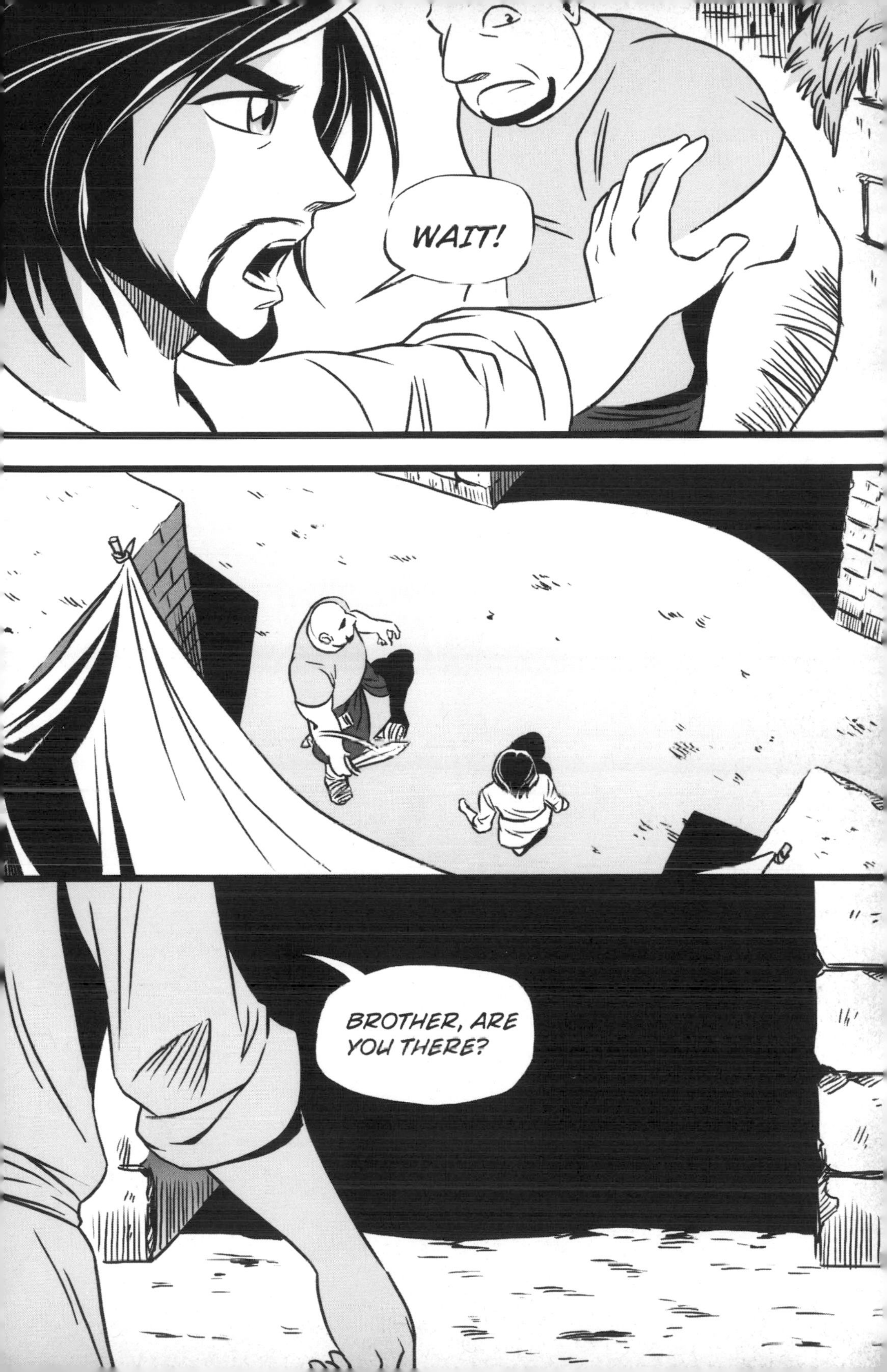
WAIT!
BROTHER, ARE YOU THERE?

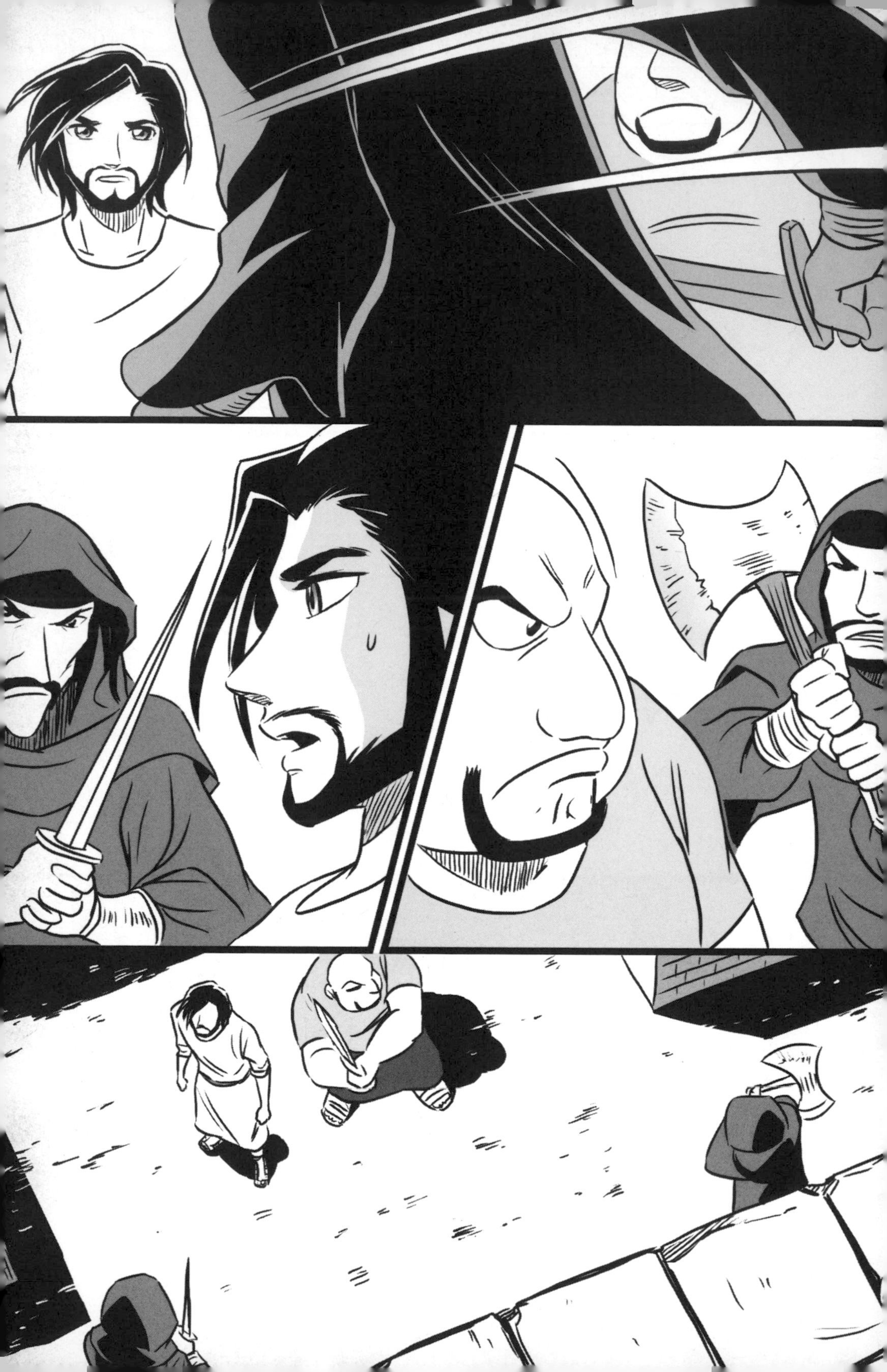

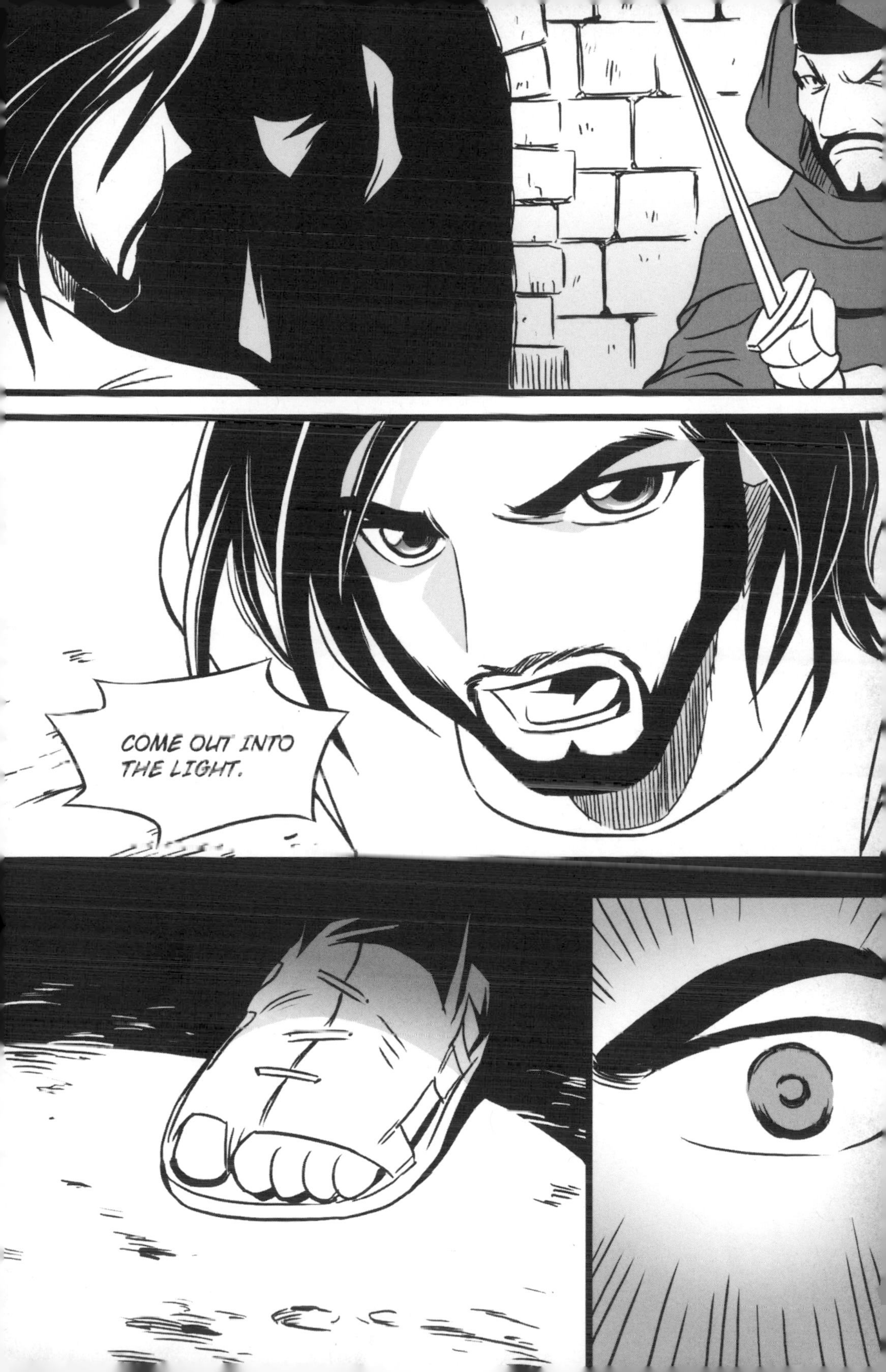
COME OUT INTO
THE LIGHT.

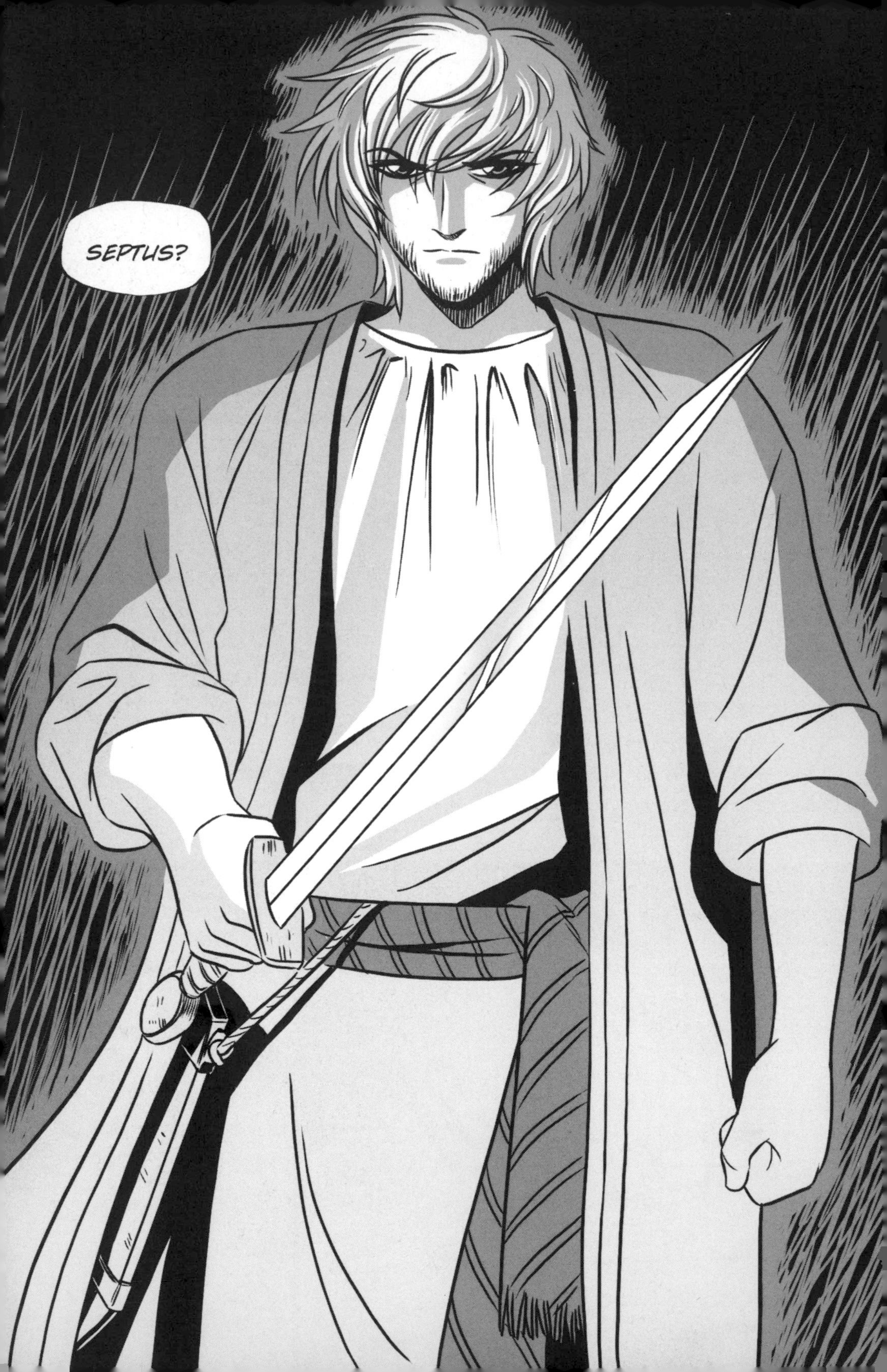
SEPTUS?

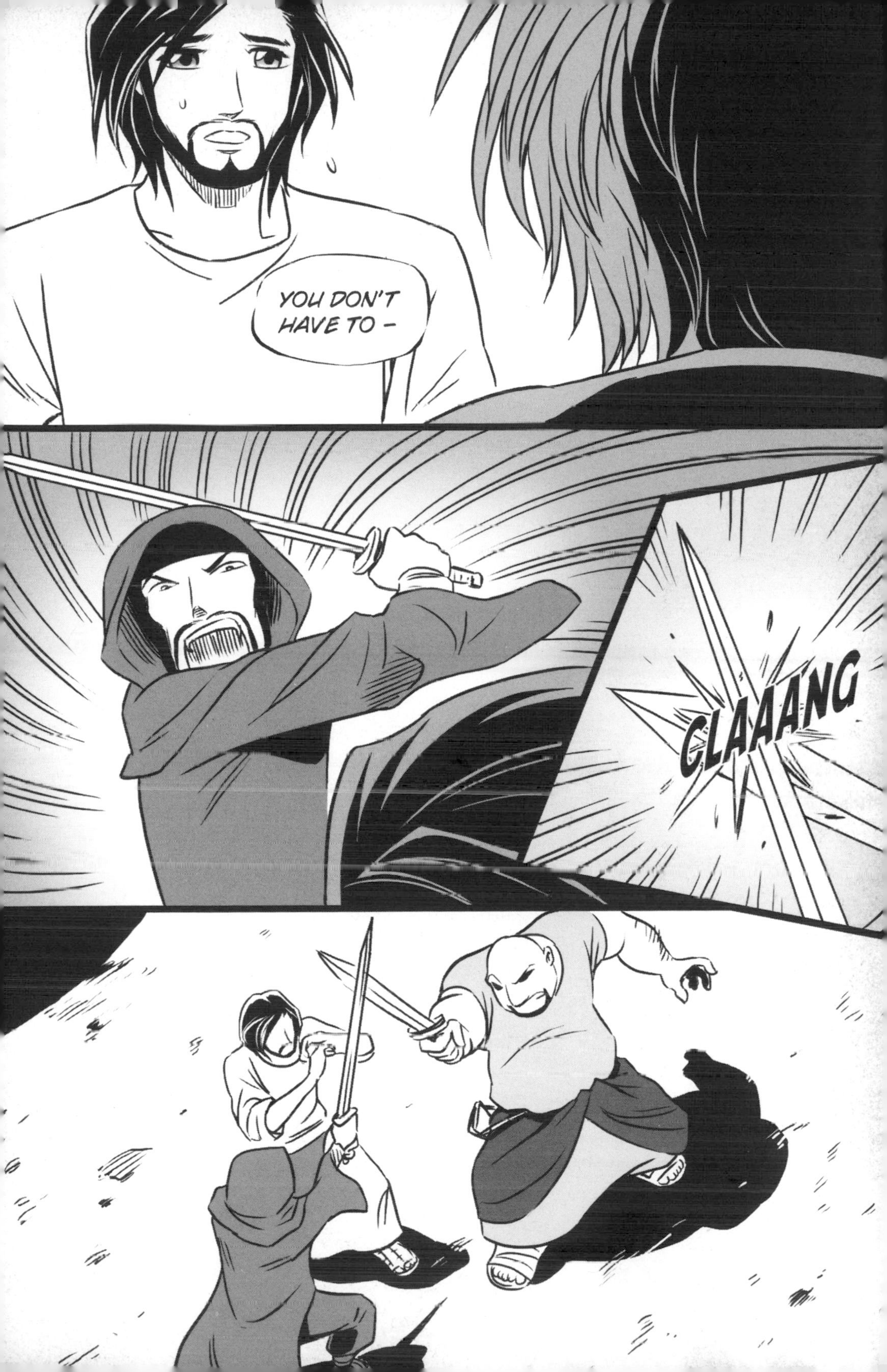
YOU DON'T HAVE TO -
CLAAANG

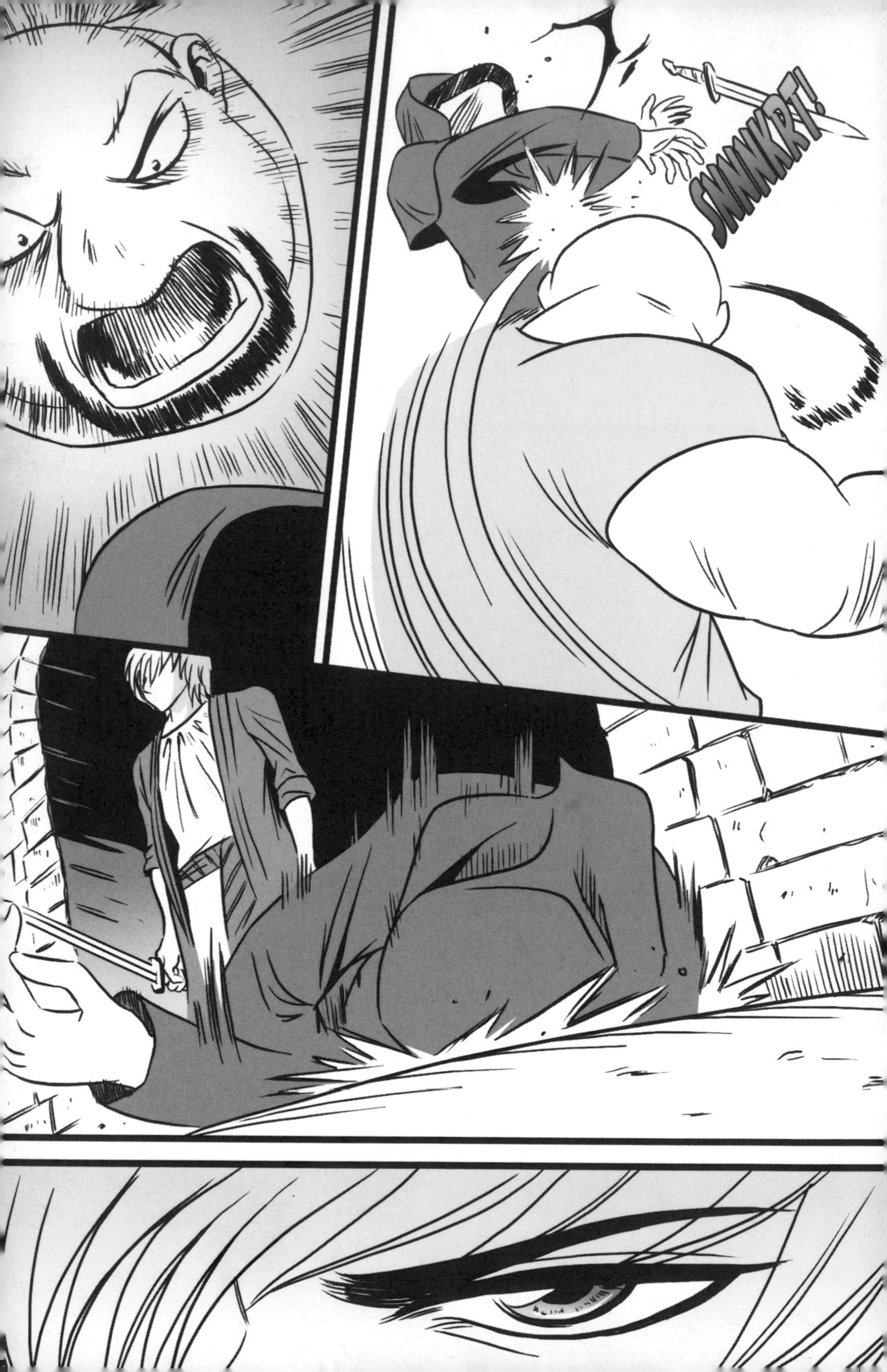
SNNNKRT!

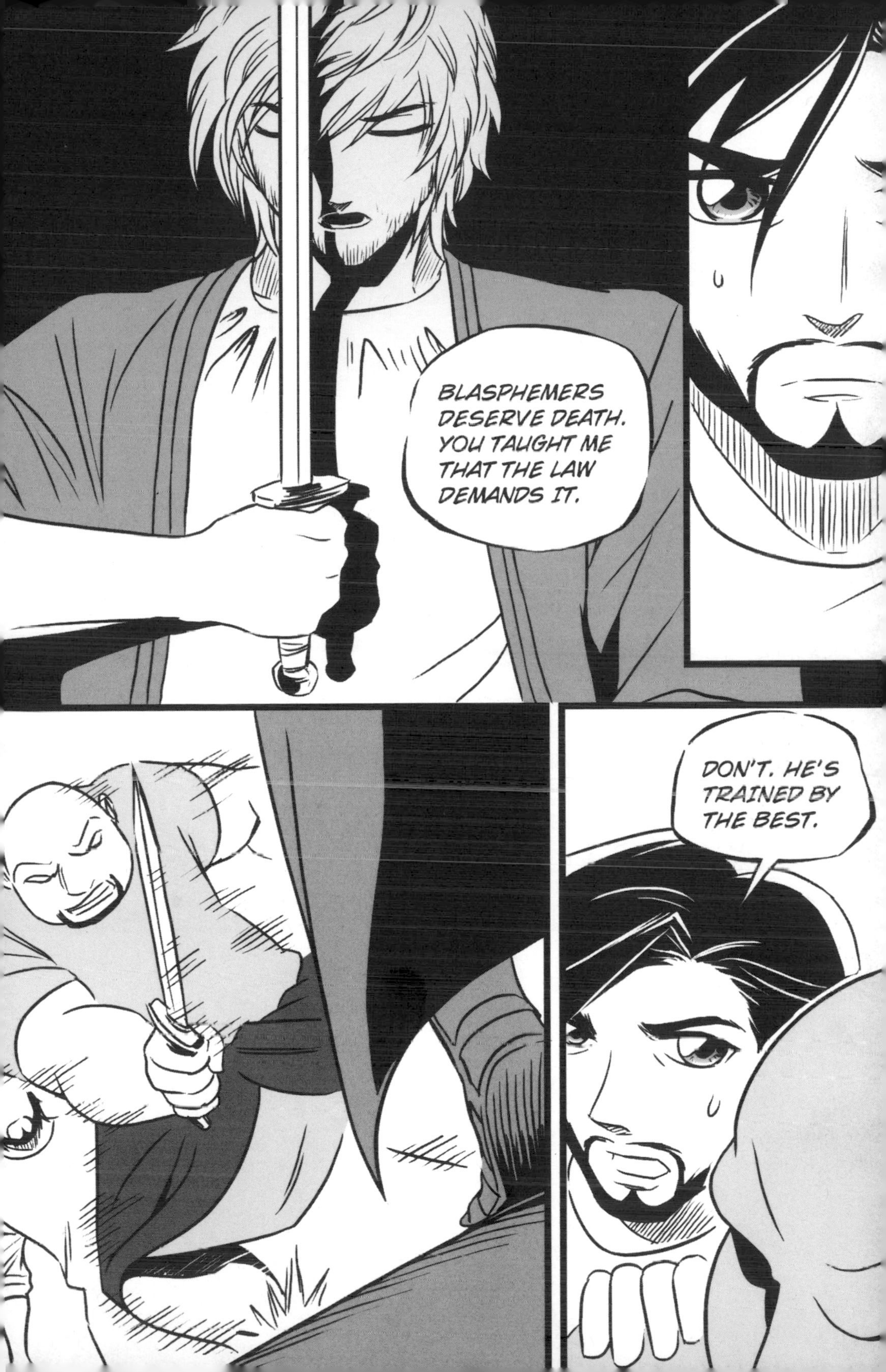
BLASPHEMERS DESERVE DEATH. YOU TAUGHT ME THAT THE LAW DEMANDS IT.
DON'T. HE'S TRAINED BY THE BEST.

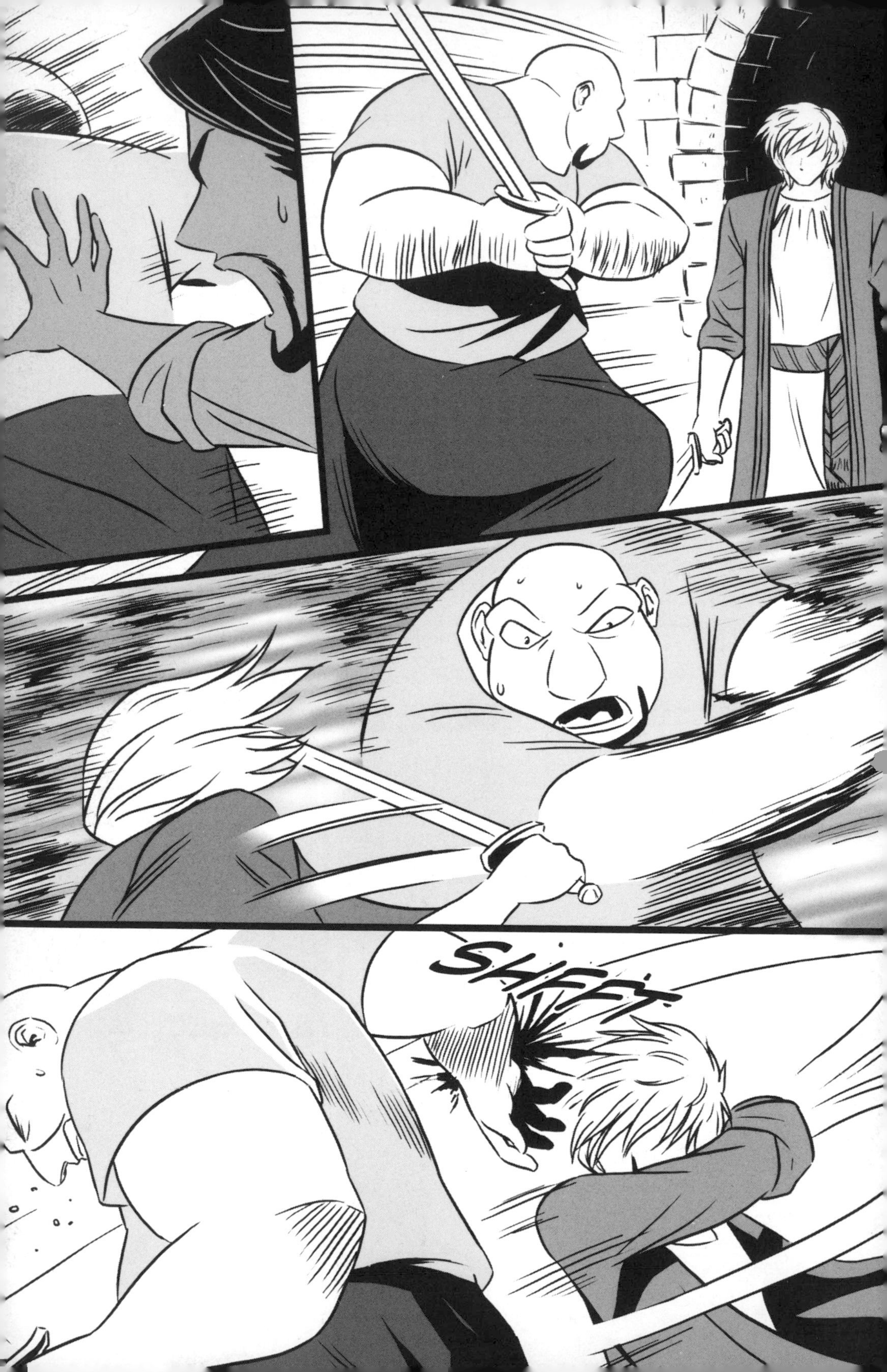
SHFFT

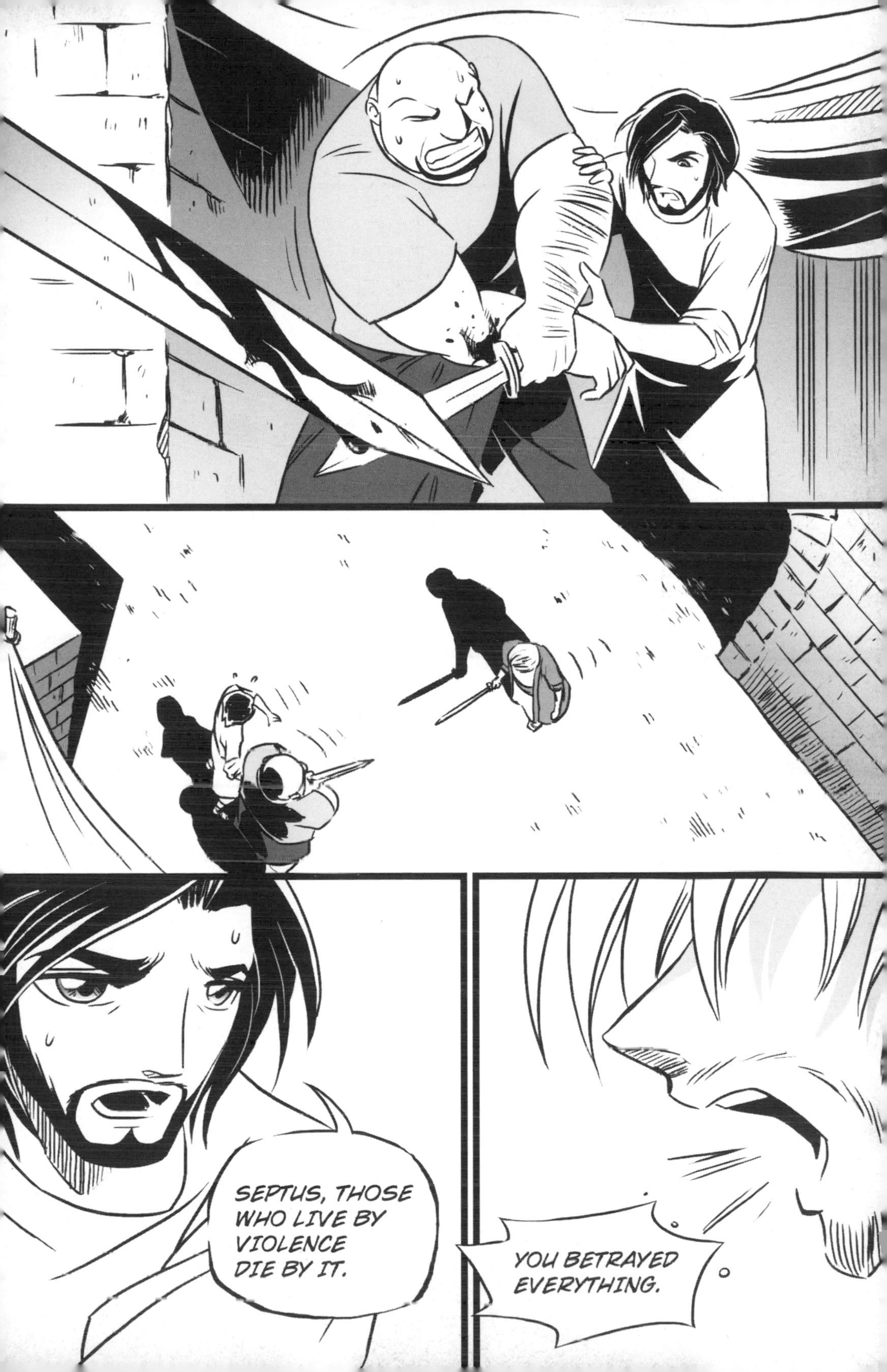
SEPTUS, THOSE WHO LIVE BY VIOLENCE DIE BY IT.
YOU BETRAYED EVERYTHING.

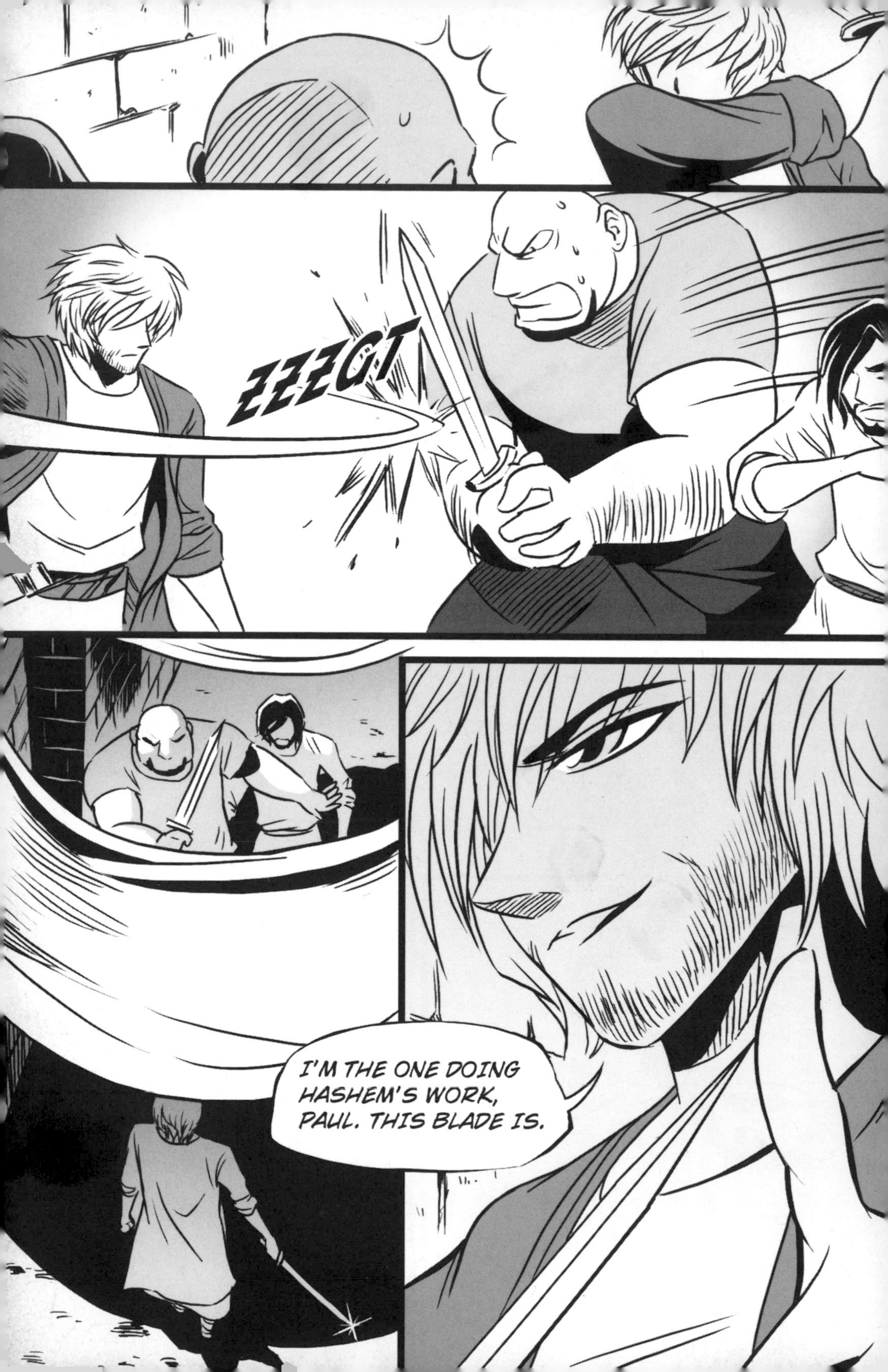
ZZZGT
I'M THE ONE DOING HASHEM'S WORK, PAUL. THIS BLADE IS.

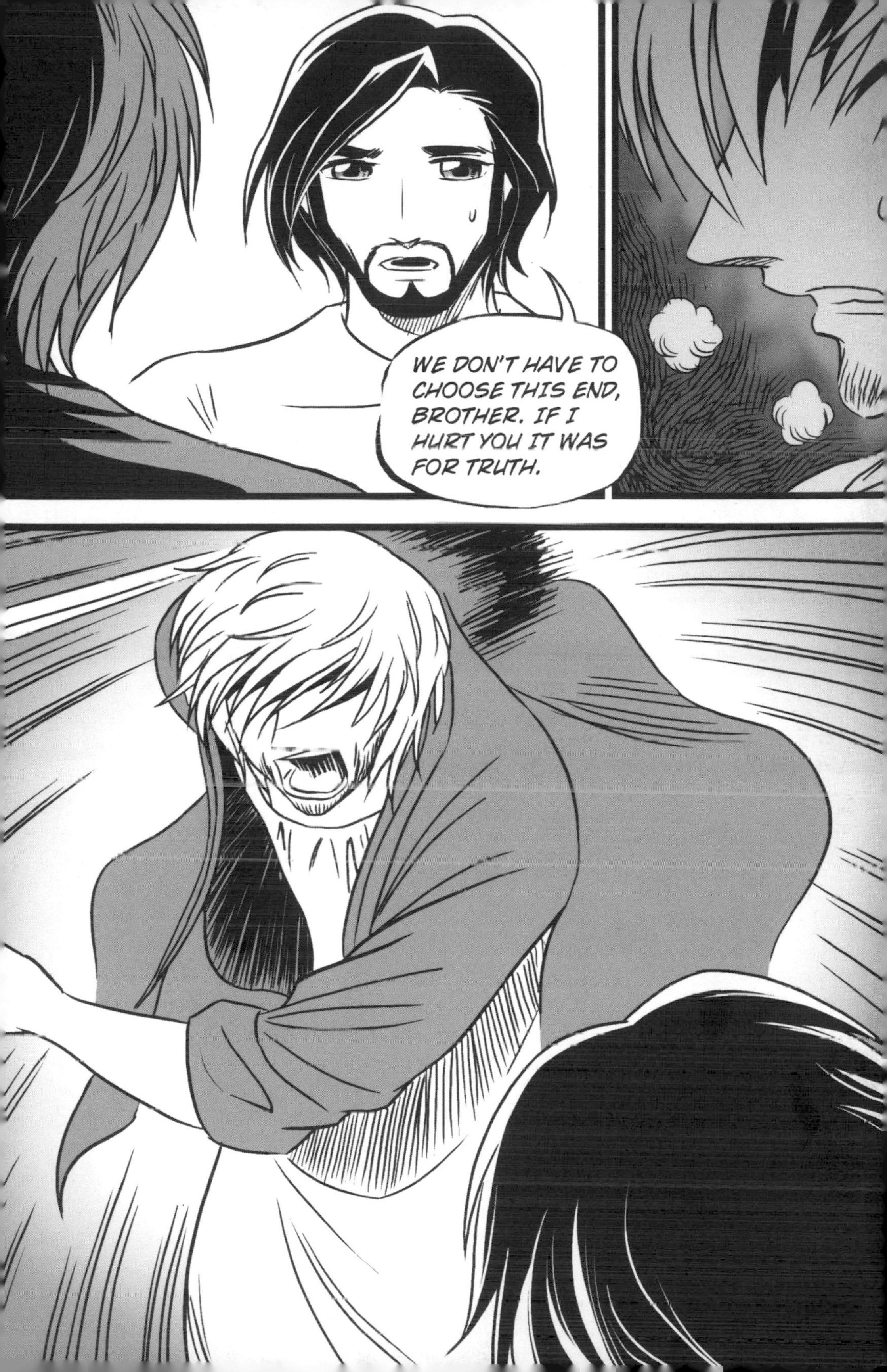
WE DON'T HAVE TO CHOOSE THIS END, BROTHER. IF I HURT YOU IT WAS FOR TRUTH.

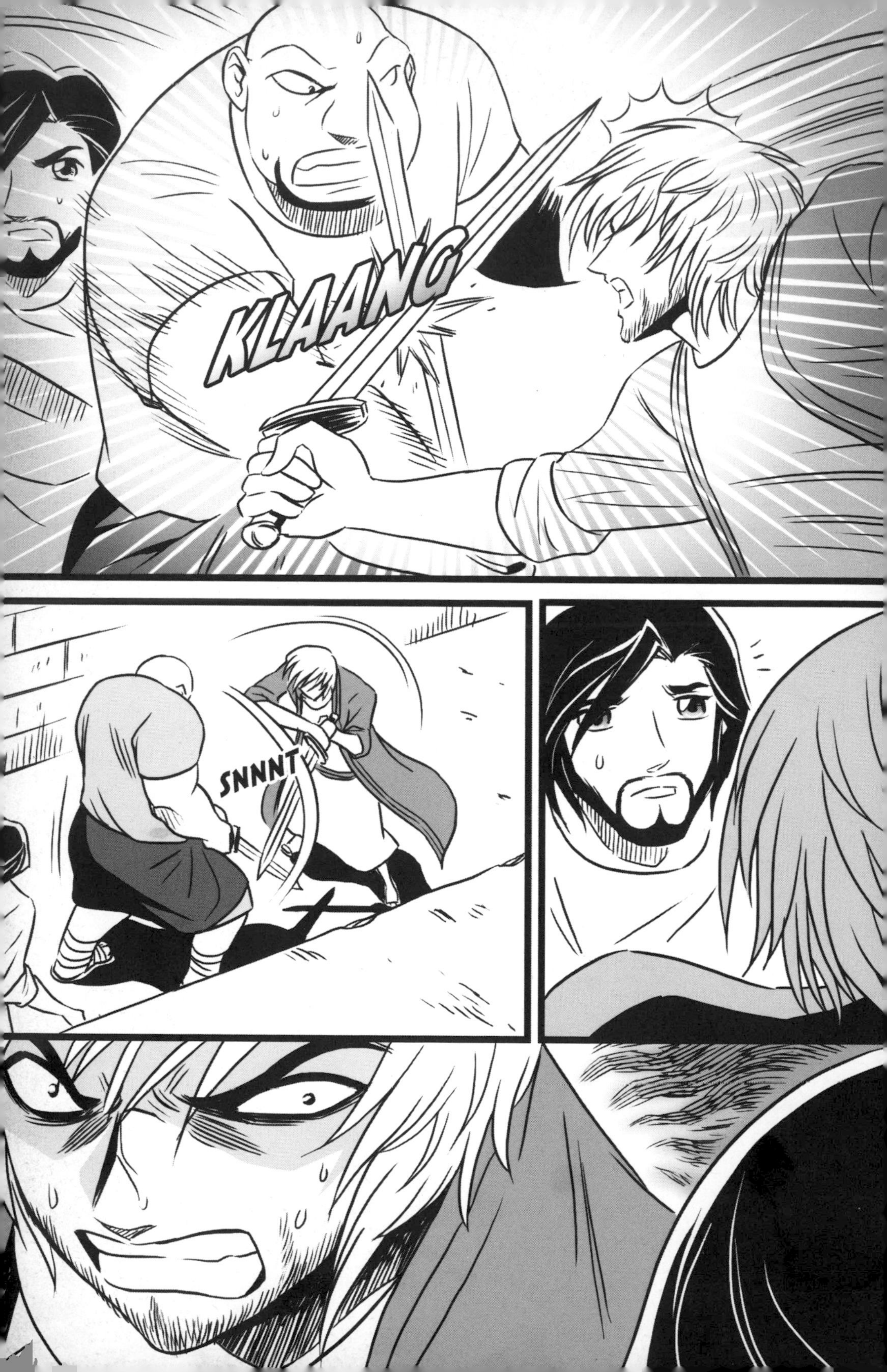
KLAANG
SNNNT

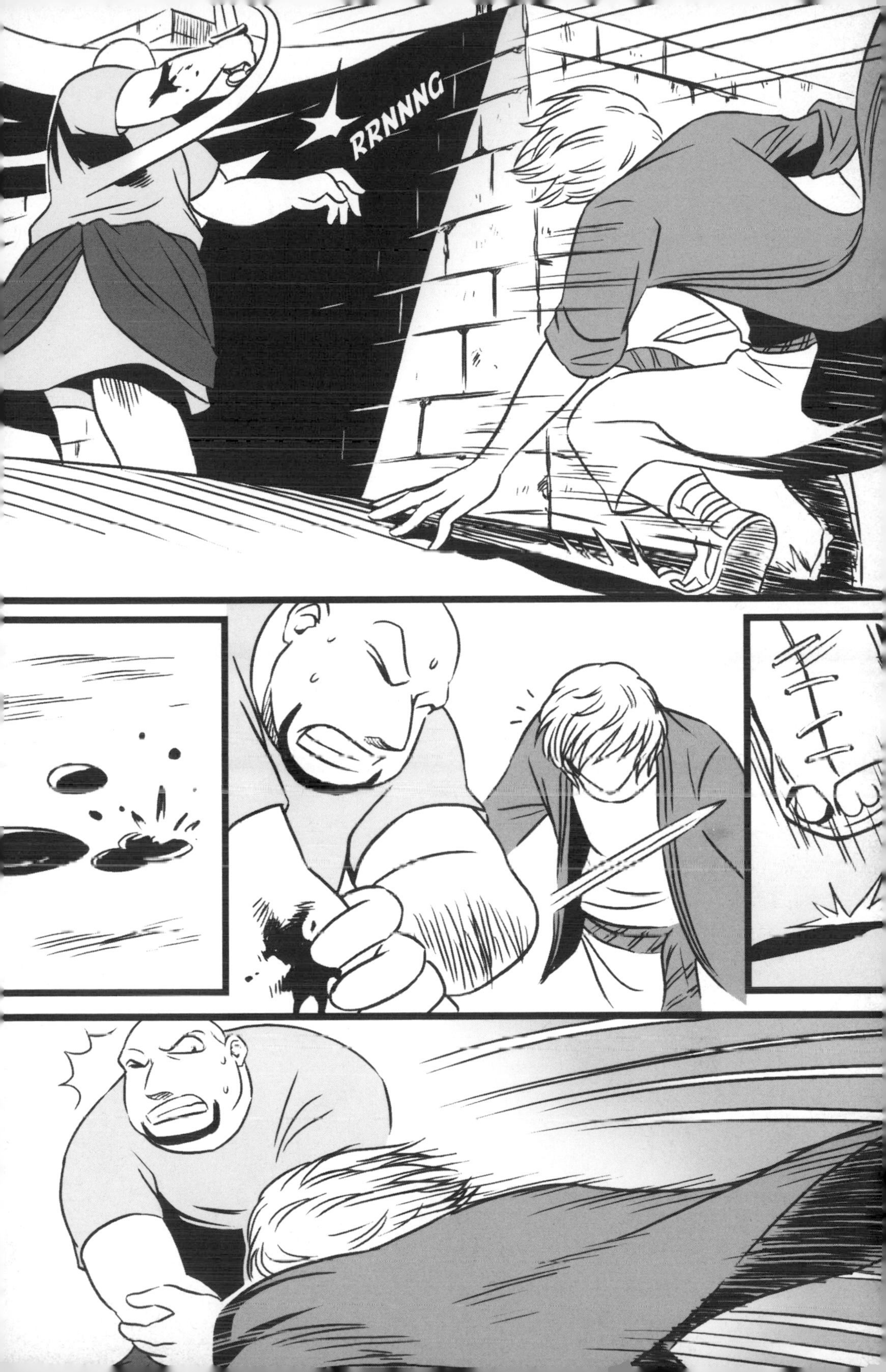
RRNNNG

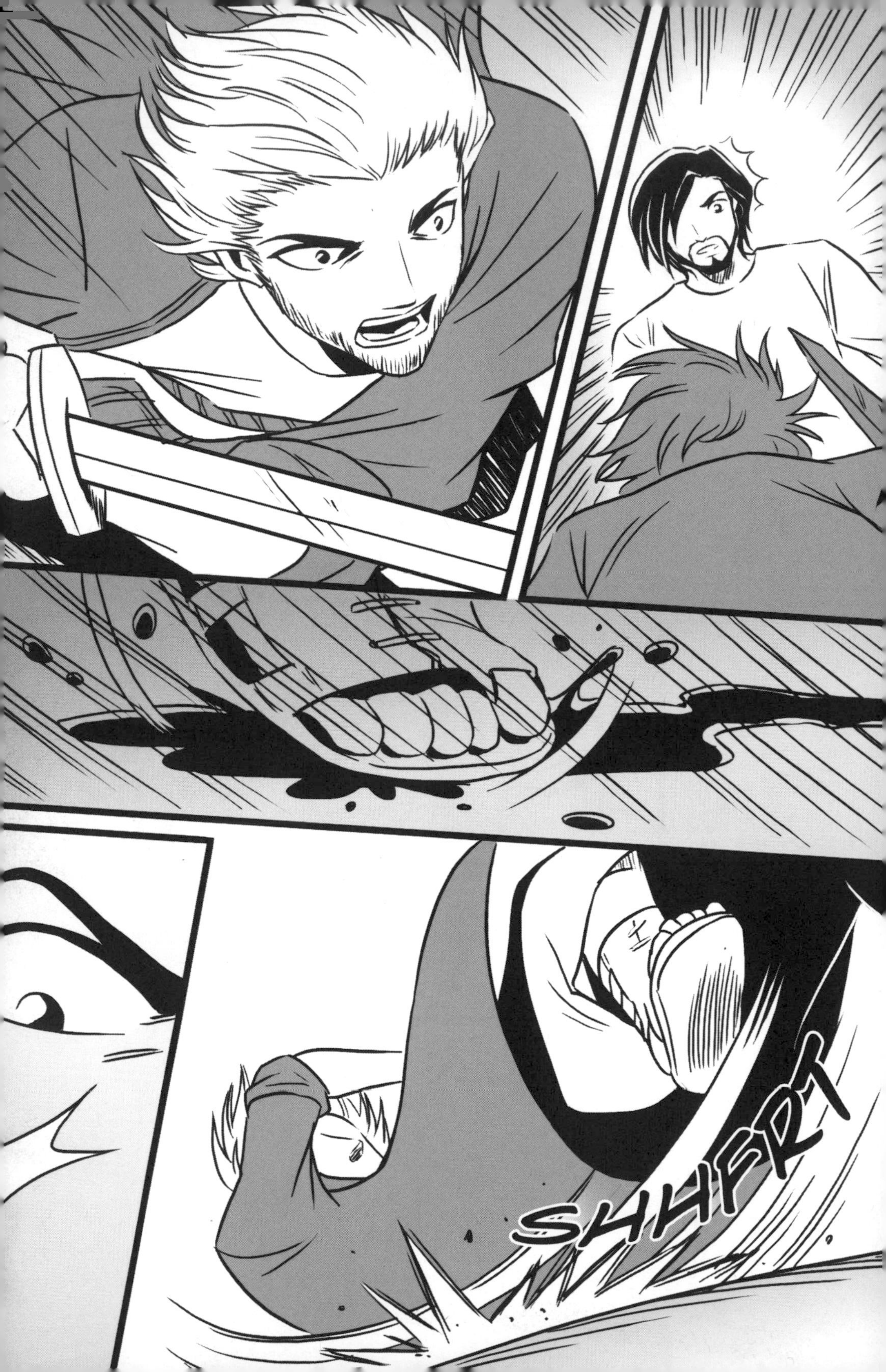
SHHFRT

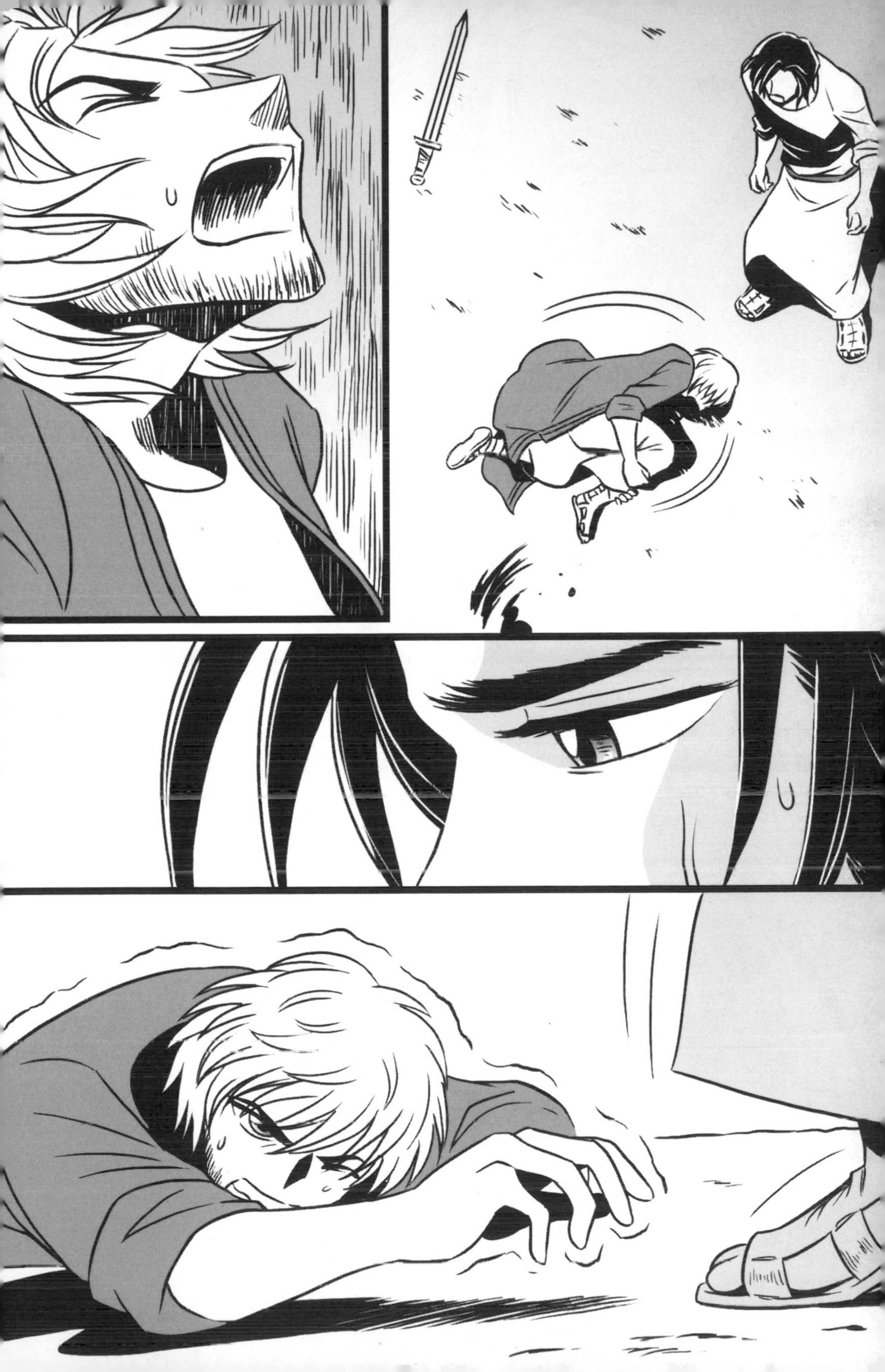

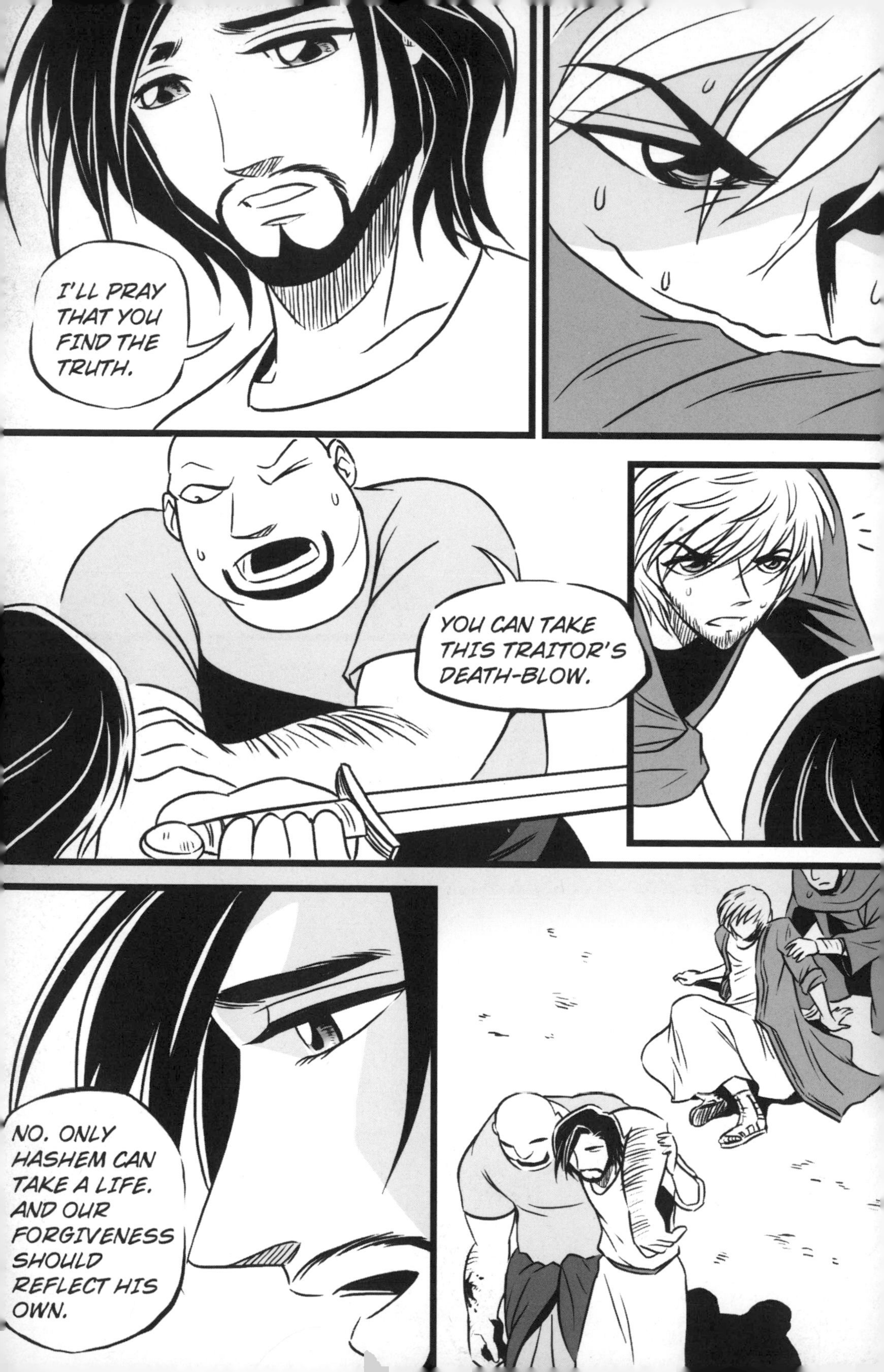
I'LL PRAY THAT YOU FIND THE TRUTH.
YOU CAN TAKE THIS TRAITOR'S DEATH-BLOW.
NO. ONLY HASHEM CAN TAKE A LIFE. AND OUR FORGIVENESS SHOULD REFLECT HIS OWN.

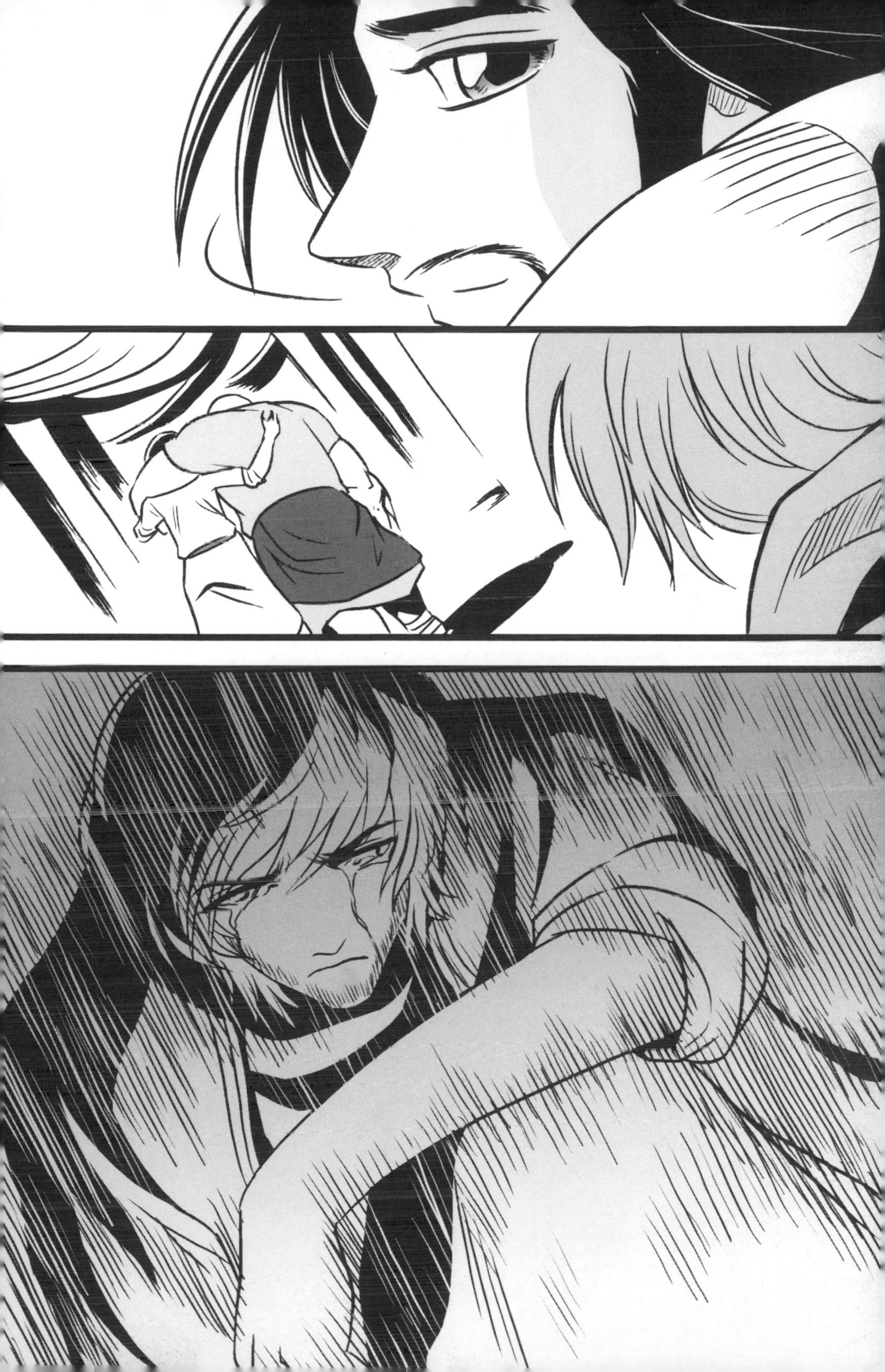

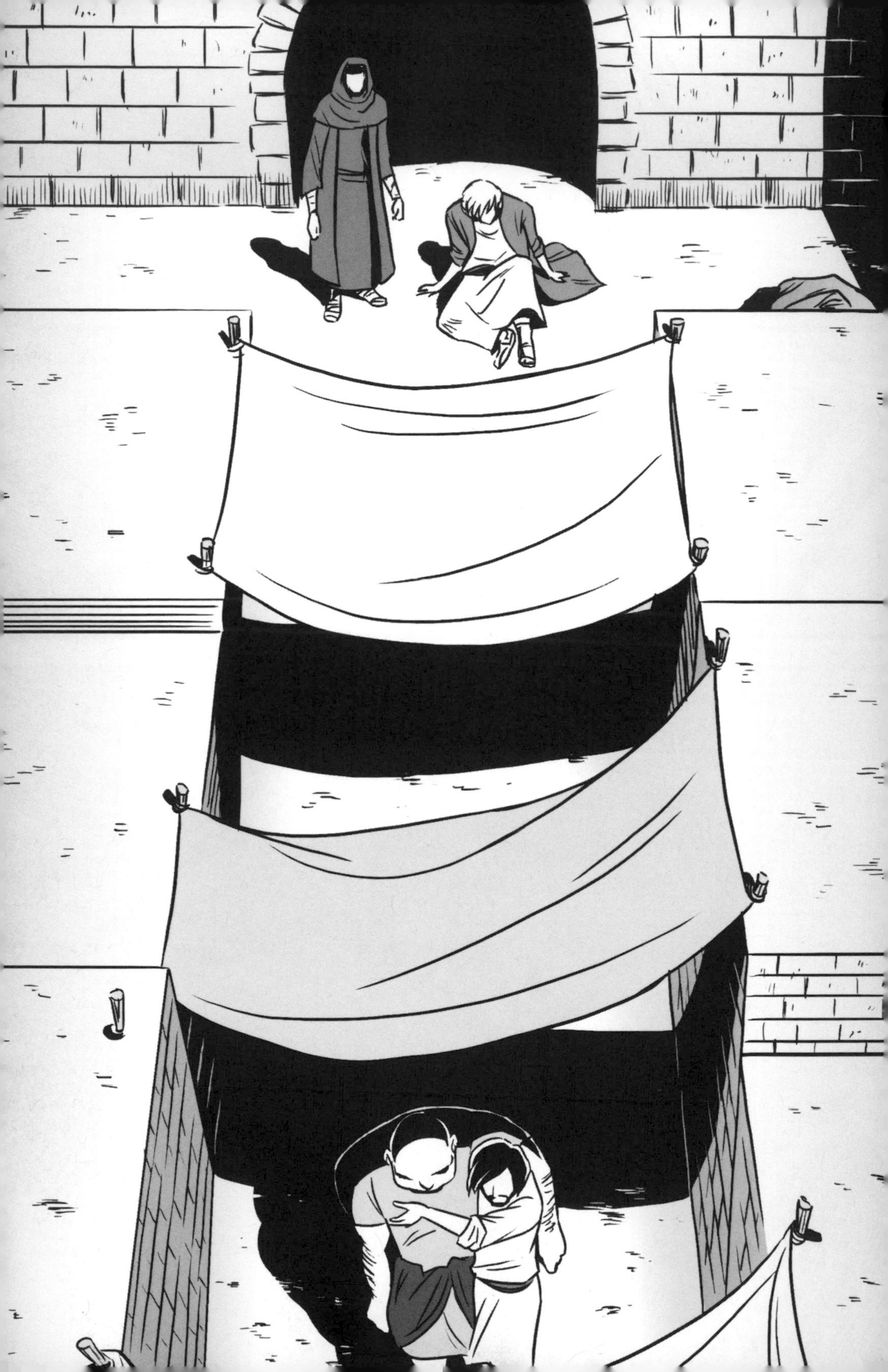

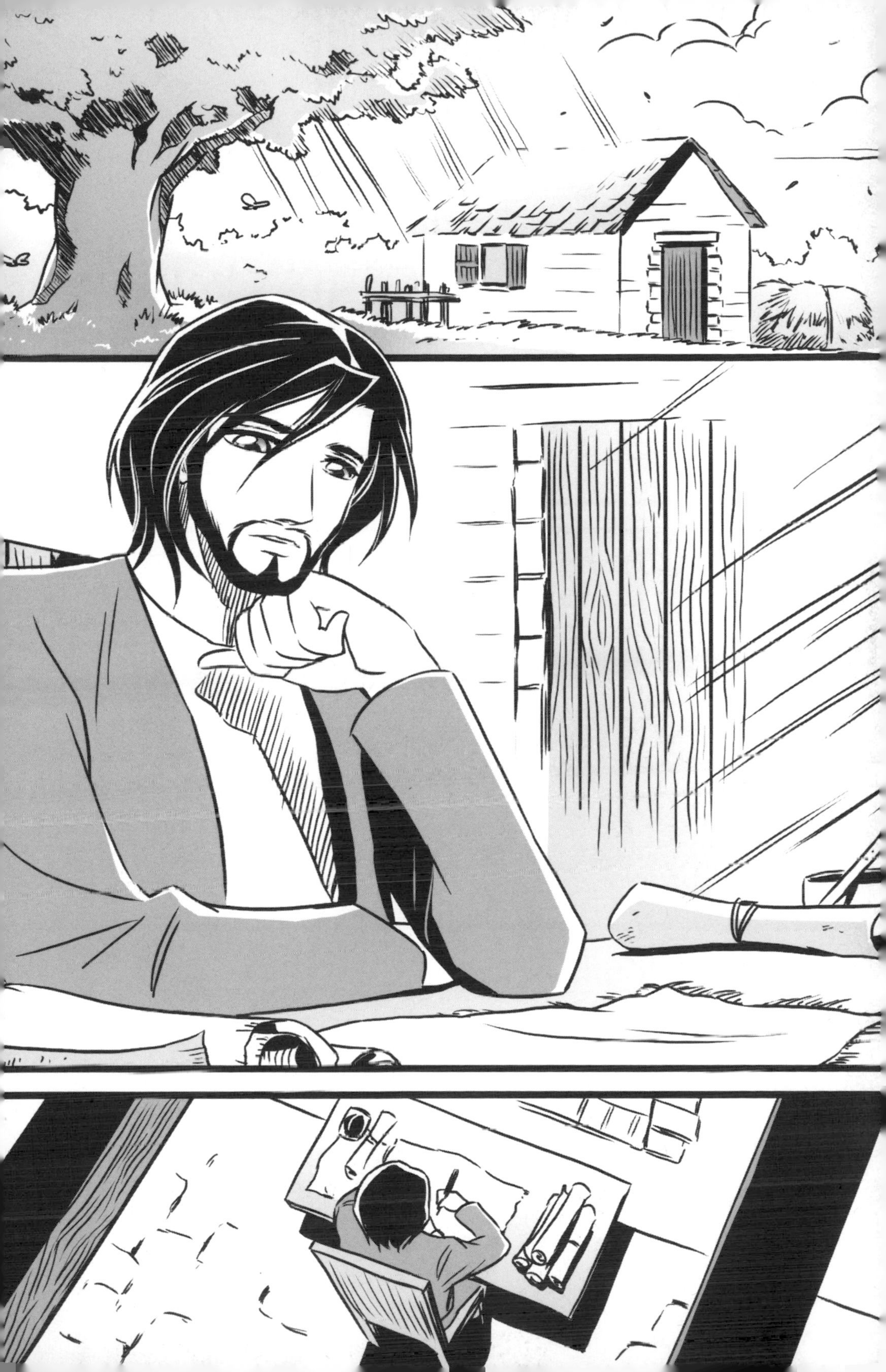

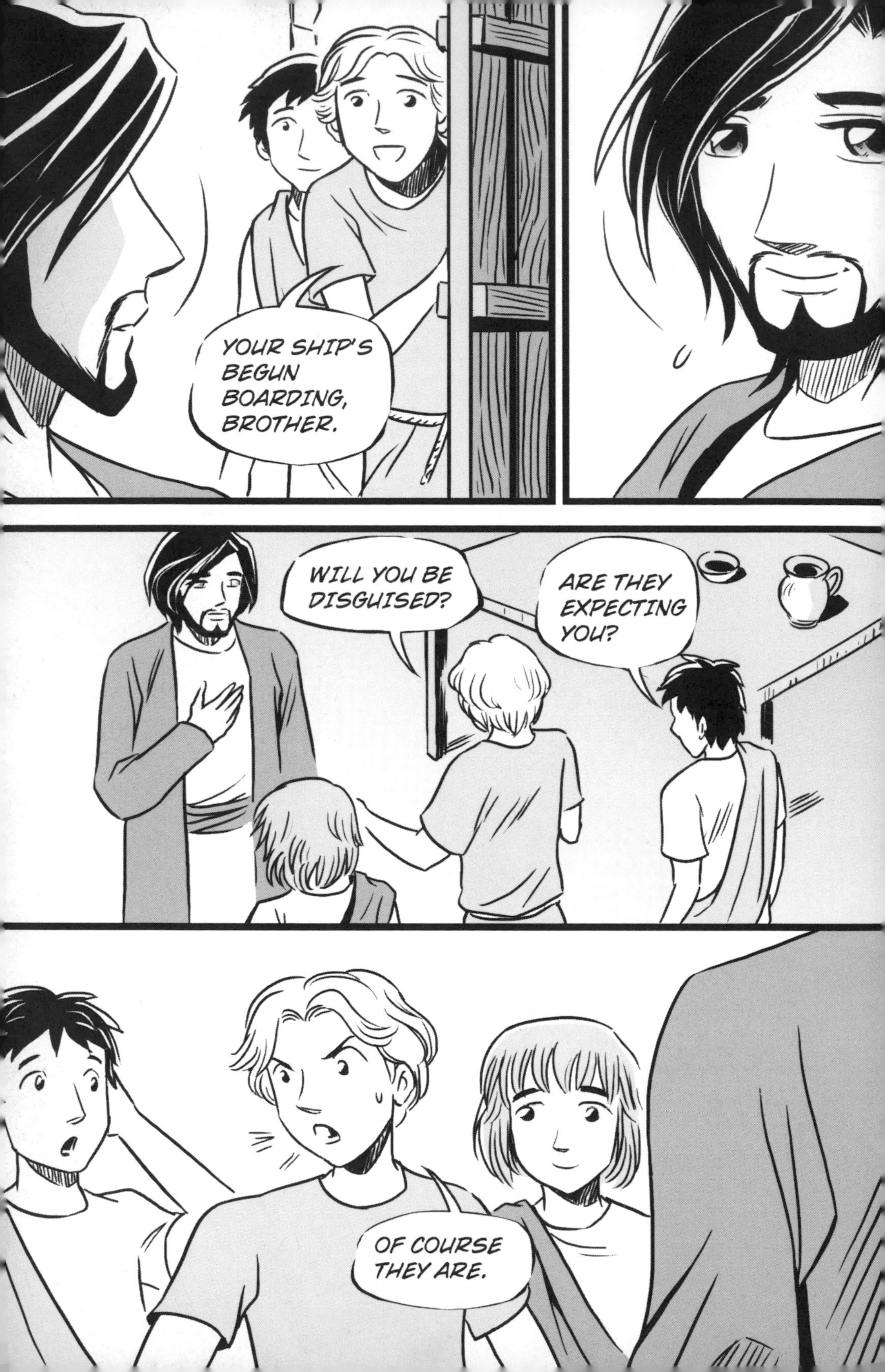
YOUR SHIP'S BEGUN BOARDING, BROTHER.
WILL YOU BE DISGUISED?
ARE THEY EXPECTING YOU?
OF COURSE THEY ARE.

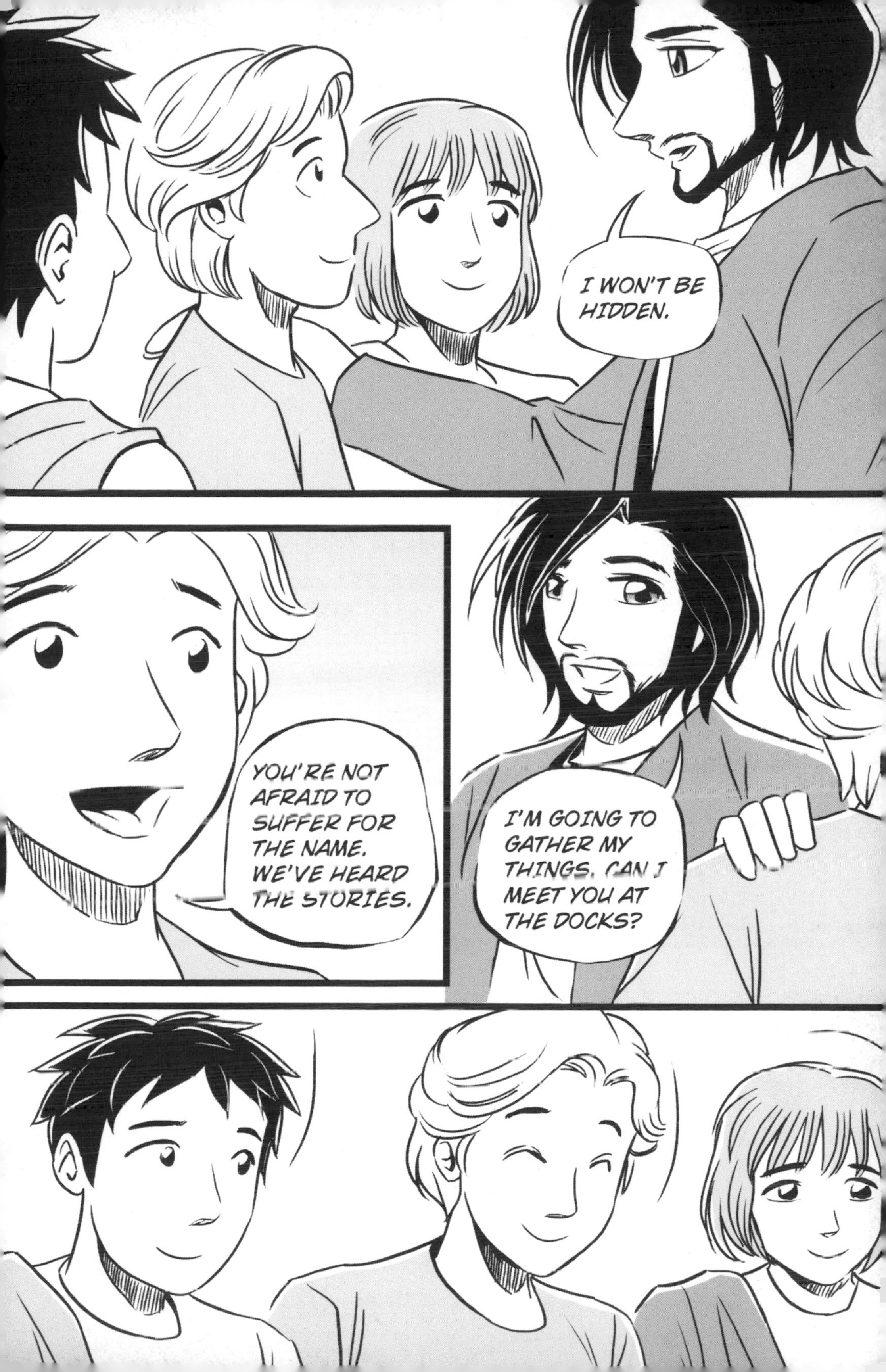
I WON'T BE HIDDEN.
YOU'RE NOT AFRAID TO SUFFER FOR THE NAME. WE'VE HEARD THE STORIES.
I'M GOING TO GATHER MY THINGS. CAN I MEET YOU AT THE DOCKS?

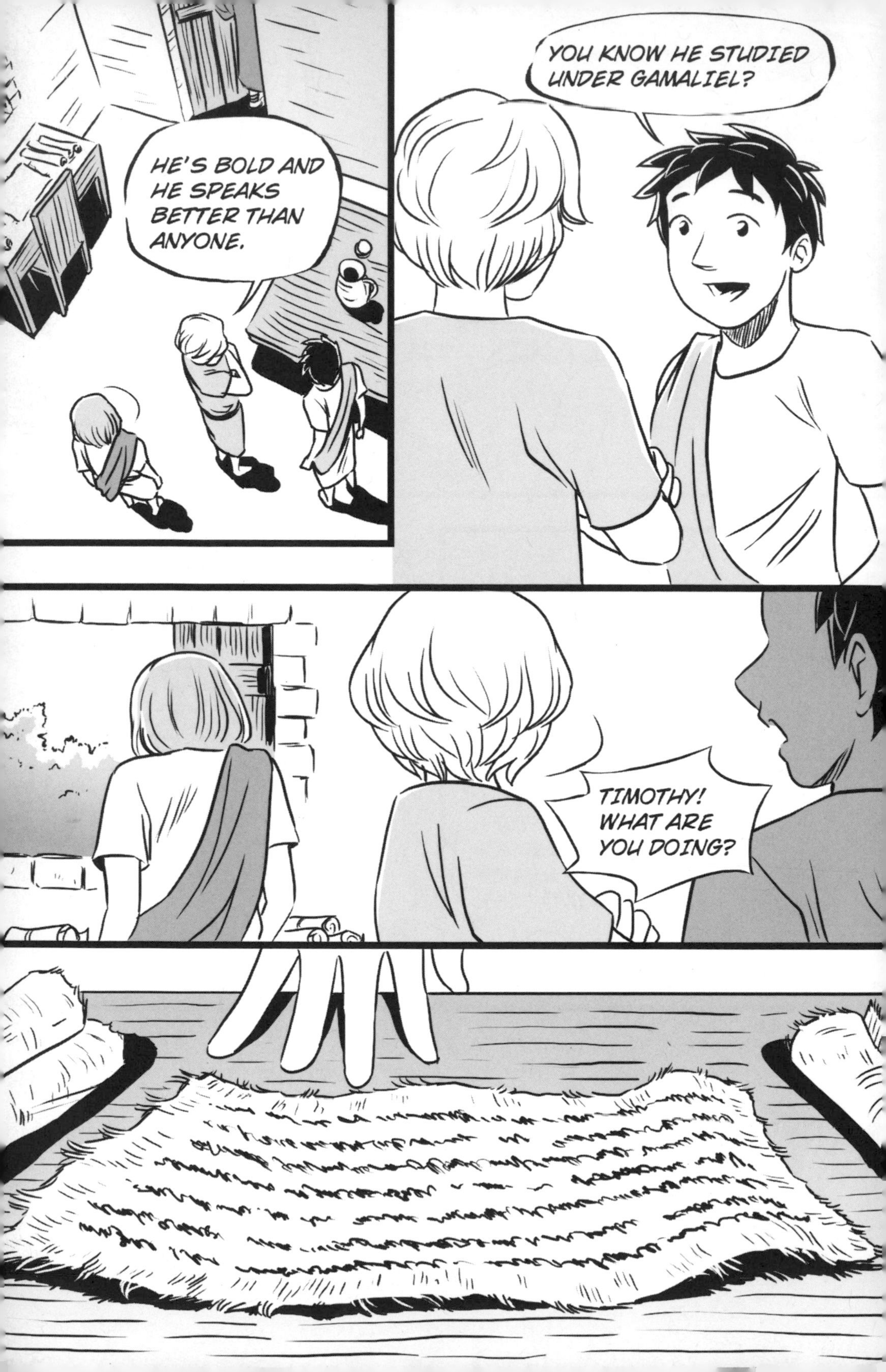
HE'S BOLD AND HE SPEAKS BETTER THAN ANYONE.
YOU KNOW HE STUDIED UNDER GAMALIEL?
TIMOTHY! WHAT ARE YOU DOING?

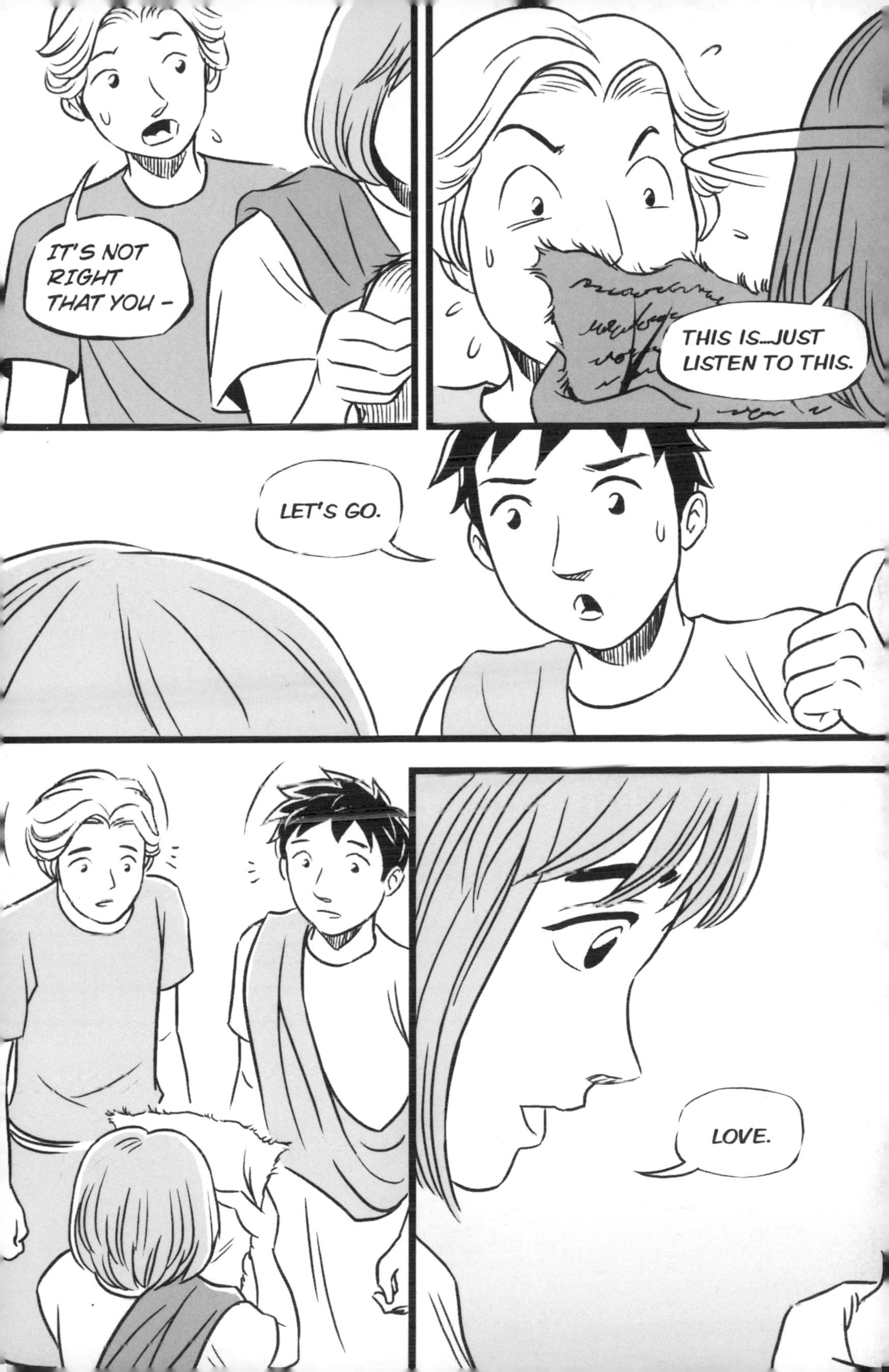
IT'S NOT RIGHT THAT YOU -
THIS IS...JUST LISTEN TO THIS.
LET'S GO.
LOVE.

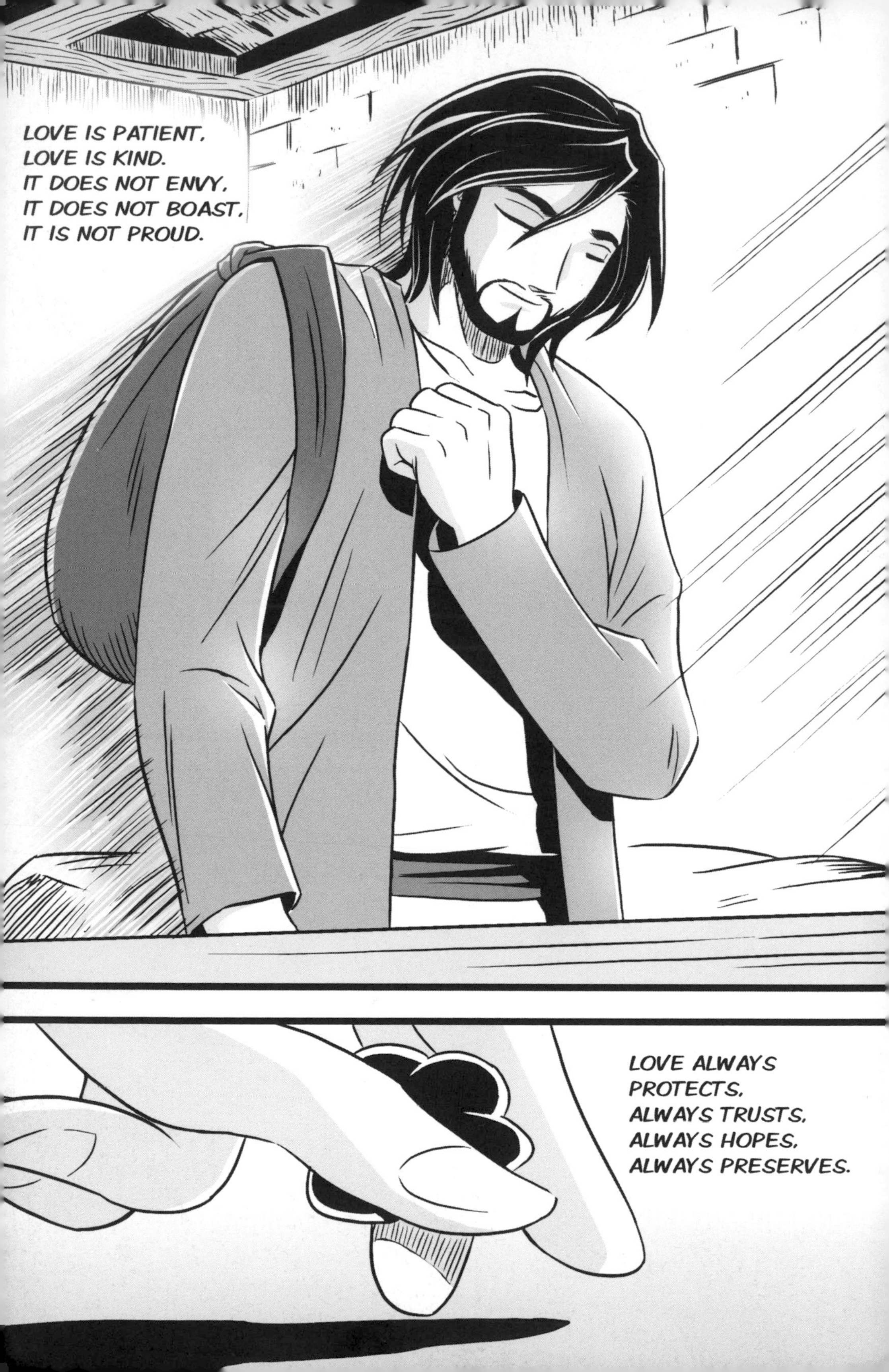
LOVE IS PATIENT, LOVE IS KIND. IT DOES NOT ENVY, IT DOES NOT BOAST, IT IS NOT PROUD.
LOVE ALWAYS PROTECTS, ALWAYS TRUSTS, ALWAYS HOPES, ALWAYS PRESERVES.

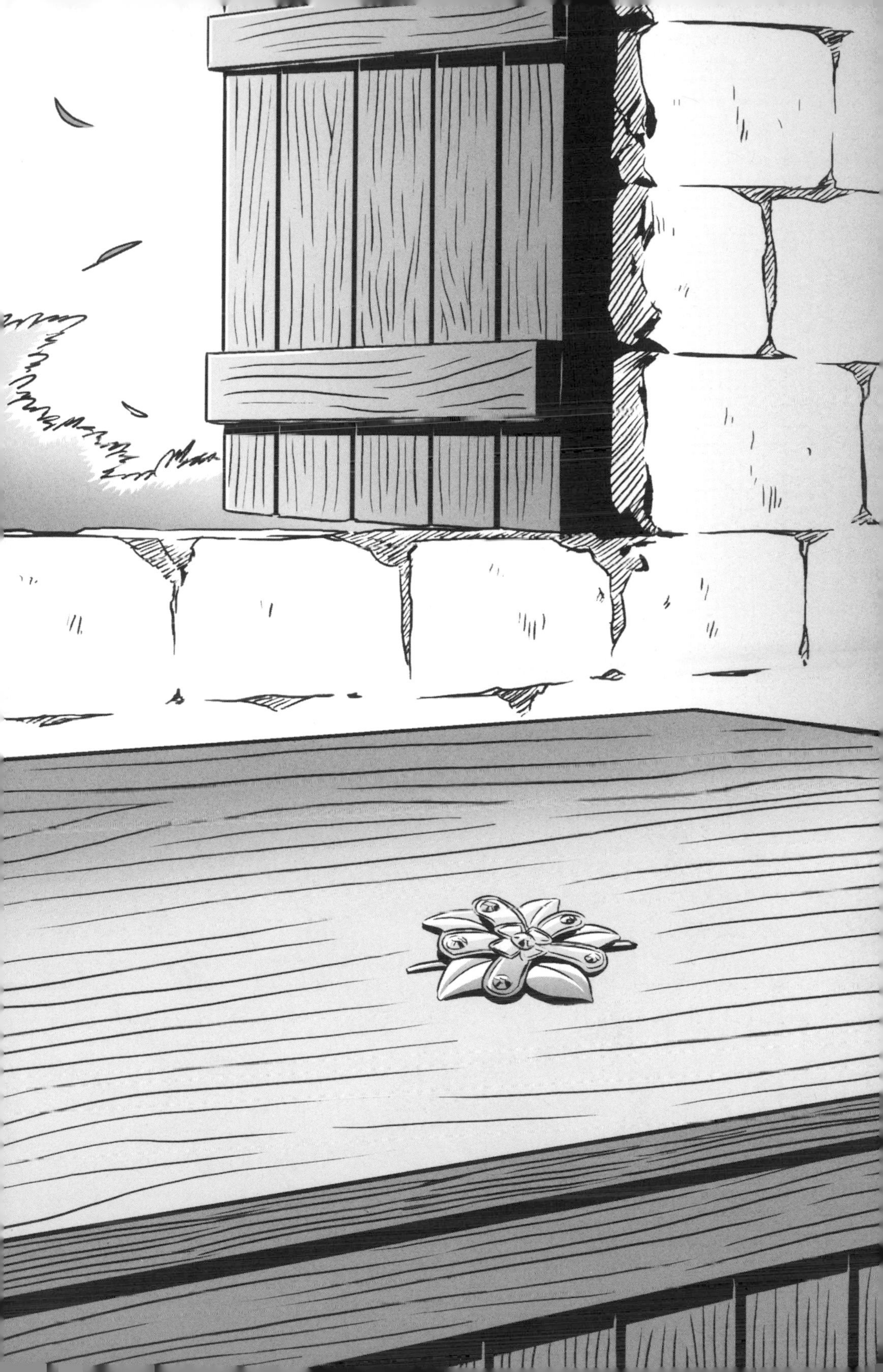

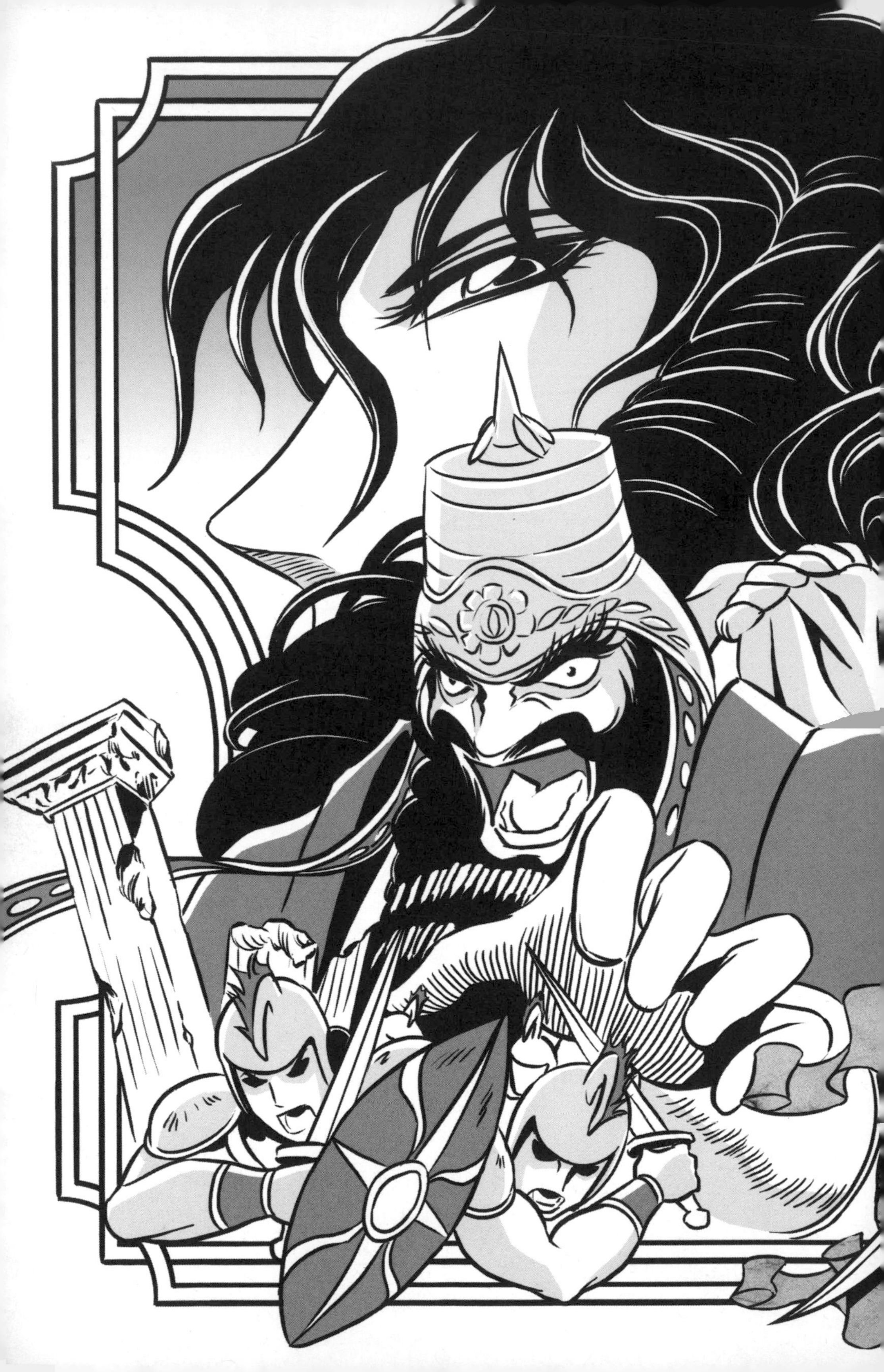

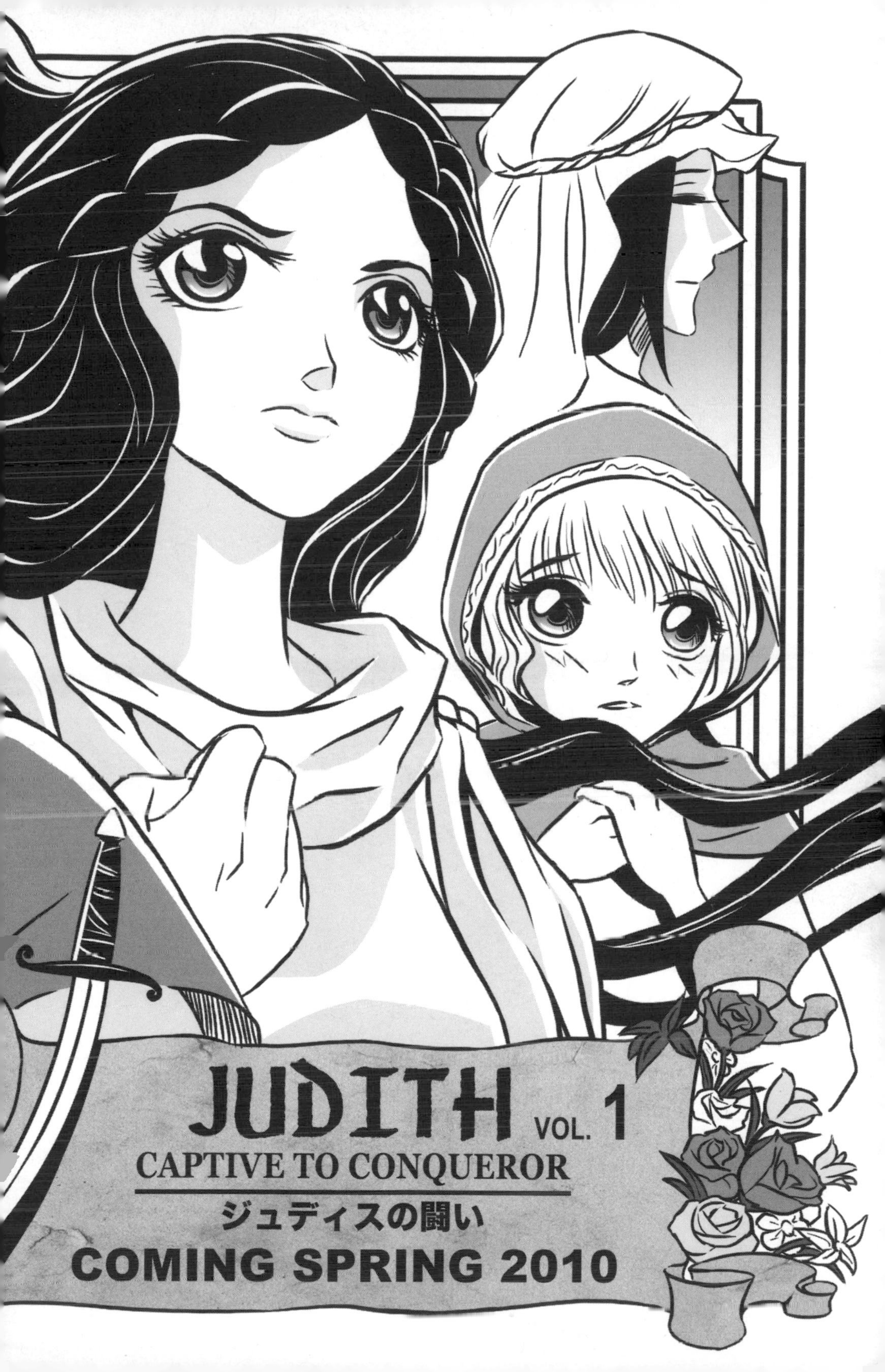
JUDITH VOL. 1
CAPTIVE TO CONQUEROR
ジュディスの闘い
COMING SPRING 2010

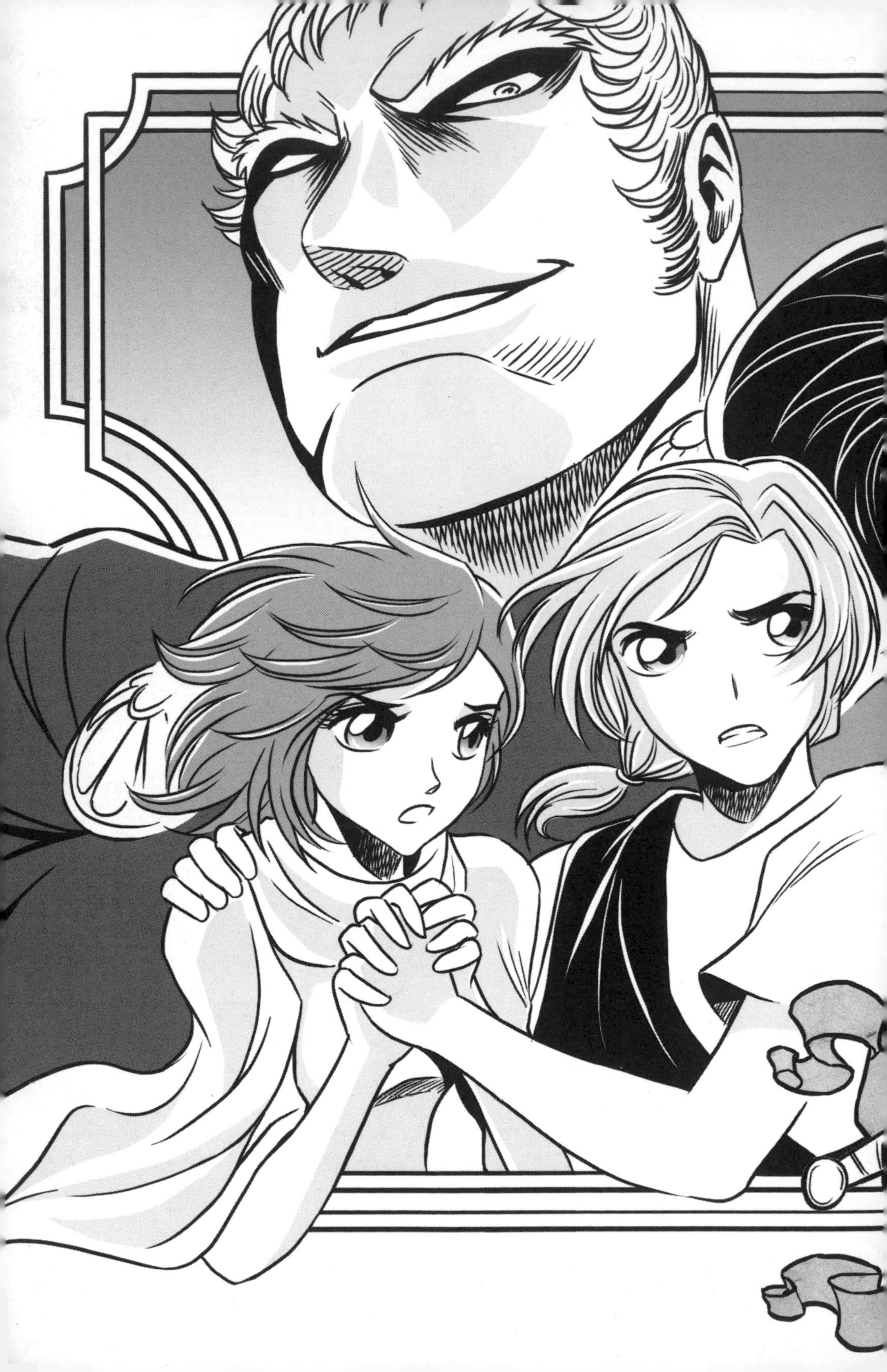

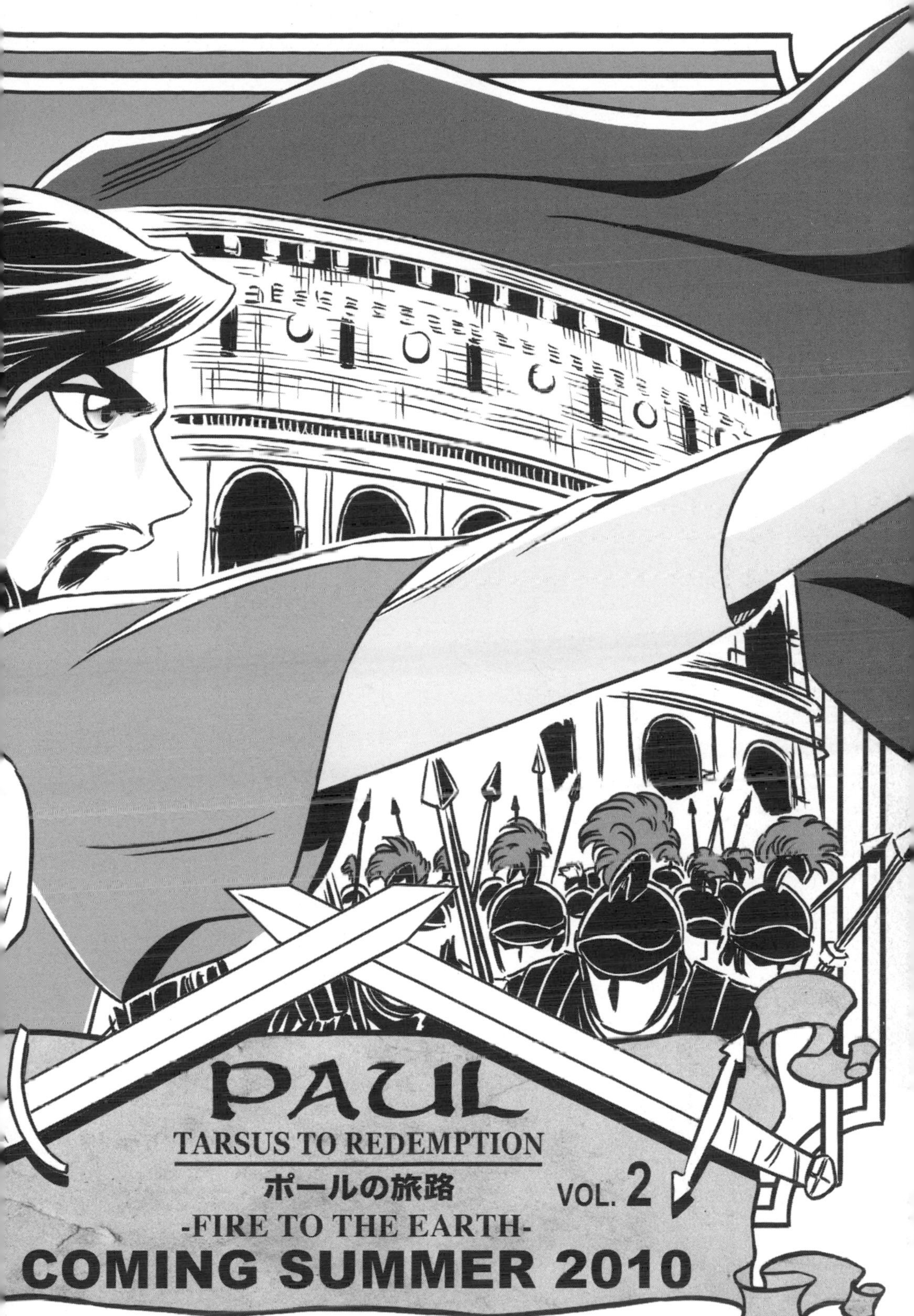
PAUL
TARSUS TO REDEMPTION
ポールの旅路
VOL. 2
-FIRE TO THE EARTH-
COMING SUMMER 2010